THE MORAL STATE

THE MORAL STATE

A STUDY OF THE POLITICAL SOCIALIZATION

OF CHINESE AND AMERICAN CHILDREN

by Richard W. Wilson

THE FREE PRESS
A Division of Macmillan Publishing Co., Inc.
NEW YORK

Collier Macmillan Publishers
LONDON

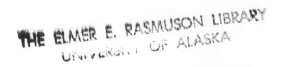

The Free Press
A Division of Macmillan Publishing Co., Inc.
866 Third Avenue, New York, N.Y. 10022

Collier–Macmillan Canada Ltd.

Library of Congress Catalog Card Number: 73–2333

Printed in the United States of America

printing number
1   2   3   4   5   6   7   8   9   10

Library of Congress Cataloging in Publication Data

Wilson, Richard W   1933-
    The moral state.

    Bibliography: p.
    1. Socialization. 2. Children in Formosa.
3. Children in Hong Kong. 4. Children in the
United States.   I. Title.
HQ783.W55   301.5'92   73-2333
ISBN 0-02-935410-2

CONTENTS

LIST OF GRAPHS

LIST OF TABLES

PREFACE

Modernization means many things. To some it is growth curves on industrial charts, while to others it is the often subtle and sometimes sudden changes in social structure. To still others it is charted in changes in demographic indicators or land distribution patterns. In this work we are concerned with yet another approach to modernization—in terms of moral outlook and the ways in which moral values come to include wider and wider ranges of people. This is a measure of modernization which need by no means coincide with the indicators more commonly cited. It is a viewpoint which looks to the quality of social life rather than the structure of social systems.

Few need to be reminded of the moral fervor which is now such a prominent feature of life in the People's Republic of China. Yet while we are able to comment on this condition, our ability to do survey research in this society is severely restricted. Whether this fervor is due at least in part to the influence of China's great tradition is a question filled with surmise. It is possible, however, to examine other Chinese communities and to witness in them the growth, change, or reduction of moral values that occurs in their own quest for change. This phenomenon defines the purpose of this study to examine socialization in Chinese and American communities in order to understand in a comparative way some of the forces in Chinese society which lead to a unique emphasis on morality as a driving force for social change and as a basis for stability and legitimacy in political life.

In carrying out this study, a debt of gratitude is owed to many, of whom only a partial listing can be made here. First of course are my own family and especially my wife, Amy A. Wilson, herself a scholar of Chinese society, who has provided both encouragement and much-needed criticism. Secondly are my colleagues at Rutgers University. This group is a large and varied one, and I can note here only a few of those whose support I sought and valued. They are Ardath W. Burks, James N. Rosenau (now at Ohio State University), Gerald M. Pomper, and Horace Andrews, among others. The Rutgers Research Council provided crucial financial support. I am also indebted to David Harrop for his constant encouragement. Three individuals provided me with invaluable research assistance. They are Mr. Siu Tong Kwok of Hong Kong, Mr. Sheng Chiang Lee of Taiwan, and Mr. James McConnell. My gratitude is also expressed to Mrs. Huei-ling Worthy, who worked to make the questionnaires comparable in both Chinese and English. Last but by no means least, special thanks is owed to the educational authorities in Taiwan, Hong Kong, Chinatown (New York City), and in New Brunswick and Princeton, New Jersey. Without their support, of course, this work could not have been accomplished.

PART I SOME THEORETICAL CONSIDERATIONS

CHAPTER I Introduction

When behavior seems different from the usual, we look to motives; when motives are at variance with the expected, we question the reason. The causes of behavior have constantly perplexed and fascinated man. Whole groups as well as individuals are subjected to scrutiny and examined for presumably common traits. Man is a measuring animal. He sets himself and his own group with its particular habits of action and thought as the standard against which to measure the world. On a range from admiration to disgust he ranks and evaluates the world in which he lives.

In assessing the behavior of individuals in the largest of social groupings, societies, it is common for stereotypes to be used in an initial evaluation. Thus the Japanese all become industrious, the British all law-abiding, and the Germans all orderly. Individuals and subgroups with all their idiosyncrasies and variations are first compared with a presumed common norm. The virtue of stereotyping is the ready and quick classification of a large number of individuals by the use of group labels. Its defect is the gross submergence of individual richness and variety and the possibility of labeling others by signs which for them may well have no meaning.

The study of Chinese society is not exempt from the urge to classify and order individuals or subgroups according to criteria which are presumed to characterize all Chinese. Work on Chinese behavior, from the earliest missionary reports to modern scholarship, has often shown a tendency to identify only salient features of a common Chinese life pattern. Some features, it is true, do appear marked in their regularity and prominence. Arthur H. Smith, for instance, the dean of nineteenth-century "sociological" observers, noted how "in China every man, woman, and child is directly responsible to someone else, and of this important fact no one for a moment loses sight."[1] A highly developed sense of mutual responsibility and a sense of identity rarely phrased in individualistic terms are two noted stereotypes concerning traditional Chinese behavior. Scholars have also noted a generalized fear and awe of those in authority, a fear best manifested, perhaps, by a hesitancy to challenge authority figures, especially fathers, and by a widely shared anxiety concerning interpersonal conflict in general.[2]

Whatever the accuracy of these stereotypic descriptions with regard to traditional China—and in a broad sense they seem generally valid—the tendency to speak of the modern Chinese in paintbrush terms is equally apparent. In many cases these descriptions attest to the persistence of traditional Chinese modes of thought and behavior. The sense of propriety and "face" and of accommodation to authority in Communist Chinese literature, for instance, has been remarked upon.[3] Hsiung has noted the very traditional emphasis by the Chinese Communists on "thought" as the basis for behavior. Quoting the *Jen-min Jih-pao*, he points out:

> Work is done by man, and *man's action is governed by his thinking.* . . .
> A man without correct political thinking is a man without a soul.[4]

The power of the family as a source of both identity and social control is nowhere more apparent than where it is *felt* to be lacking and where other social groupings, particularly the nation-state, have not been

[1] Arthur H. Smith, *Chinese Characteristics*, Fleming H. Revell Co., New York, 1894, p. 237.

[2] Richard H. Solomon, "On Activism and Activists," *China Quarterly*, no. 39, July–Sept. 1969, and "Communication Patterns and the Chinese Revolution," *China Quarterly*, no. 32, Oct.–Dec. 1967, p. 91.

[3] Ai-Li S. Chin, "Family Relations in Modern Chinese Fiction," in Maurice Freedman, ed., *Family and Kinship in Chinese Society*, Stanford University Press, Stanford, 1970, p. 119.

[4] James C. Hsiung, *Ideology and Practice: The Evolution of Chinese Communism*, Praeger, New York, 1970, pp. 128–129, from *Jen-min Jih-pao*, editorial November 11, 1960 (n.p). Italics in original.

established as creditable alternatives. Thus in Hong Kong interviews and articles alike proclaim a breakdown in family cohesiveness and discipline, especially in resettlement areas, and a need to combat the resulting anomie, or—as the Chinese so frequently put it—"individualism," by creating new, alternative social groups with positive social values. Only in this way, it is said, can "social" commitment be obtained and immediate self-gratification and psychological alienation be sublimated to the creation of an effective society. Such statements are made despite plentiful evidence that in many areas family affection and cohesiveness have declined little if any from traditional times.

As in the past, many Chinese turn to an emphasis on morals training as the panacea for the social problems they perceive. Like nineteenth-century evangelical preachers, editorialists on Taiwan thunder about the bankruptcy of moral education in a society where such training is more heavily emphasized than in most countries of the world.[5] On Taiwan the question of how to create and maintain a "moral" society seems to pervade the language and the anguish of social change. Adult corruption and juvenile delinquency are both said to manifest inadequate morality and because of this to jeopardize the education of the young. In like manner, riots and disturbances in Hong Kong and Kowloon are ascribed by commissions of inquiry at least partially to insufficient moral education.[6] The criticisms recorded by these commissions reflect the belief that proper thinking and hence proper behavior can only be achieved by intensive training in proper thought.

In China itself, morals education has been infused with political content; no action is deemed to be without political significance. An approved political morality is perceived as the basis for correct social orientation and thought. In recent years there has been a well-documented increase in emphasis at all levels of schooling on the thought of Mao Tse-tung. Mass meetings and struggle sessions ensure that the moral failure of recalcitrants will not go unnoted. From nursery school songs and plays to elaborate ballet productions, there is an emphasis on mixing political morality with art and education. Villains are arrogant,

[5] See Richard W. Wilson, *Learning to be Chinese: The Political Socialization of Children in Taiwan*, Massachusetts Institute of Technology Press, Cambridge, Mass., 1970.

[6] *Kowloon Disturbances 1966: Report of Commission of Inquiry*, The Government Printer, Hong Kong, n.d., pp. 139, 141.

cowardly, and degenerate, while heroes are persistent, brave, and pure. In China proper the family remains important, but as an alternative for loyalty there is stress on the nation, on its leaders, and on the glory of submerging one's life into sacrifice for the people. Within this societal framework there is a stress on cohesion, loyalty, and responsibility and on the disciplined working for the goals of the national group as these are defined by its leadership.

With regard to both traditional and modern China there has often been a marked tendency to characterize "the Chinese" as a people with largely homogeneous behavior. The patterns adduced are set boldly forth, often with only passing reference to their causes and interrelationships. It does not seem unreasonable to ask, however, whether there are stable and enduring core patterns which characterize the Chinese generally under the impact of modernization. If such core patterns can be revealed, it may tell us something about the strength and pervasiveness of homogeneity both past and present.

Part of the goal of this work is to investigate several modern Chinese societies in an attempt to discover where the areas of greatest behavioral and attitudinal homogeneity occur and what implications for social change these patterns reveal. We will investigate areas of congruity and incongruity among children in three separate Chinese groups where field research is possible. These areas are Taiwan, Hong Kong, and Chinatown, New York City. The patterns uncovered in these studies are compared with each other and against the patterns which emerged from a similar study of Caucasian and Negro American children from the Middle Atlantic area of New Jersey in the United States. In addition to making a comparison among these four groups we will attempt to show how training differences at the family and school level within each of these societies can help explain the political and social differences we note among them. It is our hope that this study will be an aid to better knowledge of the Chinese and will help provide a deeper understanding of some aspects of modernization in China.

Studies of geographically separated and socially different Chinese communities tend to indicate considerable homogeneity both among and within these groups. Charles Morris, for instance, found "marked intranational similarities" among four regionally defined subgroups he studied in pre–Communist China, and Rodd and Wilson found more similarity than dissimilarity between Mainlanders and Taiwanese on

Taiwan.[7] In a study covering different time periods, McClelland, working from children's stories, contrasted Taiwan and China for the period 1950 to 1959 against Republican China from 1920 to 1929. He discovered an increase for both Taiwan and China in "need achievement" with a comparatively greater increase for the People's Republic, which managed to surpass the international mean value; he found a greater increase in "need affiliation" for the People's Republic than for Taiwan, with both groups still below the international mean value; and he pointed out that there has been a decrease in "need power" on Taiwan (which, however, is still above the world average) but a great increase in this particular need on the China mainland.[8] The evidence is not conclusive, but certainly suggests strongly that Chinese communities are similar in a number of interesting and significant ways. The data also implies, however, that caution should be exercised with regard to what is "typical" or "nontypical" in Chinese society and that such beloved terms as "Chinese culture" should be viewed at best as abstractions of a much more complex reality.

Each of the three Chinese groups analyzed in this study is geographically and politically distinct from the others. Chinatown in New York City is a small enclave surrounded by a dominant European culture that penetrates the enclave in a number of ways, not least of which through the requirement that children be educated in an American public school system. Learning about China is therefore largely a family enterprise, supplemented for those who can afford it by a late-afternoon Chinese school, where Chinese language and related topics are taught. Hong Kong, on the other hand, is a southern Chinese city composed largely of people referred to loosely as Cantonese, and is governed as a British Crown Colony. The school system, dominated administratively by the British, allows training in either English or Chinese. Taiwan, an island approximately 100 miles from Fukien

[7] Charles Morris, *Varieties of Human Value*, University of Illinois Press, Chicago, 1956, noted in Kenneth W. Terhune, "From National Character to National Behavior: A Reformulation," *Journal of Conflict Resolution*, vol. 14, no. 2, June 1970; William G. Rodd, "A Cross-Cultural Study of Taiwan's Schools," *Journal of Social Psychology*, vol. 50, first half, August 1959; Richard W. Wilson, "A Comparison of Political Attitudes of Taiwanese Children and Mainlander Children on Taiwan," *Asian Survey*, vol. 8, no. 12, Dec. 1968.

[8] David C. McClelland, "Motivational Patterns in Southeast Asia with Special Reference to the Chinese Case," *Journal of Social Issues*, vol. 19, no. 1, January 1963, pp. 9–12.

province, is an authoritarian political system under the control of the Kuomintang or Nationalist Party. The educational system is highly centralized under the direction of a Ministry of Education and is compulsory through the ninth grade.

Basically, this study is an interpretation and analysis of aspects of the political socialization of approximately 1100 children from Chinatown (90 children), Taiwan (335 children), Hong Kong (362 children), and the eastern United States (294 children). These children, of both sexes, divided among third, fifth, and seventh grades, are not a rigorously matched sample, except that generally all are middle- to low-income children of both sexes from large urban areas. The exception to this is the group of children from Princeton, New Jersey, about one-half of the Caucasian and Negro American sample, who are predominantly from middle- to upper-middle-class families. One assumption of this work is that modernization occurs most rapidly in urban areas—or, in the case of the United States, in its affluent suburbs—and that tests of attitudinal and behavioral change during modernization should therefore take place in these areas. It was in this sense that an attempt was made to develop "units of comparability" in the selection of samples. Tighter controls, however, were not employed.

The sample of Chinatown was the smallest and was a portion of the approximately 2600 children who attend the New York Chinese School. This school is situated within a geographically small ethnic Chinese community in which about 25 percent of the 45,000 residents have arrived within the last half decade. Partly for this reason there has been a decrease in internal cohesion in Chinatown and a rise of social problems, some associated with criminal activity. The dropout rate from the American public high school in the area is a surprising 15 percent, much of this reportedly due to an inadequacy in the use of English.[9]

The social problems found in Chinatown are writ large in Hong Kong. Chinese respondents there uniformly tend to report breakdowns in social cohesion and in individual sense of purpose. These comments include remarks concerning corruption, growing teen-age delinquency, overcrowding (in the resettlement areas most families live with five adults—meaning anyone over ten years of age—in a room ten feet by twelve feet), opprobrium directed against status based on commercial

[9] Murray Schumach, "Neighborhoods: Chinatown is Troubled by New Influx," *New York Times*, June 16, 1970, p. 49.

success, and fear to cooperate with others (because, it is said, these others will actually only be working for their own advantage). Regardless of the truth of these statements, there is indicated a considerable sense of rootlessness. Elementary education in Hong Kong has increased from a decimated post-war figure of 4,000 in 1945 to over 380,000 in primary school in 1970. There are now 450,000 primary school places for all of the approximately 650,000 children of primary school age, although as noted, 70,000 of these places are not filled. The Hong Kong sample selected for this study was from government-aided Chinese language primary and secondary schools at North Point.

The nature of the political and social system in Taiwan has tended to reduce the extent of the social problems manifest in Chinatown and Hong Kong. Urbanization, however, has been rapid, with all the attendant ills of dislocation and overcrowding which this may cause. Visitors traveling to Taiwan from Hong Kong quickly notice a distinctly greater drabness and lack of flamboyance. This is due partly to differences in life style and partly to the atmosphere which prevails in Taiwan as a result of the long-term civil war with the Communists. Hostility between Mainlanders and Taiwanese appears, on the whole, to be abating but still remains the major impediment to internal social cohesion. Family orientations are strong but are giving way before the combined onslaught of urbanization, industrialization, and mass education. The children from Taiwan selected for this study were of mixed Taiwanese and Mainlander backgrounds from public primary and middle schools in Taipei, the capital city.

Lastly, the "American" sample was drawn from two areas of the most urbanized state in the United States, New Jersey. These two areas were New Brunswick and Princeton. Neither of these two mini-cities has the same high incidence of crime and dislocation that characterizes larger cities in the United States, although New Brunswick tends toward this pattern to a greater extent than Princeton. New Brunswick is a largely working-class, small city with a heterogeneous white population and a black ghetto. Of the sample of children from New Brunswick approximately one-half by head count were black, giving the entire New Jersey sample, including Princeton, an approximately 25 percent black representation, or slightly more than double the national black representation. The tests in both Princeton and New Brunswick were made at public primary and secondary schools. These schools are controlled by

local boards of education and are under the direction of school adminis-
trations headed by superintendents.

While the Chinese on Taiwan and those on the mainland live under
antagonistic political regimes with markedly different goals, it is still our
judgment that the social patterns of these two systems have a closer
correspondence in terms of this analysis than the People's Republic has
to either Hong Kong or Chinatown. This is an assertion of considerable
complexity which it is impossible to prove adequately, since survey
research is currently impossible in the People's Republic. Our major
contention is that the *styles* of learning in both areas, while different in
some respects, have considerable congruence despite the mutually hostile
stance of the two regimes. Lack of opportunity to observe a mainland
school system and administer standardized tests precluded the inclusion
of a sample from this area. Despite this drawback we strongly contend
that the patterns we observed in this study for our Chinese samples are
relevant to the Chinese Communist case and are suggestive of similar
patterns and trends within that society.

POLITICAL SOCIALIZATION

Political socialization is a new field with an old history. The essence of
its fundamental question—does adult society in some way reflect the
training of the young?—has been asked in a variety of ways for as long
as man has hypothesized about his social existence. Plato, Confucius,
Bodin, Filmer, and Locke are but a few of those who in one form or
another have been interested in childhood experience as an explanation
for adult thought and behavior. Yet while rigorous within these thinkers'
own frames of logic, much of this body of theory remained in the realm
of conjecture until the advent of modern social science, with its more
precise canons of proof and procedure.

At issue is no longer a search for a will-o'-the-wisp entity known as
"national character," a construct which assumes a congruity among
individuals within a society which we now know to be nonexistent. We
still do ask the question, however, whether personality distributions
among nations vary significantly. This latter query is related to a methodology in which presumably standardized child-rearing practices of a
given social unit are analyzed in order to determine the extent to which

associated patterns of childhood personality development limit the probable range of adult personalities that can develop. In other words, as LeVine points out, personality traits are statistical characteristics of populations and there is no contradiction in assuming both intrapopulation variability and cross-population differences in central tendency.[10] These personality traits arise from a complex interaction between goals, some of which are socially acquired (as preeminence in archery might be in a hunting tribe), the socially acceptable way to achieve one's goals, and punishments for failure to conform to appropriate norms of role performance.[11] There is then a process of adaptation between the personality of an individual and the social structure in which this person lives. A man has neither total free will nor the absence of it but a scale of possibilities relating to his own dispositions, to events, and to the needs of others who are in the same general situational context.

Just as an individual may change over time, so also may the personality distributions which characterize larger populations. These latter changes are primarily generational in origin, for although all individuals grow and develop throughout life the general value orientations of any given individual are generally fairly stable in adulthood unless subjected to massive shock and disorientation. The most stable psychological attributes within a population personality distribution are values—or modal attitude clusters—but these may show significant intrapopulation variability as frequently as every twenty-five years. Some reasons adduced for this are that older generations die, thus allowing the possibility for a change in overall value orientations; that older generations may not wish to perpetuate certain patterns with their children; and that new generations may have experiences which incline them to reject what older generations may value.[12] In modern times, in many societies, it has been the exception rather than the rule for succes-

[10] Robert A. LeVine, "Culture, Personality, and Socialization: An Evolutionary View," in David A. Goslin, ed., *Handbook of Socialization, Theory and Research*, Rand McNally and Co., Chicago, 1969, p. 510.

[11] *Ibid.*, p. 511.

[12] Kenneth W. Terhune, "From National Character to National Behavior: A Reformulation," *Journal of Conflict Resolution*, vol. 14, no. 2, June 1970, pp. 237–238; and David Easton and Jack Dennis, *Children in the Political System*, McGraw-Hill Book Co., New York, 1969, p. 38. See also Don D. Smith, "Modal Attitude Clusters: A Supplement for the Study of National Character," *Social Forces*, 44, 1966, noted in Terhune, *loc. cit.*, p. 252. As partial proof that cultures may have idiosyncratic qualities Marvin K. Opler has noted how certain types of mental disorder vary among cultures and even within the same culture

sive generations to face similar events, be motivated to achieve a similar set of goals, be presented with the same conditions for social acceptance, and be activated to conformity by similar types of punishment. There is, however, greater likelihood for variability in events and goals than in training practices, which tend to be remarkably conservative. The gestures and phrases used toward children constitute a pattern of influences that is frequently unknown to the users and is highly stable among generations.

Within any given social system it is not necessary that all members have either the same cognitive structure or even the same motives in order to enjoy stable social interaction. Nevertheless, even common-sense observation indicates that members of a social system, be such a unit the family or a national grouping, frequently exhibit idiosyncratic mannerisms peculiar to that particular system. It is quite proper, in fact, to view the group "as a selective, normative environment which exerts pressures in favor of those personality traits which facilitate optimal performance in social roles. Such pressures, operating through socializing agents who influence the developing individual, act to skew the distribution of personality traits in the population toward the socially valued norms for role performance."[13] In this manner, therefore, there is a linkage between personality distribution within a population, prevalent childhood training practices, parental values which legitimize these practices, and the overall value and normative structure of the socio-cultural system as reflected by parents within the family.[14] However, while family or other small-group child-rearing practices may show a similarity related to a common inclusion in a larger socio-cultural system, it is also true that any given family is only partially representative of general norms and values and will only partially reflect what at a higher level of generalization appear to be uniform patterns of child training. In addition, individual traits, sex type, and sibling position all affect the interaction of any individual with the larger social structure and preclude the possibility of uniformity of development and response. We would expect, therefore, to find considerable variability around any

over time. See Marvin K. Opler, *Culture Psychiatry and Human Values*, Charles C. Thomas, Publisher, Springfield, Illinois, 1956, pp. 64–114.

[13] Robert A. LeVine, *Dreams and Deeds: Achievement Motivation in Nigeria*, University of Chicago Press, Chicago, 1966, p. 12.

[14] *Ibid.*, p. 18.

given cluster of traits which at the socio-cultural level appears to characterize a population as a whole.

An individual may hold a number of private values, but a social system has, by one definition, shared values and goal orientations which serve as standards for evaluation of others who are either in or out of the group. During learning, certain expected modes of behavior are acquired which serve as measures of the predictability of another's actual behavior in a given "standard" situation. Furthermore, a person becomes a member of a social structure by learning

> . . . to play a role complementary to those of other members in accord with the pattern of values governing the collectivity. The new member comes to be *like* the others with respect to their common membership status and to the psychological implications of this—above all, the common values thereby internalized. Psychologically, the essential point is that the process of ego development takes place through the learning of social roles in collectivity structures. Through this process, in some sense, the normative patterns of the collectivity in which a person learns to interact become part of his own personality and define *its* organization.[15]

Although one frequently hears of the social structure as determined by the socialization of its members or of the socialization process as a function of the necessities of the social structure, there is, in fact, a complementarity between these positions. To the extent that the individual acquires the normative patterns associated with social roles held by older members of the collectivity his socialization will be a response to the social structure, but to the extent that his learning is not related to specific roles or has idiosyncratic qualities then the future social structure will be derivative of the socialization process.

Social scientists have had considerable difficulty in using psychological explanations in sociological studies. A one-to-one relationship between the individual and social levels has so far been unsubstantiated, although there has been fruitful use of psychological explanations as suggestive shorthand expressions for social phenomena. As Greenstein has so aptly pointed out, reductionism is the usual criticism against the

---

[15] Talcott Parsons, "Social Structure and the Development of Personality: Freud's Contribution to the Integration of Psychology and Sociology," in Neil J. Smelser and William T. Smelser, eds., *Personality and Social Systems*, John Wiley and Sons, New York, 1963, p. 42. Italics in original. (Originally published in *Psychiatry*, vol. 21, 1958, pp. 321–340.)

use of psychological studies of character to explain social events.[16] Yet the difficulty lies in our capacity to conceptualize rather than in any intrinsic lack of complementarity between individual idiosyncratic factors and the forces of the social structure in which the individual lives. In the attempt to relate individual behavior to societal phenomena, various notions have been advanced, ranging from biological determinism (as, for instance, that the possession of a double male chromosome predisposes certain males to aggressive activity), to the influence of instinctual, nonrational forces (the id and superego), to free will and cognitive steering, and finally to the individual as a respondent to external stimuli.[17] Except for the two cases at either end of the spectrum, some psychological data is often deemed necessary to explain or predict behavior. Whether one is engaged in typological study, in aggregate analysis, or in single case study, social and psychological characteristics are not mutually exclusive but are complementary, in that the individual's psychological predispositions are to some extent related to the socialization experience in which the individual has learned to relate to the social environment in approved ways.[18]

Part of the difficulty in using psychological concepts arises from an undifferentiated use of psychological terms and concepts. It has been suggested that for studies of aggregate behavior it is wise to distinguish between core personality, which refers to properties such as needs and defense mechanisms, and social personality, which refers to beliefs, attitudes, and values.[19] This type of dual conceptualization allows the analyst to use personality-related concepts for populations as a whole while remaining cognizant of the linkage between these aggregated personality characteristics and the multitude of core personalities from which they derive.

Many experiments which "prove" social psychological points take place in highly contrived situations which are often unrelated to anything that the subjects do or perceive themselves as actually doing under normal conditions.[20] Real-life situations can vary from those with a

[16] Fred I. Greenstein, *Personality and Politics: Problems of Evidence, Inference, and Conceptualization*, Markham Publishing Co., Chicago, 1969, p. 19.

[17] Jonas Langer, *Theories of Development*, Holt, Rinehart, and Winston, New York, 1969.

[18] Greenstein, *op. cit.*, pp. 16–17.

[19] Terhune, *op. cit.*, p. 208.

[20] David Marlowe and Kenneth J. Gergen, "Personality and Social Interaction," in

complex set of interacting variables to single-life experiences where some factor such as death, insight, or tragedy overpowers other influences and deeply affects the individual's later development. Scholars working in the area of socialization who are analyzing situations where high degrees of control are impractical attempt to impose some measure of order on their data through various conceptual and methodological schemes.

Childhood is often segregated in the study of socialization because previous work has indicated the preeminence of learning during this period. Attitudes, values, and behavior related to political learning are established by twelve to fourteen years of age and closely correspond to those held by adults. Contrary to much popular belief, high school is not a period of great learning in these areas (with the exception of the development of cynicism) but is rather a period of transition.[21] These and other findings emphasize the importance of segregating childhood as a field of inquiry. They underline the importance for behavioral studies of acquiring an insight into the content and process of early learning.

Political socialization, as a subcategory of more general studies of socialization, deals specifically with those attitudinal and behavioral characteristics of individuals which relate to situations where hierarchy and authority are to some degree present. In this general form, "political" refers to authority situations as they may occur in any of the many group contexts in which an individual lives. We use this definition rather than one more narrowly related to politics per se because our own conception of political socialization is that attitudinal dispositions and behavior patterns specifically relevant to politics cannot be understood without reference to and grounding in an understanding of authority situations which are not specifically relevant to politics in context. It is our contention that much work in political socialization has been both

Gardner Lindzey and Elliot Aronson, eds., *The Handbook of Social Psychology*, 2nd ed., vol. 3, Addison-Wesley Publishing Co., Reading, Mass., 1969, p. 607.

[21] M. Kent Jennings and Richard G. Niemi, "Patterns of Political Learning," in Edward C. Dreyer and Walter A. Rosenbaum, eds., *Political Opinion and Behavior: Essays and Studies*, 2nd ed., Wadsworth Publishing Co., Belmont, Ca., 1970, pp. 140, 156–157. Also Elisabeth Ruch Dubin and Robert Dubin, "The Authority Inception Period in Socialization," *Child Development*, vol. 34, no. 4, Dec. 1963; Robert D. Hess and David Easton, "The Child's Changing Image of the President," *Public Opinion Quarterly*, vol. 24, 1960, pp. 237–238; Fred I. Greenstein, *Children and Politics*, Yale University Press, New Haven, 1965, p. 56; and Robert D. Hess and Judith V. Torney, *The Development of Political Attitudes in Children*, Aldine Publishing Co., Chicago, 1967, pp. 23–26.

too narrowly defined and focused at too high a level of generalization. The results from these studies have been interesting and informative but too often appear truncated and lacking in explanation of how political attitudes and behavior patterns relate to the total complexity of a person's attitudinal and behavioral characteristics.

Political socialization as a field is being increasingly utilized by those who have been impressed with the analytic strength of the notion of "political culture." These scholars see in theories of socialization hypotheses subject to empirical verification and disproof which can explain why changes may occur over time in politically related cognitions, affective orientations, and evaluations. Yet while there has been much broad reference to political *culture*, there has often been a tendency to place greater emphasis on specific political patterns and orientations and to be much less explicit concerning the larger cultural context. Too frequently the division between political socialization as a process whereby authority-related attitudes are acquired and as a process whereby attitudes and behavior relevant to politics are acquired is not clearly made.[22]

Recently there has been an increasing effort to deal with aspects of political socialization which are not specifically "political" in content. At one level of generalization this has led some observers to look at the preparatory or anticipatory aspects of induction into a social system, wherein certain values, attitudes, and role performance characteristics relating to authority situations are acquired in anticipation of later application.[23] At another level, learning related to authority situations has been conceptualized as *direct* (learning political symbols, institutions, etc.) and *indirect* (where political learning derives from nonpolitical relationships, activities, and beliefs).[24] In this framework much political learning is seen as unorganized, varied, nondeliberate, and decentralized, precisely because much socialization concerning authority relationships takes place in highly personalized primary relationships such as in the family and in peer groups. Strictly political relationships, on the other hand, are perceived as being largely secondary, involving less total, personalized commitment but more structure. The dissimi-

[22] William R. Schonfeld, "The Focus of Political Socialization Research," *World Politics*, vol. 23, no. 3, April 1971, p. 551.

[23] Hess and Torney, *op. cit.*, pp. 6–7.

[24] Richard E. Dawson and Kenneth Prewitt, *Political Socialization*, Little, Brown and Co., Boston, 1969, pp. 67–73.

larity between direct and indirect political learning helps explain some of the discontinuities of political socialization.[25] At another and more abstract level of generalization, scholars have begun to conceptualize on how to connect psychological antecedents to politically-related attitudes and behavior. Terhune has discussed how the cognitive structure of authority figures—universalistic (doctrine and dogma) versus case-particularistic—may affect decision-making.[26] Merelman has described how work by Jean Piaget and others on the stages of moral development in children may lead to a better understanding of the political ideologies of various social systems.[27] The interaction of the psychological and situational determinants of political behavior has been examined by Greenstein. He has determined that concern must be given to both factors, although in any given circumstance one may provide a more appropriate explanation than the other.[28] In these and other instances, an increasing attempt is being made to define and order the complex variables involved in socialization in general and political socialization in particular.

To understand the attitudes and behavior patterns of people in authority situations is a goal toward which, as yet, only limited achievements have been made. The deficiencies are largely related to the youthfulness and complexity of the field. There has, for instance, been little emphasis on comparative political socialization.[29] The studies which have been conducted have been almost totally concerned with single social units at either the national or subnational levels. Moreover, the emphasis in these studies has been largely on the formal, explicit aspects of political socialization—attitudes toward the President or policeman or the learning of political roles. And finally, as we have already noted, there has been a persistent difficulty in integrating sociological and psychological variables. This problem is manifested in our continuing

[25] *Ibid.*, pp. 100–101.

[26] Terhune, *op. cit.*, p. 249.

[27] Richard M. Merelman, "The Development of Political Ideology: A Framework for the Analysis of Political Socialization," *American Political Science Review*, vol. 63, no. 3, Sept. 1969, pp. 750–767.

[28] Greenstein, *Personality and Politics*, p. 143. See his diagram on p. 63, adapted from M. Brewster Smith, "A Map for the Analysis of Personality and Politics," *Journal of Social Issues*, vol. 24, no. 3, 1968, p. 25.

[29] The most notable exception to this general condition is the pioneering work by Gabriel A. Almond and Sidney Verba, *The Civic Culture: Political Attitudes and Democracy in Five Nations*, Little, Brown and Co., Boston, 1965.

inability to state in a strict causal way that the personality characteristics of individual members of social systems define and delimit aggregate states of political attitudes and behavior. We have instead suggestive leads and more or less probable statements which are as yet largely unverified in a rigorous way.[30]

In the following pages, we shall attempt a comparative study concerning internalization of values. This analysis will encompass aspects of political socialization that relate directly to the "political;" our major emphasis, however, will be directed toward *authority-related* attitude and behavioral stances. This focus has been selected because it is our belief that only with a thorough understanding of this aspect of socialization can we adequately begin to comprehend what motivates people in specifically political contexts. An attempt will also be made to suggest how certain psychological variables relate to the ways in which people learn to behave and feel in authority situations and to examine how such behavior and feelings affect social stability and the legitimacy of authority in social systems.

In the chapters that follow we shall approach socialization in a somewhat different manner from what has usually been done. Initially we shall discuss a particular psychological variable, shame, which appears to be an important factor in the motivation and inhibition of behavior, especially in the learning of moral codes that serve as guidelines and prompters for specific actions. Secondly, we shall briefly examine the learning process of Chinese and American children in order to assess how situational factors may influence behavior. We shall attempt to ascertain how certain behavioral dispositions may be heightened or muted by the interaction of both psychological and situational factors. On the basis of this analysis, we shall present data showing how attitudes regarding behavior may be differentially internalized on the bases both of age and of development in a distinctive learning environment. Finally we will discuss how and why internalized attitudes concerning behavior vary in intensity depending on the particular type of behavior and the social context.

Clearly what will be presented here is only an approach to the subject and by no means solves the limitations which still confront those who engage in socialization studies. The complexity of variables, the lack of precision in testing devices, and the difficulty of uncovering

[30] Greenstein, *Personality and Politics*, pp. 120–128.

crucial linking points still limit us to only gross descriptions. But to paraphrase Goffman, it is better to begin even in a speculative way with regard to this fundamental area of knowledge than to continue a rigorous blindness toward it.[31]

[31] Erving Goffman, *Behavior in Public Places*, The Free Press, New York, 1963, p. 4.

CHAPTER 2 Shame

In the study of socialization, major emphasis is placed upon understanding the influence of the environment upon the behavior of the organism. Behavior is perceived to be a dependent variable with respect to environmental influence. It is the task of the analyst to determine what sets of positive reinforcers and aversive stimuli from the environment lead to particular behavioral outputs. Furthermore one must determine which outputs become stable for a population (aspects of culture) beyond the lifetime of any individual and how these sets of outputs are institutionalized as role performance in a social structure, in addition to the relative rankings of goodness or badness (values) that are attached to various behavioral forms.

In a strict sense, what are often termed "inner" psychological forces in socialization can be viewed as by-products of external influence rather than as causes for what we observe. That these forces are so frequently spoken of in a causal sense is attributable to the complexity of the relationships and to imperfections in our present knowledge.[1] As we develop a better knowledge of socialization, these "inner" forces become less adequate as explanations. They do maintain an enormous utility, however, as concepts which describe the feelings and experience which a person has acquired in interaction with environmental influences and

[1] B. F. Skinner, "Beyond Freedom and Dignity," *Psychology Today*, vol. 5, no. 3, August 1971, pp. 37–40, 59, 63. (Since published by Knopf, New York, 1971.)

the as yet imperfectly understood ways in which a person's innate drives (hunger, sex, sleep, etc.) and experience mediate with any given unit or set of external stimuli. We can therefore look at concepts such as guilt or shame as labels for feelings related to certain stimuli and to certain behavioral outputs. Until we are more knowledgeable concerning socialization, there may also remain a tendency to conceive of such factors as autonomous determinants of behavior. They are apt to maintain this characteristic as long as our understanding of observable cause-and-effect phenomena is imperfect, that is, as long as we go beyond controlled laboratory research into realms where the operational definitions of the variables involved cannot be rigorously set forth. Finally, this imperfection will persist as long as we remain ignorant of the ways in which particular sets of feeling and experience become attributes of any given individual and statistically significant aspects of populations.

For our purposes we will place emphasis on the primary importance of the influence of external stimuli but will also rely on certain conceptions of "inner forces" as convenient concepts at our present stage of development for understanding the ways in which individuals mediate with their environment. In discussing our conceptual framework we do not intend in this work to set forth a full explication of personality—such an explication can be more adequately found in a voluminous literature specifically pertaining to the subject—but rather to discuss as sparingly as possible those personality attributes which we feel pertain to the particular aspects of socialization studied here.

Cultural studies are full of attempts to use shame as an analytical tool. While shame has been generally recognized as common to the socialization process in all societies, some scholars have postulated that certain social systems could be identified through a presumably special shame characteristic. That this categorization also tended to delineate Western from non-Western and developed from developing societies was, no doubt, not the least of its attractions. Although lately quiescent, these studies did stimulate considerable debate concerning the utility of using shame—and guilt—as criteria for classifying the attitudinal and behavioral complexes of social systems.

Perhaps nowhere has the use of shame been more prevalent than in the study of Oriental societies. For this reason, then, and because we feel that shame as a concept has a certain usefulness, it is pertinent here to review briefly some of the ways in which this concept has been handled. We shall then develop some further thoughts concerning shame and its place in the socialization process.

It is one thing to perceive instances of the operation of shame within the socialization process of a given social system, but quite another to differentiate or measure social systems solely by such criteria. In the broadest and crudest characterizations shame-oriented societies are usually held to be many in number, to be generally static and industrially backward, and to have a prevalence of "external" sanctions. Guilt-oriented societies, on the other hand, are supposedly characterized by "internal" sanctions and are few in number and progressive in nature. However, not only are such facile descriptions questionable but in fact societies are never without some admixture of shame and guilt. The whole problem is heightened by differences in language meanings and moral codes and in the theoretical criteria used by scholars, and by the limitations of testing devices.[2]

Ruth Benedict, in *The Chrysanthemum and the Sword*, was among the first to attempt a systematic exploration of one East Asian society, Japan, in terms of shame and guilt criteria.[3] Her study was extraordinarily provocative and served the very useful function of underlining the possibilities of this form of analysis. Her characterization of Japan as a shame culture was based on a model whereby certain individuals (the father, emperor, etc.) utilize shaming sanctions to obtain approved behavior from subordinates. In her analysis external stimuli are critical, for, as she says, "shame cultures rely on external sanctions for good behavior, not, as true guilt cultures do, on an internalized conviction of sin."[4] For a person to "know no shame" is equivalent to saying that he has no decency, and a person may be aroused to aggression if it is felt that some insult or detraction has been tendered. On the other hand, sincerity, an utter devotion to codes of conduct, is considered to be one of the highest virtues.[5]

[2] Gerhard Piers and Milton B. Singer, *Shame and Guilt*, Charles G. Thomas, Publisher, Springfield, Illinois, 1953, pp. 65–66.

[3] Ruth Benedict, *The Chrysanthemum and the Sword*, Houghton Mifflin Co., New York, 1946.

[4] *Ibid.*, p. 223.

[5] *Ibid.*, pp. 270, 293. See also Douglas G. Haring, "Aspects of Personal Character in Japan," in Douglas G. Haring, ed., *Personal Character and Cultural Milieu*, Syracuse University Press, Syracuse, N.Y., 1956, pp. 419, 427.

Wolfram Eberhard, in *Guilt and Sin in Traditional China*, has utilized a concept of shame similar to Ruth Benedict's. According to him, "A shame society, by definition, is based upon a system of exclusively social values,"[6] and shame is experienced when "social obligations or rules, even simple formal rules of manners, are violated."[7] Eberhard feels, perhaps rightly, that shame has been overstressed in the analysis of Chinese society, although he admits there is "meager information" on the subject. Toward the end of his analysis he makes the statement that for the traditional elite, at least, well steeped in Confucianism, shame "was a moral concept and was internalized, together with the precepts of the code of social behavior. In essence, then, shame and guilt operate in the same way."[8] Nowhere else, however, does Eberhard speak of shame and guilt in this manner, and the comment seems as though it were appended in perplexity about behavior which exhibits shame characteristics but which seems related primarily to internalized sanctions.

The main body of Eberhard's analysis attempts to prove a guilt versus shame orientation in traditional Chinese society. Sin, he says, is expressed by the same term in Chinese as guilt, and sin is defined as "actions, behavior and thoughts that violated rules set up by supernatural powers."[9] Guilt for the average traditional Chinese was based on the rules embodied in popularized Buddhism and folk Taoism and arose from the transgression (a sin) of some specific supernatural code. The guilt orientation which Eberhard finds is related to his belief that internal sanctions are extremely important in Chinese society. This assumption of course, follows directly from the belief that shame is operative only when the presence of external sanctions can be verified.[10]

Against the view—derived from an emphasis on the importance of religion in Chinese life—that guilt rather than shame existed in traditional Chinese culture is the opinion expressed by F. W. Mote that in

[6] Wolfram Eberhard, *Guilt and Sin in Traditional China*, University of California Press, Berkeley and Los Angeles, 1967, p. 121.

[7] *Ibid.*, p. 123.

[8] *Ibid.*, p. 124.

[9] *Ibid.*, pp. 12–14.

[10] It is, perhaps, interesting to note that in one of the hells—the shaving prison—whose punishments are presumably internalized ". . . the faces are cut off from persons who did not care about honesty and moral cleanliness. . . ." This punishment is strikingly reminiscent of the "loss of face" pertaining to shame rather than guilt. *Ibid.*, p. 33.

the Chinese world view there was no concept of sin as an offense against divine will, but rather "in its place, there existed the much less serious error of human wrongdoing, a deflection of harmony, a source of shame but not of danger to the soul."[11] Even in traditional times a popular fear of the supernatural was always accompanied by an equal fear of losing face before one's ancestors. In any case, in modern times, which are our concern, there has been a spectacular growth of purely social values in both China and the West, values without reference to religious sanction or association with the supernatural.

In studies of modern Chinese society there have been a number of efforts to define shame and to use it as an operational concept.[12] One such analyst, Lucian W. Pye, does not adhere to a model whereby guilt and shame are differentiated on the basis of internal versus external sanctions. For Pye, internalization is compatible with shame: "In the Chinese political culture, shame and humiliation are fundamentally associated with the feeling that the self has been unjustly treated."[13] He does not hesitate to characterize a whole culture as dominated by shame (humiliation), and is quite explicit that the arousal of shame in modern Chinese society is due to a perception of the discrepancy between the actuality of social conditions—particularly during the late nineteenth and early twentieth centuries—and the collective ideal of what China should be.[14] Pye hypothesized that the inability of authority figures, especially fathers, to carry out their respective role functions during this period generated a frustrated hostility which became one of the major forces in modern Chinese politics. This hostility is related to shame over the supposed failure of the parental or more generalized authority figures to approximate the social ideal of what authority should be.

Not all analysts of modern Asian societies concede the field to the shame theorists. Like Eberhard with reference to the traditional

---

[11] F. W. Mote, "Chinese Political Thought," in David S. Sills, ed., *International Encyclopedia of the Social Sciences*, vol. 2, Macmillan Co. and The Free Press, 1968, p. 396.

[12] See Hu Hsien-Chin, "The Chinese Concepts of Face," in Haring, *op. cit.*; also Richard W. Wilson, *Learning to be Chinese: The Political Socialization of Children in Taiwan*, Massachusetts Institute of Technology Press, Cambridge, Mass., 1970.

[13] Lucien W. Pye, "Hostility and Authority in Chinese Politics," *Problems of Communism*, vol. 17, no. 3, May–June 1968, p. 12.

[14] See Lucian W. Pye, *The Spirit of Chinese Politics*, Massachusetts Institute of Technology Press, Cambridge, Mass., 1968.

Chinese, George De Vos has advanced the thesis that guilt has been undervalued as an explanation of aspects of modern Japanese behavior.[15] One of the major problems in analyzing guilt in Japanese society, it is said, is the difficulty in drawing parallels between the absolutes of a family-oriented morality and those associated with a more universalistic moral system. This problem is heightened by the Westerner's predilection for relating guilt to transgressions of sexual codes, a relationship which is presumably attenuated in Japanese society.[16] One of the successes of De Vos's analysis is his delineation of guilt in a society where the underlying social factors are dissimilar from those normally considered essential within the Western context for the generation of guilt. His major contribution, however, is in pointing out the difficulties of strictly differentiating shame and guilt behavior. As he notes:

> When shame and guilt have undergone a process of internalization in a person during the course of his development, both become operative regardless of the relative absence of either external threats of punishment or overt concern with the opinions of others concerning his behavior. Behavior is automatically self-evaluated without the presence of others.[17]

Exclusive emphasis upon either shame or guilt has been strongly criticized by P. M. Yap as detrimental to the study of Oriental societies. He has noted from his work in Hong Kong with Chinese patients that in terms of affective disorder ideas of guilt and unworthiness are extremely rare and mild when expressed and there is no mention of sin at all.[18] Yap, however, is uncertain concerning the general view that Chinese behavior is motivated by little or no guilt, feeling that at best this is a half-truth and that the usual notions of face which are used to describe behavior are of little help. He feels that the opposition of shame to guilt is "intellectualistic, arbitrary, and without empirical justification," and,

[15] George De Vos, "The Relation of Guilt toward Parents to Achievement and Arranged Marriage among the Japanese," *Psychiatry*, vol. 23, no. 3, August 1960. See also Kazuko Tsurumi, *Social Change and the Individual: Japan before and after Defeat in World War II*, Princeton University Press, Princeton, N.J., 1970, p. 148.

[16] De Vos., *op. cit.*, pp. 288, 300.

[17] *Ibid.*, p. 290.

[18] P. M. Yap, "Phenomenology of Affective Disorder in Chinese and Other Cultures," in A. V. S. de Reuck and Ruth Porter, eds., *Transcultural Psychiatry*, Little, Brown and Co., Boston, 1965, p. 93.

further, that it is not the content of moral religious feeling which is important for understanding behavior but rather the social forces operating in early child training that mold self-control responses.[19]

There is some reason to believe that many of the problems of differentiating guilt from shame derive from semantic and conceptual difficulties related to these terms. Clearly the use of shame or guilt as criteria for the study of Asian societies has foundered from lack of uniform conceptualization. Our task, therefore, will be to sketch a coherent model of shame, this being the concept we are primarily concerned with. To begin with, however, we shall make some comments concerning guilt, since shame is so often—and erroneously—conceived to be the antithesis of that concept.

GUILT

Guilt is presumed to be related to a violation of internalized rules and taboos. The regulatory mechanism that acts as the "force" which alerts the individual to a possible or actual violation and which triggers an aversive sensation—guilt—is conceived of as the superego. According to Freud, the superego is not just the internalized qualities of the parents but is everything that has had an effect on an individual, including the tastes and standards of his social class and the characteristics and traditions of the race.[20] Internalization is inferred from the ways in which people behave and from the appearance of guilt anxiety in situations which are described by the individual and/or others as ones of transgression. Guilt occurs either in situations where one has acted inappropriately in terms of identifiable social regulations or where one has failed to be true to some aspect of an internalized code of behavior.

Guilt has been described as painful feelings of "self-blame, self-criticism, or remorse which result from deviation (real or imagined) from

[19] *Ibid.*, pp. 100–101. Also P. M. Yap, "Ideas of Mental Health and Disorder in Hong Kong and Their Practical Influence," in *Some Traditional Chinese Ideas and Conceptions in Hong Kong Social Life Today*, Brochure of the Hong Kong Branch of the Royal Asiatic Society, Hong Kong, 1967, p. 75.

[20] Sigmund Freud, *An Outline of Psychoanalysis*, [first published in 1938] W. W. Norton and Co., New York, 1949, pp. 122, 123, from Erik H. Erikson, *Identity Youth and Crisis*, W. W. Norton and Co., New York, 1968, p. 47.

proper behavior."[21] When experienced it activates a search for self-punishment or attempts at restitution or undoing of the act.[22] There is a corollary assumption that guilt is related to anxieties acquired in childhood, especially in interaction with parents, and that these anxieties gradually become generalized to other individuals and to supernatural forces and taboos. Generally speaking the fear involved in guilt appears at the unconscious level to be one of mutilation (castration). Some analysts have posited a relationship between the development of guilt and early socialization in which the threatened or actual denial of love by parents is an important stimulus for the development of a tendency toward guilt feelings.[23] More recent work supports the notion that the development of guilt is rarely found in studies of young children but is found in a majority of older children, and that love withdrawal as a training technique does not relate to self-critical guilt.[24] Rather, self-critical guilt has been found to relate to parental warmth and induction training. In the induction learning context the parent teaches a child to feel remorse by reasoning with him and pointing out the harm caused to others by his actions. In this way, the child increasingly with age learns to put himself in the place of someone else in an internalized sense even if the other person does not know it.[25]

In its barest form the essence of guilt appears to be a feeling of intense remorse generated by a failure to live up to a more or less articulated set of codes and prompted by a fear of mutilation for transgression. The relationship between guilt feelings and anticipation of external punishment is statistically significant although not at a high level.[26] It is hypothesized that punishment may be perceived as emanating from threatening parents and then, through the mechanism of displacement, from the supernatural. Strong guilt and a consequent strong sense of threat are related to the time of onset of rigorous rule training—the earlier the socialization the stronger the superego—and to the extent and

[21] John W. M. Whiting and Irvin L. Child, *Child Training and Personality: A Cross-Cultural Study*, Yale University Press, New Haven, 1953, p. 219.

[22] *Ibid.*, p. 219.

[23] *Ibid.*, pp. 241–242, 254–255, 258.

[24] Lawrence Kohlberg, "Development of Moral Character and Moral Ideology," in Martin L. Hoffman and Lois W. Hoffman, eds., *Review of Child Development Research*, vol. 1, Russell Sage Foundation, New York, 1964, pp. 411–412.

[25] *Ibid.*, p. 413.

[26] Whiting and Child, *op. cit.*, p. 259.

severity of the shift from indulgence for aggressive behavior to non-permissiveness with a concurrent fixation on the perceived threats involved in the transition period to non-permissiveness.

Although guilt need not be associated with the supernatural, its classic form involves rules based on religious sanction. To the extent that the forces of the supernatural are perceived of as all-seeing and universal —such that punishments apply regardless of the status of the individual —we may expect the internalization of rigid sets of universal codes and taboos regarding feeling and behavior. It is important to point out, however, that to the extent that supernatural power can be bargained with, cajoled, or intimidated we have neither an absolute sense of threat nor a non-deviating code of rules and to that extent we do not have pure guilt but rather an admixture of guilt with other forms of anxiety.

GUILT AND SHAME

The notion of a lack of complementarity between shame and guilt would seem to have its origins in the early definitions given to these concepts. The prevailing criterion for differentiation was felt to be the distinction between external and internal sanctions operating to induce desirable and inhibit undesirable behavior. This assumption has a direct relationship to the differentiation of Freud among fear, shame, and guilt—on the basis of the conditions that cause them—in which conscience anxiety is guilt and shame is social anxiety induced by anticipated ridicule or social criticism.[27] In this type of conceptualization guilt is presumed to be based on violation of internalized values, especially parental values, whereas shame is based on actual or potential criticism or disapproval from other persons.[28] Because of these different bases guilt has been described as inhibiting transgression whereas shame is said to relate to the failure to achieve some goal; shame motivates a person to achievement of some desired end. Helen Lynd has noted that:

[27] Irving L. Janus, George F. Mahl, Jerome Kagan, and Robert R. Holt, *Personality: Dynamics, Development, and Assessment*, Harcourt, Brace and World, New York, 1969, p. 112.

[28] Daniel R. Miller and Guy E. Swanson, *Inner Conflict and Defense*, Henry Holt and Co., New York, 1960, p. 136.

Guilt is centrally a transgression, a crime, the violation of a specific taboo, boundary, or legal code by a definite voluntary act. Through the various shadows of meaning there is the sense of the committing of a specific offense, the state of being justifiably liable to penalty. In the usual definitions there is no self reference as there is in shame.[29]

In shame, on the other hand, there is a definite element of self-consciousness. This has been best described by Erikson, who counterposes shame in the development process to a sense of trust in one's environment. Shame is defined as:

> that sense of having exposed [one] self prematurely and foolishly. . . .
> Shame is an infantile emotion insufficiently studied because in our civilization it is so early and easily absorbed by guilt. Shame supposes that one is completely exposed and conscious of being looked at—in a word, self-conscious.[30]

In terms of learning, shame and guilt have usually been differentiated by varying sets of criteria. It has been posited that one of the ways in which a shame orientation is acquired is by learning sets of "ought not" proscriptions (ought not to make one's mother angry; ought not to bring disgrace to the group), which are obtained from a number of socializing agents who stress punishment by other social agents.[31] The basis of shame anxiety is said to be acquired partly in a process of comparing and competing with peers (siblings, schoolmates, gang members, members of one's social class, etc.) in which conformity with expected social standards is achieved through a process of identification with other group members. This learning process is distinct from that involved in development of a guilt orientation, where socialization is through internalization of parental images and where conformity is achieved through submission, that is, fear of transgression.[32]

There is a tendency in the literature on guilt and shame to define these emotional states according to whether the sanctions to which a person responds originate from within or from others. Shame is said to

---

[29] Helen Merrell Lynd, *On Shame and the Search for Identity*, Science Editions, New York, 1961, p. 23.

[30] Erikson, *op. cit.*, p. 110.

[31] Eberhard, *op. cit.*, p. 2.

[32] Gerhart Piers and Milton B. Singer, *op. cit.*, p. 36.

be "the you in relationship to others" while guilt is hypothesized as "the you in relationship to internalized principles;" shame is presumed to exist where conformity is achieved by orienting behavior and values in accordance with others whereas guilt exists where conformity is to a set of internalized principles or codes of behavior. There is clearly a certain neatness to this conceptualization and, as a first approximation, even some validity. Unfortunately the reality of actual behavior and feeling impels us to go beyond this simple dichotomization; indeed, we are impelled to reject the dichotomy as a false one and to seek a reformulation of the conceptualization which can retain what is valid in existing work while explaining the anomalies we view in empirical data. It has become too apparent that guilt and shame are similar in fundamental ways, that they are not antitheses but rather have different focuses and modes, and that both embody moral evaluation and the placement of the individual in relation to an internalized ideal. A further examination of shame is therefore called for.

SHAME

Shame and guilt both embody a moral obligation to conform and an acceptance of a moral standard. They have traditionally been differentiated on the basis that conscious and unconscious guilt feelings have a greater degree of internalization than shame feelings, that shame is presumed to be related to anticipated discovery by others whereas guilt can be aroused either with no witnesses or through observation by fantasied gods or spirits.[33] Yet even if we accept this definition it is clear that both shame and guilt can be associated with virtually any class of acts. Therefore the fundamental differentiating criterion has been in practice whether an act evokes a sense of transgression by an individual (guilt) or a sense of failure (shame). But transgression must have an observable quality vis-à-vis others, and it is not always clear how much a given transgression has this effect. Shame appears to cover a wider variety of behavior than guilt, since the actions associated with shame do not always have perceivable consequences for others and may thus be conceived of as personal failure rather than transgression. The consequences of a lack of cleanliness, for instance, do not impinge on others

[33] Yap, "Phenomenology of Affective Disorder," from Table VI, p. 101.

in the same way as an act of aggression.[34] However, one may conceive of cases of failure that have the consequence of causing shame to one's family or others as types of transgressions against these others for which one feels guilt.[35] For failure to be thought of as transgression, socialization must emphasize the consequences which one's acts may have for others. In this sense shame and guilt are subtly blended, with moral evaluation a component of both. The result of such blending, however, unless one abolishes a strict dichotomy between guilt and shame, is a lack of clarity as to which set of criteria are operative. Moreover, it has been noted in comparative analyses that

> transgressions for which guilt appears to be the primary reactive affect in our own society, and which are clearly positive acts of commission . . . may be more closely associated with shame in other societies.[36]

Perhaps the most exhaustive work on shame has been done by Silvan Tomkins.[37] For Tomkins guilt is but another form of shame humiliation, a conclusion we support. Shame has a broad variety of meanings, whereas guilt embodies qualities of internalized contempt and is therefore merely an expression for shame that concerns moral matters which have been internalized and are thus distinguishable from other aspects of shame.[38]

Shame socialization is related to many different types of sanctions. These may be delayed, indirect, direct, unintended, etc., with varying levels of intensity. Shame may be experienced when no one else has evoked sanctions—and, again, it may not be felt when someone has. There is a distinct likelihood of feelings of shame being generated whenever another person—particularly a significant other person—is bipolar in display of affect. In this case, both the positive affect and shame are intensified. For instance, in the bipolarity praise–contempt the contempt produces shame due to a continuing need for praise, but

[34] Justin Aronfreed, *Conduct and Conscience: The Socialization of Internalized Control over Behavior*, Academic Press, New York, 1968, p. 253.

[35] *Ibid.*, p. 251.

[36] *Ibid.*, p. 252.

[37] Silvan S. Tomkins, *Affect Imagery Consciousness*, Volume 2: *The Negative Affects*, Springer Publishing Co., New York, 1963. The remarks which follow are largely derived from this work.

[38] *Ibid.*, pp. 138, 151–152.

after the shame is over the wish for praise is likely to increase over its original level. In developing motivation for action toward the attainment of certain goals an authority figure may thus be both lavish in praise and harsh in contempt.[39]

When shame and self-contempt are compounded a person may be induced into trying again and again. If ultimately successful, the individual may learn to tolerate these emotions and harness them toward the attainment of objectives. Certain affects must be used sparingly, however. Too much anger will cause fear or counter-anger rather than shame. Distress must usually not be overwhelming in order to be a source of shame.

Physical punishment and shame are compatible in the discipline of the child, and, indeed, physical punishment is especially likely to be used where the parents' pride is involved and where the child during punishment does not give a sufficient indication of shame. Shame can also be experienced vicariously through the mechanism of identification. This identification may include a wide range of individuals or groups and can be aroused by a multiplicity of situations or actions involving these others.[40]

Shame may be compounded. When one blushes one may be ashamed of being ashamed. Because of the attention called to the reddening of the face self-consciousness and shame are tightly linked. In fact, many affects are socialized by shaming techniques. Thus shame may be experienced in many situations if a particular context activates affects which are associated with shame. The result is an indirect and powerful control of behavior. For instance, if socialization has associated shame with excitement (sexual, etc.), enjoyment, distress, anger, fear, etc., then a person may experience shame when these affects are experienced. Where shame is controlled and bound by negative affects, any attempt by a child to deny, minimize, or escape from shame will result in an experience of distress, anger, or fear. Activation of these feelings whenever there is a wish or action to do something shameful is a powerful inhibitor. The result is a feeling of "impotent, angry, fearful [sic] anguished humiliation rather than [of] shame *per se*."[41]

[39] *Ibid.*, pp. 154–155, 220–222.
[40] *Ibid.*, pp. 219, 224–225, 361, 407.
[41] *Ibid.*, pp. 136, 227, 408. Quotation from p. 408. Italics in original.

For a shame orientation to become truly dominant in a personality, humiliation must develop from the experience of a single situation to a perception of this experience as part of a class of similar situations. From this point it is but a short step to perceiving this class as but one among several classes. For an ultimate shame orientation, reinforcement of shame in terms of duration, intensity, and frequency is also an essential component.[42] For shame to be truly operative in a person or population, therefore, we would expect several socialization experiences which embody shame to be reinforcing in content and style.

In the socialization process shame can be an aspect of both punishment and reward through the relationship to bipolar affects. Shame may be a powerful factor motivating the individual to conform and achieve, and it may be an equally powerful sanction against actual or potential deviance. This point must be especially stressed, as there is a common tendency to view shame purely in its punishment aspects.

The attachment of shame to various affects may greatly complicate a person's emotional expression. Where fear, love, or other types of affect are associated with shame their expression may be inhibited—giving rise to an apparent stoicism or inscrutability. Authority figures may deliberately cause dependency in hierarchical relationships by shaming independence; they may praise certain classes of behavior and show contempt for others in such a way that conformity to set ways of role performance is powerfully buttressed, with the direct effect of maintaining power and authority relationships. In reverse manner, dependency may be shamed and an impetus given to initiative and competitiveness. Expressions of shame may also be used as communication signals intentionally informing others of a person's evaluation of the situation. They may also serve as warnings to ward off hostile reactions. Because expressions of shame do serve a communication function there is no necessary one-to-one relationship between the expression of shame and the actual emotional level experienced by an individual.

Finally, what is the feeling of shame? Tomkins defines it as an inner torment "activated by an incomplete reduction of excitement or joy."[43] It is a sense of nakedness, defeat, alienation, and a lack of dignity or worth. It is different from contempt and disgust, but like these affects it

[42] *Ibid.*, pp. 403, 419–420. Tomkins frequently speaks of shame in a pathological sense. We have utilized shame as a component of the socialization process generally.

[43] *Ibid.*, pp. 98, 118.

involves humiliation.[44] For sociologists it is an embarrassment that occurs when an assumption related to a social situation has been unexpectedly discredited, when rules of "relevance and irrelevance" break down and one talks or moves wrongly and awkwardly as "a dangerous giant."[45]

Shame is the feeling of being small and powerless in relation to others. It is this aspect of shame which makes it such a potent force during socialization and which makes experiences of shame in adulthood so humiliating. The deepest shame is above all the sense of weakness and failure in one's own eyes, a questioning of one's own adequacy and even of the adequacy of the world in which one lives, an experience of unexpected and sudden exposure of one's intimate self in which one's trust in the dependability of oneself and others is destroyed. At times the feeling of revelation of vulnerable aspects of the self may be so shattering as to make the experience almost impossible to communicate. Shame may involve the transgression of a code or taboo (guilt), but it goes beyond mere transgression to include a self-conscious awareness of oneself. As such the sense of shame is one of falling short, and the result is "a wound to one's self-esteem" in which ultimately there is a "feeling of a crumpling or failure of the whole self."[46]

What makes the sense of falling short, of failure, so particularly devastating in some circumstances is the fear of rejection and isolation, which one dreads may result from the inability to perform one's role in the expected way. Others, and especially important others, may cast one away for an inadequate response. The fear of losing others is a "primal, terrifying danger" which is one of the earliest and most powerful anxieties, affecting, as it does, especially in childhood, one's very capacity to exist.[47] In the case of guilt the "unconscious" fears punishment in the form of mutilation for transgressing internalized prohibitions, but in our opinion this fear must be subsumed under the more

[44] *Ibid.*, pp. 118, 261.

[45] Erving Goffman, *Encounters: Two Studies in the Sociology of Interaction*, Bobbs-Merrill Co., Indianapolis, 1961, pp. 80–81; and Edward Gross and Gregory P. Stone, "Embarrassment and the Analysis of Role Requirements," in Gregory P. Stone and Harvey A. Faberman, eds., *Social Psychology Through Symbolic Interaction*, Ginn-Blaisdell, Waltham, Mass., 1970, p. 175.

[46] Lynd, *op. cit.*, pp. 23–24, 27, 31–32, 43, 47, 50, 64–65. Quotations from pp. 23, 52.

[47] Abraham H. Maslow, *Toward a Psychology of Being*, D. Van Nostrand Co., Princeton, N.J., 1962, p. 49.

encompassing and comprehensive dread of abandonment. To be mutilated is to have the larger lose the smaller, as in castration, but the more frightening case is when the larger intentionally leaves the smaller as in abandonment, the actuality of the symbolic fall from grace. In shame one has not lived up to the internalized ideals of parents, teachers, and other respected and loved authority figures, and the unconscious fear is that they will then cut themselves away.

> Behind the feeling of shame stands not the fear of hatred, but the fear of contempt which, on an even deeper level of unconscious, spells fear of abandonment, the death by emotional starvation. The parent who uses as educational tools the frequent exposure of the child's immaturity ("Look how foolish, dumb, clumsy you are!") will be the one to lay the foundation of such fear of contempt. We suspect, however, that the deeper rooted shame anxiety is based on the fear of the parent who walks away "in disgust," and that this anxiety in turn draws its terror from the earlier established and probably ubiquital separation anxiety. . . . On a higher, social and more conscious level of individual development, it is again not fear of active punishment by superiors which is implied in shame anxiety, but social expulsion, like ostracism.[48]

The fear of rejection and abandonment shows itself in many ways. A twelve-year-old American boy in seventh grade said it to me in the following way during an interview:

> If in school a kid is being blamed and other kids see him—or parents or anybody—he'll be afraid of other kids thinking he's queer and then other kids won't want to hang around with him. The kids would be mad at him and reject him.

A nine-year-old third-grade American girl was more descriptive:

> I just think it's bad if you're standing up in front of a class being scolded. It's embarrassing. I just don't like it. I don't know why, I just feel embarrassed. You feel it inside, your stomach hurts. Being hit by a group would be better than being abandoned by them.

[48] Piers and Singer, *op. cit.*, p. 16.

EGO-IDEAL

The formation of identity appears to arise from a series of related judgments, one wherein the individual sees himself in a way in which he believes others judge themselves and him and another wherein he assesses the way in which he feels he is being judged in the light of his own self-perception and in comparison both with those who judge him and with other role models. The process is largely unconscious and involves both the core of the self and the groups of which one is a member.[49] Identity arises from acting out various roles so that a person learns to "place himself" in social situations. A notion of self is very early established in relation both to parents and to other authority figures and also in relation to groups of which one is a member. To a greater or lesser extent this identity comes to be felt as uniquely idiosyncratic; some components are felt to be unshared with others even though the number of such components in some situations may be very small.

Judgments of the self in identity formation require some capacity for self-criticism, for being able to say one is wrong. The ability to do this depends on having learned from others values and attitudes attached to categories of behavior, thought, and feeling.

Self-criticism is a developed capacity in which evaluations which initially come from others are used eventually by the self to correct and modify behavior in accordance with what comes to be an esteemed ideal model. It is this capacity which makes self-esteem an aspect of almost all activity, and it is the knowledge that others evaluate by the same or a similar set of criteria which makes failures perceived by others a source of shame. Once these evaluative criteria have been internalized the same feeling of failure can be aroused even when the transgression has not been witnessed. In the latter case shame anxiety may be aroused both in situations wherein one perceives an actual discrepancy between one's expectations and one's performance and in those situations, particularly those which are unstructured and uncontrolled, wherein an inconsistency is possible despite one's best efforts.

Self-esteem is associated with the idealized aspects of one's identity. These aspects of the personality may become a relatively conscious set of ideals. The process of acquiring this set is largely unconscious, how-

[49] Erikson, *op. cit.*, pp. 22–23.

ever, since an ideal self is a composite of a number of attributes, which are not all incorporated at the same time or to the same relative degree. Among other characteristics, an ideal image will encompass content (as intelligent or kind), intensity (strength of the image), importance, salience (how often the image or aspects of the image are in the conscious), consistency (degree of contradiction), stability (whether the image is shifting or stable), and clarity (whether it is hazy or unambiguous).[50]

In psychoanalytic terms the notion of an idealized self has not been an easy concept to label or define. Freud, in the *New Introductory Lectures* (1933), described the principal aspects of the superego and gave each a name. The name for the positive standard against which the conscience measures the ego, the ideal of capability, knowledge, and morality, was "ego-ideal," a term first used in the 1914 paper "On Narcissism."[51] In more recent times the ego-ideal has been defined as "a set of to-be-striven-for but forever not-quite-attainable ideal goals for the Self."[52] The ego-ideal is an internalized standard which in our terms is composed of ideal self-images and may also include internalized rules and taboos.

To fail to meet the standards of the ego-ideal will cause shame anxiety, and the intensity of this shame will be directly related to the strength of the ego-ideal. This anxiety will be experienced as a failure to live up to the ego-ideal. Although it does not follow that there will be an automatic shift in behavior following an experience of shame, there is a usual presumption that such an experience will be followed by increased efforts toward conformity with the ego-ideal.

In interaction with the social environment individuals frequently test themselves in certain situations, both to determine the actual nature of the environment and to assess the acceptability of one's thought and behavior with regard to others and with regard to the self. There is thus a certain tension between reality as it is perceived and ideal conceptions

[50] Adapted from Morris Rosenberg, *Society and the Adolescent Self-Image*, Princeton University Press, Princeton, N.J., 1965, pp. 6–7.

[51] Roger Brown, *Social Psychology*, The Free Press, New York, 1965, p. 376.

[52] Erikson, *op. cit.*, p. 211. Erikson differentiates the ego-ideal from the ego-identity—the "actually attained but forever-to-be-revised sense of the reality of the self within social reality"—and the body-self, which he describes as the ideas, images, and configurations provided by the experience of one's body that serve as a persistent comparison with an ideal self.

of the self within this reality. This tension may at times relate only to some particular aspect of the self, as, say, to content or saliency, and at other times may relate to a whole cluster of ideals. Shame arises from an awareness of having done something unworthy in terms of one's ego-ideal; since this ego-ideal is essentially the product of a long period of interaction with others, shame may also occur (but need not) when one senses that some aspect of the self has incurred the contempt of others. In either case an awareness of self is central, although in the second example the feelings or actions of others may play a part.[53] It is for this reason that one cannot speak of shame as solely related to external sanctions.

While shame is primarily related to the self, to a measurement of the reality of one's self against an ideal, this ideal goes beyond a core of narcissistic omnipotence to embrace learned attitudes of the social groups of which one is a member. These attitudes both are incorporated into the ego-ideal and serve as an external standard against which behavior can be measured. In the truest sense, then, other family members, peers, etc., as well as other models in the socialization process, such as legendary heroes or sages, come to constitute a reference group. Besides the idealized images which one has for oneself it is, therefore, quite appropriate to speak of ideals held in common by a family or larger social unit; the individual's sense of identity thus comes to be more or less associated with his membership in particular groups. An individual can thus feel shame if another individual or group with whom he is associated commits actions which fail to live up to an expected ideal.

The ego-ideal is a composite of the positive identities which a person would like to acquire and manifest. These positive identities are always counterposed with negative identities. Part of the task of socialization agents is to develop in a conscious way an awareness of the attributes of a positive identity and to inculcate disapprobation toward aspects of a negative identity when found in oneself or others. Not all failure, of course, is of an extreme nature, and both individuals and groups have reasonably well-articulated gradations of response to levels of behavior, in oneself or others, that manifest some aspect of a negative identity. Neither individuals nor groups react in the same way to cases of simple embarrassment as they would in a situation of utter mortification. In the

53 Lynd, *op. cit.*, pp. 23–24.

latter case an individual's response may be one of extreme self-hate or contempt and a group's response toward an erring individual or group might be ostracism or extreme hostility. Whatever the level of reaction, and in most social situations it is not of the extreme form, there is an aversive response toward negative identity elements and a positive reinforcement of positive attributes of the ego-ideal. In learning, there-fore, through repeated evaluation, one slowly acquires interlocking conceptions of right and wrong, a set of more or less well-articulated and more or less well-internalized moral standards with regard to categories of behavior, thought, and feeling. When the behavior of the self is identified with that of a contemptuous other or a generalized con-temptuous other a critical transformation will occur. The remembered contemptuous other and the remembered contemptuous self are merged as a negative element and reinforce the development of an internalized judicial system enforced by both the self and the other.[54] Finally, as Tomkins notes, "Eventually, both the self and the other may be re-placed by a generalized other and finally by a completely impersonal norm."[55]

MORAL DEVELOPMENT

The anxiety of shame is not generated unless the positive norms and values associated with the ego-ideal have been transgressed or insuffi-ciently invoked in the control of behavior. When shame is avoided and behavior is in accordance with internalized cultural rules we say that behavior is "moral" and that the individual is acting according to "conscience." Involved in the development of an internalized moral orientation are habits of self-evaluation which, we have tried to point out, are aspects of behavior having to do with shaming socialization.

The notion of moral orientation that we imply has no relationship to any one institutionalized ideological definition, but is simply the sets of norms and values which are learned during socialization and have positive value in a given cultural context. We would expect, therefore, that moral orientation would vary in direction and intensity among populations (in an aggregate sense) as well as among individuals.

[54] Tomkins, *op. cit.*, p. 256.
[55] *Ibid.*, p. 256.

Values as standards of desirability are attached to a number of behavioral modes, not all of which are complementary. There are work values, achievement values, sex values, survival values, etc., and these may vary in intensity according to physiological state and environmental conditions. Individuals may violate values at one level of generalization in order to conform to a value orientation at another level of generalization. The moral evaluation of behavior by others and the degree of shame anxiety experienced by the evaluated individual will depend upon the relative ranking of the value judgment.

Levels of morality have usually been divided according to an "internal–external" orientation, a pattern which we have also noted in traditional shame and guilt studies. Conscience, for instance, has been defined as progressing from the most primitive stage—a collection of crude don'ts—to rule conformity, where authority resides in others; to an organized body of internalized moral rules; to the highest stage, consisting of internalized moral principles accessible to rational questioning and testing.[56] The higher stages of morality are presumed to imply reasoning and interpretation of rules in conflict situations rather than just a knowledge of and rigid belief in such rules.[57]

The notion of stages of moral development derives from hypotheses concerning differences in levels and rates of internalization and from observations concerning presumably subsequent and related differences in the style and intensity of adherence to norms and values. These theoretical and empirical statements are then correlated with known physiological and cognitive changes, involving development of a capacity for conceptual differentiation and hierarchic integration, which occur during maturation.[58] It is an assumption occasionally advanced that the later stages of moral development may not develop or may be restricted in development in certain social systems which do not provide the appropriate and requisite training. In any case the later stages are often difficult to differentiate, being as they are an amalgam, to some extent, of the characteristics of preceding steps. Moral learning is specific rather than generalized (one does not begin by learning some inclusive moral code but rather by learning the values associated with discrete

[56] Robert F. Peck with Robert J. Havighurst, *The Psychology of Character Development*, John Wiley and Sons, (Science Editions), New York, 1960, pp. 170–171.

[57] Kohlberg, *op. cit.*, p. 394.

[58] Elizabeth Hall, "A Conversation with Jean Piaget and Bärbel Inhelder," *Psychology Today*, vol. 3, no. 12, March 1970, p. 26.

acts) and proceeds in terms of the development of evaluative capacity, appropriate role behavior, and knowledge. There is no invariant pattern of development which characterizes the acquisition of these three dimensions, however. We cannot, therefore, speak of a universal and inclusive process of moral development applicable in all particulars to every individual or every social system.

Despite the fact that an invariant sequence of development cannot be posited, a broad categorization of moral growth has been set forth by a number of scholars. Peck and Havighurst speak of amoral and expedient character types during infancy and early childhood, of conformist and irrational-conscientious types during later childhood, and finally of the development of a rational-altruistic type during adolescence and into adulthood.[59] Such models are usually related, in one form or another, to the typologies of moral development developed by Jean Piaget and his disciples over the last four decades. Piaget conceptualized that two overarching moral stages could be used to organize a theory of moral development. In the first stage, that of "egocentrism," the child considers his own point of view as the only possible one but conceives of his parents as all-knowing, perfect, and sacred and of the rules emanating from these authority figures as demanding unquestioning respect and obedience. The child is unaware that others have a point of view, and rules are interpreted literally in terms of oneself. In Piaget's own words:

> . . . the child has no idea of his own ego [relative to others]; external constraint works upon him and he distorts its influence in terms of his subjectivity, but he does not distinguish the part played by his subjectivity from that played by the environmental pressure. Rules therefore seem to him external and of transcendental origin. . . .[60]

This unquestioning respect for external authority, known as the stage of heteronomy, is replaced by a stage of autonomy at about eight to ten years of age, when a concern for reciprocity and equality begin to develop. The morality which develops during this latter stage is based on

[59] Peck with Havighurst, *op. cit.*, p. 3. See also Robert E. Lane, *Political Thinking and Consciousness: The Private Life of the Political Mind*, Markham Publishing Co., Chicago, 1969, p. 197.

[60] Jean Piaget with the Assistance of Seven Collaborators, *The Moral Judgment of the Child*, trans. Marjorie Gabain, Collier, New York, 1962, p. 95.

cooperation. Piaget hypothesized that increasing intellectual growth and experience with roles combine with increasing interaction with peers to change moral orientation from one based exclusively on external authority as the source of law (rules) to one based on internalized principles subject to reciprocity.[61]

Rather unfortunately for comparative analysis, some of the features of Piaget's theory of moral development have been considered as applicable to large-scale social units. The distinction assumed is that there is a greater development of "moral character" in civilized societies than in primitive ones. Piaget himself hypothesized that the type of constraint imposed on individuals in the western world was a form of "cooperative solidarity" whereas it would remain a "compulsory conformity" in primitive communities.[62] A child in western society was presumed to free himself more and more from adult authority, whereas "in the lower grades of civilization" puberty supposedly marked the beginning of increasing subjection to elders and to tradition.[63]

In the years since Piaget's theories were first put forth, research has not supported many of his initial assumptions. Peer-group participation, for instance, has not been found to be associated with intentionality and reciprocity.[64] It has not been proven that there is a trend from obedience-serving acts to need-serving acts, nor have findings supported the hypothesis of a general trend from an authoritarian to a democratic ethic. There is some support, however, for the notion of an orientation in early childhood to obedience, punishment, and impersonal forces and subsequent development toward more internalized and subjective values.[65]

Perhaps the most intensive work at the present time on stage theories of moral development is being carried out by Lawrence Kohlberg. Piaget's stages have been elaborated into a series of six-step progressions, and an attempt has been made to test empirically the

[61] Kohlberg, *op. cit.*, pp. 394–396.

[62] Piaget, *op. cit.*, pp. 346–347.

[63] *Ibid.*, pp. 250–251.

[64] Eleanor E. Maccoby, "The Development of Moral Values and Behavior in Childhood," in John A. Clausen, ed., *Socialization and Society*, Little, Brown and Co., Boston, 1968, pp. 234–235. Kohlberg is cited as the authority for this assertion.

[65] Kohlberg, *op. cit.*, p. 399 and Kohlberg, "Development of Children's Orientations toward a Moral Order," in Richard C. Sprinthall and Norman A. Sprinthall, eds., *Educational Psychology*, Van Nostrand–Reinhold, New York, 1969, p. 76.

validity of the steps themselves and the accuracy of the development thesis.[66] Briefly stated, these six steps are as follows:

LEVEL I   PRE-MORAL LEVEL.

Value resides in external quasi-physical happenings, in bad acts, or in quasi-physical needs rather than in persons and standards.

Type 1   Obedience and punishment orientation.
Egocentric deference to superior power or prestige. Motivational aspect: punishment by another.

Type 2   Naively egoistic orientation.
Right action is that instrumentally satisfying the self's needs and occasionally others'. Motivational aspect: manipulation of goods; rewards by another.

LEVEL II   MORALITY OF CONVENTIONAL ROLE-CONFORMITY.

Moral value resides in maintaining conventional order and the expectancies of others.

Type 3   "Good boy" orientation.
Orientation to approval and to pleasing and helping others. Motivational aspect: disapproval by others.

Type 4   Authority- and social order-maintaining orientation.
Orientation to "doing duty" and to showing respect for authority and maintaining the given social order for its own sake. Motivational aspects: censure by legitimate authorities followed by guilt feelings.

LEVEL III   MORALITY OF SELF-ACCEPTED MORAL PRINCIPLES.

Moral value resides in conformity by the self to shared or sharable standards, rights, or duties.

Type 5   Contractual legalistic orientation.
Recognition of an arbitrary starting point of rules or expectations for the sake of agreement. Motivational aspect: community respect and disrespect.

Type 6   Conscience or principle orientation.
Orientation not only to actually ordained social rules but also to prin-

[66] The data that follows is derived from Kohlberg, "Development of Children's Orientations," pp. 76–87.

ciples of choice involving appeals to logical universality and consistency. Motivational aspect: self-condemnation.

While we recognize the achievement involved in the development of this scheme, we need not accept in an absolute sense the validity of each of these categories. There is a certain lack of clarity in differentiating the various types and in some cases an arbitrary conceptualization at a given level. It is also difficult to accept completely Kohlberg's assertions that the higher levels replace or inhibit lower levels rather than being additions to them, and that the attainment to each new level involves a reorganization of thought processes.[67] This is, in our opinion, an overly internalized notion of development. We may also seriously question whether self-condemnation as a motivational aspect is operative solely at the type 6 level as is asserted. While it may be predominant in type 6 it is certainly a major factor even in type 4. There is also in Kohlberg the same effort we have noted elsewhere to ascribe motivational influences to either internal or external forces, with a bias toward the former as a higher stage of development. Contrary to these assumptions, our concept of shame implies a complementarity of such forces and the impossibility, except under very special conditions, of a normal life experience dominated solely by one pole or the other. In fact, our notion of shame as it functions in the socialization process leads us to support generally a theory of a moral continuum but to reject Kohlberg's type 6 as an attainable social reality in terms of a population as a whole. Rather we would see some *amalgam* of types 3, 4, and 5 as the more probable social reality in modern societies, with type 3 indicating the importance for behavior of the approval of others and type 5 the importance of internalized norms. Which type is predominant in a given social context will depend upon the circumstances and especially on the degree of social participation involved and the values which are operative at that time.

Tests of Kohlberg's stage theory with a predominantly male sample aged ten, thirteen, and sixteen showed that the first two types decreased in salience with age, types three and four increased in salience until age thirteen and then stabilized and types five and six increased with age until age sixteen.[68] Cross-cultural analysis of Kohlberg's stages generally

---

[67] *Ibid.*, p. 83.
[68] *Ibid.*, p. 77. Most children know the basic moral rules and conventions of society by

shows a universality of sequence. Either type three or type four or both tend to be highly important by age sixteen in all societies, although the percentage distribution of other types varies rather markedly.[69] The major difference is the relatively greater salience of type five with age for U.S. samples and its rather minimal salience in four other social systems (Mexico, Taiwan, Turkey, Yucatan). When children ages ten, thirteen, and sixteen on Taiwan are compared with a comparable U.S. sample they exhibit the same general aspects of moral judgment. At age ten approximately forty percent of Taiwan children give type-one statements, compared to thirty percent for the U.S. By age sixteen this percentage has dropped to eight percent in Taiwan and ten percent in the U.S. Between ages ten and sixteen type-four responses increase from ten to sixty percent in Taiwan and from fifteen to thirty-five percent in the U.S. This is the most salient type for both groups by age sixteen. But the U.S. has about twenty percent type-five statements by age sixteen versus only six percent at the same age in Taiwan. At age sixteen adolescents on Taiwan show a roughly similar pattern to their American counterparts but exhibit a far greater concentration in type four than the Americans, who are more evenly distributed among the various types. The ranking of types for both groups by age level is as follows, the highest ranking occurring at the left.[70]

Age	Taiwan	US
10	1–3–2–4–5–6	1–2–3–4–5–6
13	3–4–2–1–5–6	4–3–5–2–1–6
16	4–3–1–5–2–6	4–3–5–1–2–6

first grade. See also Robert D. Hess and Judith V. Torney, *The Development of Political Attitudes in Children*, Aldine Publishing Co., Chicago, 1967, pp. 215–221.

[69] Lawrence Kohlberg, "Stage and Sequence: The Cognitive–Developmental Approach to Socialization," in David A. Goslin, ed., *Handbook of Socialization Theory and Research*, Rand McNally and Co., Chicago, 1969, pp. 382, 384–385.

[70] These figures and the preceding remarks are from Kohlberg, "Development of Children's Orientations," pp. 84–85 (see esp. Figure 2, p. 85). There is some discrepancy in the rankings reported here and in the Kohlberg citation of footnote 69. There is also a discrepancy with the results set forth in Lawrence Kohlberg and Carol Gilligan, "The Adolescent as a Philosopher: The Discovery of the Self in a Postconventional World," *Daedalus*, Fall, 1971, p. 1070. In this latter work type three is predominant with sixteen-year-old adolescents from Taiwan, followed by type four. For the American sample at the same age, type five is predominant, followed closely by types four and three. While the percentage distributions differ somewhat, the major point is relatively clear. Children from Taiwan are heavily oriented toward type-three and type-four morality, while American children are more evenly distributed among several types, most notably three, four, and five. Several

MORALITY AND THE EGO-IDEAL

Strict behaviorists point out that a number of hypotheses concerning moral development by stages have not been confirmed.[71] Bandura and Walters tested children aged five to eleven and found considerable discriminative moral judgment responses, including both objective and subjective categories. They concluded that Piaget's categories were neither predetermined nor invariant.[72] According to these analysts there is no need to assume some inner moral agent such as the superego. They feel that inhibition of deviant behavior is related to anxiety reduction associated with punishment or self-punitive responses. In their opinion, consistency in moral behavior is obtained when parental models have a "generalized resistance to deviation or self-punitive responses and at the same time use reinforcement patterns that are consistent with the behavioral examples they provide."[73]

Non-behaviorists strongly dispute the evidence for morality as a function of imitation of authority figures. The conformity conception, as Kohlberg calls it, is not well defined, and he asserts that no consistent relationship has been found between earliness and amount of parental demands and/or training in good habits and measures of children's obedience, responsibility, and honesty. Direct training and physical punishment are said to produce only short-run conformity, not generalized and long-term habits of inhibition and resistance to deviation.[74]

At our present level of knowledge there may well be no clear-cut and final resolution concerning what actually constitutes moral development. Piaget's work has elicited criticism, as there is no strict uniformity concerning age-related changes. Yet there is considerable evidence that

other investigations have tended generally to support the results reported here. See Jacqueline J. Goodnow, "A Test of Milieu Effects With Some of Piaget's Tasks," *Psychological Monographs*, vol. 76, no. 36, whole no. 555, 1962, pp. 1–22. There were some departures from Piaget's Geneva results. See also Peck with Havighurst, *op. cit.*, p. 197.

[71] Duncan MacRae, Jr., "A Test of Piaget's Theories of Moral Development," *Journal of Abnormal and Social Psychology*, vol. 49, no. 1, January 1954, pp. 14–18.

[72] Albert Bandura and Richard H. Walters, *Social Learning and Personality Development*, Holt, Rinehart, and Winston, New York, 1963, pp. 185, 207.

[73] *Ibid.*, pp. 209–210.

[74] Kohlberg, "Development of Moral Character," pp. 388–389. Also Maccoby, *op. cit.*, p. 243, citing just in Aronfreed, "The Effects of Experimental Socialization Paradigms upon Two Moral Responses to Transgression," *Journal of Abnormal and Social Psychology*, Vol. 66, no. 5, May 1963.

thought processes change between infancy and middle childhood, and Kohlberg has presented evidence from no less than eleven societies controlled for sex group, social class, and subculture showing age trends toward increased intentionality. Kohlberg has critically noted how empirical work with Piaget's theses on heteronomy and autonomy has indicated that these moral stages do not meet the criteria of stage as Piaget's cognitive stages do; Kohlberg's own work on stages of moral judgment has attempted to meet these criteria. He has further pointed out how some of the developmental sequences of the Cognitive–Developmental model correspond with developmental aspects from neo-psychoanalytic work.[75] Some scholars have argued that stage theory and social-learning theory are not mutually exclusive but are, in fact, explanatory at different levels of generalization.[76]

For our purposes we shall avoid adherence to a concept of an autonomous internal moral agent or to the notion that strict stages govern the moral growth process. We do, however, adhere to the notion of changes in cognitive capacity. We believe that there are crucial socializing influences, such as induction training, whose effects are critically dependent upon the development of cognitive capacity. We further feel that the pattern of moral development is related to the learning of roles and role behavior and to the amount and type of affect that exist within the learning environment. In other words, moral development, as it is called, is in our terms a process involving cognitive growth that takes place within an affective environment that favors or inhibits the learning of certain types and standards of role behavior.

During childhood there is an increasing cognitive complexity and integration of the evaluations which are applied to role behavior. These changes, we feel, account for the similarity across social systems which is noted by Kohlberg in the apparent stage development of evaluative systems. There is no need, however, to posit any autonomous internal agent which operates without reference to the social milieu. When we speak of the ego-ideal as a body of standards against which actual behavior is measured (failure to meet this standard evoking an anxiety termed shame), we do not refer to some autonomous internal entity but

[75] Kohlberg, "Stage and Sequence," pp. 374–375, 456–458.

[76] Maccoby, op. cit., p. 252; Edward Zigler and Irvin L. Child, "Socialization," in Gardner Lindzey and Eliot Aronson, eds., The Handbook of Social Psychology, 2nd ed., vol. 3, Addison-Wesley Publishing Co., Reading, Mass., 1969, pp. 456–457.

to a structure of *learned dispositions invested with value orientations* that change over time with cognitive development in both complexity and integration and which contain the positive (and by reverse analogy the negative) values regarding role behavior that structure a person's sense of identity. The differences we note across social systems relate to the fact that the pace and extent of ego-ideal development may be affected by differing patterns of socialization, which are such that learned dispositions are acquired in different ways and with different degrees of intensity. Moral dispositions may be learned as sets of formal rules related to specific others or as general principles which are presumed to supersede any cultural base. Cognitive complexity may be equal in either case. Clearly different social systems and different categories of individuals (sex, class, subculture, etc.) may have evaluative systems which differ in type and intensity. What we need to know is what kinds of social experience involving role learning produce different evaluative structures.

PART II SOCIALIZATION SETTING

CHAPTER 3 The Learning

Environment

Individuals in any social system learn behavior and attitudes appropriate to their culture, social class, family, sex, sibling position, etc. They learn not only what is appropriate but also what is inappropriate. Most belief and attitude patterns concerning social interaction are not "natural" but must be acquired, and this is true of the most basic as well as the most complex patterns. For beliefs and attitudes regarding behavior to become internalized requires a learning context in which there is at least minimal participation by the learner, familiarity with the demands of others is assured, and ways are provided both for emotional dissonance to be avoided and for rewards to be obtained for appropriate responses.

Social learning is a group phenomenon and, especially in childhood, frequently takes place within a clearly hierarchical context. The nature and structure of the group and its hierarchy, as well as the general environment in which the group exists, are of critical importance in influencing the learning context. The status of the group relative to others may affect conceptions of the self as a group member as well as the group's external behavior and internal atmosphere.[1]

Within a group both the structure of the hierarchy and the ranges of behavior associated with any given hierarchical position will influence

[1] Lewis A. Coser, *The Functions of Social Conflict*, The Free Press, New York, 1956, p. 103.

51

learning. In all groups members are tied both horizontally and vertically, and these ties may be both instrumental and expressive; the severance of ties may cause fear and anxiety. To some extent leaders are presumed to be exemplars of ideals and as such are sources of identity and legitimizers of behavior for followers, so that loss of or severance from leaders has emotional ramifications. Leaders can act, through personal motivation or from social constraint, in a manner that either may inhibit and make dependent those in subordinate positions, or may foster expression and self-assertiveness in others. The prescribed role behavior of leaders or followers or both may have some inherent flexibility and allowance for maneuver or may be so tightly restrained that deviation beyond a narrow range causes loss of face and the imposition on the offender of negative sanctions. Finally, leader and follower roles are linked and legitimized by sets of values defining given positions. These values act to stabilize relationships when conflict occurs and even to suppress conflict when hostility exists.

Regardless of the benignity or lack of it in leader-follower relations some amount of mutual dependency will exist, with the heavier share usually held by the subordinate. In socialization the attributes of a superordinate may become positively valued, at least partially owing to the dependency involved; leadership will retain its right to authority as long as it continues to evoke positive evaluations that legitimize dependency on the part of followers.

To a great extent, the capacity of a leader to instill in others a positive evaluation of his actions depends ultimately on his power to control resources. However, his role-competence, his capacity to dispense nurturant and vicarious rewards, and the desirability of the results of his actions are also important. A child discriminates between good and bad leaders, and through a process of increasing generalization learns the correct responses to good and bad authority and is able to imitate "good" leaders and reject the example provided by the "bad." To the extent that various leaders use similar cues, it becomes possible for the child to imitate and follow leaders at progressively higher levels of social generalization. It is this type of process that is the basis for the persistent observation that political leaders are looked upon by their followers as embodying the ideals of the earliest authority pattern, that of the parental model.[2]

2 David Easton and Robert D. Hess, "The Child's Political World," in Leroy N.

The effectiveness of modeling in socialization depends, to some extent, on its explicitness. In social systems where human beings are assumed to have innate predestined characters there may be little conscious or overt sense of the efficacy of modeling, even though, of course, modeling will still be a prevalent aspect of learning. In other types of social systems, explicit modeling may be considered highly effective. In the case of the Chinese, there is a long tradition, going back 2500 years ago to the sayings of Mencius, of both the efficacy and necessity of "appropriate" modeling. Mencius, as Chinese children today learn, was impressed by the capacity of dyes to change white cloth into whatever color it contacts, and concluded that the same principle applied to human beings. The learning paradigm adduced was that association with good people would make a man good while association with evil would inevitably lead to bad character. In this tradition overtly proper behavior is considered of extreme importance, for it is presumed to be the ultimate indicator of one's own worth as well as the best guarantor of the proper behavior of others.

Actually, children learn certain behavior patterns and values and accept historical or living people as models of good or bad behavior through a process of multiple exposures to both animate and inanimate patterns of the culture. Rather than simply learning a discrete meaning or pattern, the child is the continuous observer of and ultimate participant in situations where important others show very small degrees of pride, anxiety, elation, love, fear, or tension with regard to some situation. In the end, even some originally neutral stimulus in a chain of cues and responses may acquire a culturally idiosyncratic value such that in itself it becomes a stimulus for a consequent act and a reinforcer of a preceding action. This entire process may be accomplished largely unconsciously.

A high degree of perceived similarity with a model appears to result in a relatively greater degree of imitation; it apparently facilitates the acquisition of certain response patterns in addition to enhancing levels of performance.[3] With increasing age response patterns are selectively

Rieselback and George I. Balch, eds., *Psychology and Politics*, Holt, Rinehart, and Winston, New York, 1969, pp. 103–104.

[3] Mary A. Rosekrans, "Imitation in Children as a Function of Perceived Similarity to a Social Model and Vicarious Reinforcement," *Journal of Personality and Social Psychology*, vol. 7, no. 3, November 1967, p. 307.

restricted to an increasingly narrow range of appropriate roles and actions. Maximum socialization influence occurs when the model and the reinforcing agent are the same. By repeated association of imitative behavior with reward the child becomes motivated to behave like the socializing agent and ultimately rewards himself by expressions of self-approval and self-love.[4] Similarity between the model and the child serves to remind the child that approximations to model behavior in the past were rewarding as similarity increased. True modeling, however, is more than imitation. In Bronfenbrenner's words, it "goes beyond mimicry in implying the adoption of behaviors which are *symbolic equivalents* of the behavior engaged in by the model."[5] True modeling implies the capacity not merely to copy behavior but also to learn and support the values which legitimize a given action, so that explicit modeling becomes no longer necessary as an antecedent to a given type of response.

An act has been defined as internalized "to the extent that its maintenance has become independent of external outcomes—that is, to the extent that its reinforcing consequences are internally mediated, without the support of external events such as reward or punishment."[6] Some scholars reject the notion of internalization as meaning the development of an inner "moral" guidance system, and prefer to speak only of sanctions, potential or actual, as being internalized.[7] Others, while noting that there is no simple and direct process of internalization, do feel that the self does mediate incoming information in terms of an internal structure that is constantly being developed through reorganization.[8] For our purposes we shall largely support the former interpretation, while noting that, in our opinion, both the positive and the negative valences associated with a given act are internalized and cognitive

[4] Albert Bandura and Richard H. Walters, *Adolescent Aggression*, Ronald Press Co., New York, 1959, pp. 253–254.

[5] Urie Bronfenbrenner, *Two Worlds of Childhood: U.S. and U.S.S.R.*, Russell Sage Foundation, New York, 1970, p. 130. Italics in original.

[6] Justin Aronfreed, *Conduct and Conscience: The Socialization of Internalized Control over Behavior*, Academic Press, New York, 1968, p. 18.

[7] Eleanor E. Maccoby, citing the positions of Albert Bandura and Richard H. Walters, "The Development of Moral Values and Behavior in Childhood," in John A. Clausen, ed., *Socialization and Society*, Little, Brown and Co., Boston, 1968, pp. 259–260.

[8] Lawrence Kohlberg, "Stage and Sequence: The Cognitive–Developmental Approach to Socialization," in David A. Goslin, ed., *Handbook of Socialization Theory and Research*, Rand McNally and Co., Chicago, 1969, p. 423.

development will cause these valences to be elaborated by association with other acts in a discriminative hierarchy. What is not implied is any internal mechanism beyond the increasing capacity of the brain to store and organize data. It is this "storage" factor, we feel, which makes it possible for us to study individuals in different social systems and by use of appropriate categories of analysis to differentiate such individuals on the basis of their different perceptions of reality.

The nature of a response in a given situation is partly a function of the type of external stimulus and partly a function of internalized response strategies. An "internal" orientation is the result of instrumental or operant training, where an act and its outcome are frequently paired. The affective change experienced by the individual from the outcome may become attached to the cues or thoughts associated with the act. Later, even without the outcome, the affect may be elicited by the cues.[9] This type of process, resulting from both rewarding and punishing cues, appears to motivate much behavior.

A response largely based on an internal orientation derives from the affects attached to certain acts but is not independent of external stimulus. Even when an internal orientation appears dominant an external orientation can often still be noted, as in the case when, even though one is alone, certain courses of action are followed because of a sensed perception by real or imaginary others. Often there is a subtle mixture of direct external cues, sensed perception by some nonpresent other, and orientation of conduct to internalized, abstract standards transmitted by esteemed models. Reward and punishment (positive and negative sanctions) are not always related to direct external stimuli but may be mediated by cognitive processes in such a way that both internal and external orientations are engaged. This is especially the case with those who have experienced induction training, where there may be no direct consequences for oneself in a given situation but one's behavior is governed rather by the expected consequences for others.[10]

External orientations appear to arise from interaction with relatively cold and power-assertive parents whose use of physical punishment engenders a concern for external discipline. An internal orientation, on the other hand, where there is an emphasis on interpersonal

[9] Aronfreed, op. cit., p. 49.

[10] The arguments in this paragraph were largely drawn from Aronfreed, op. cit., pp. 66, 268–269.

values and a concern about the consequences of one's acts for others, appears to arise from warm parents who minimize power assertion and who use induction training.[11] Yet while certain general outcomes may be posited as deriving from certain affectively oriented experiences with socializing agents, it is actually *change* of affect within the learner which is fundamental. It has been found, for instance, that verbal reinforcers are more effective in molding the performance of a young child in a simple task after the child has been exposed to a brief period of social isolation. When the existence of some minimal intensity of affective attachment to nurturant authority figures is challenged by an aversive experience of punishment, the resulting anxiety about maintaining the affective relationship constitutes an effective force in internalizing behavioral controls.[12]

Sears, Rau, and Alpert have suggested that strong, rapidly internalized orientations are related positively to five variables: (1) high early dependency, (2) high parental nurturance, (3) high parental standards of conduct, (4) high use of love-oriented techniques of discipline, and (5) clear presentation of models and of labels of appropriate behavior.[13] Much attention has been focused on love-oriented techniques of discipline as a crucial factor in the development of conscience.[14] In fact, however, the use of withdrawal-of-love techniques of discipline has not been found to be invariably related to the development of a strong moral orientation. It is not withdrawal of love alone that creates conscience but love withdrawal combined with warmth; that is, some amount of love (warmth) must have been given for the threat of withdrawal of love to be effective. Mothers who are generally warm are more likely to have children with strong consciences than are mothers who are cold but who also seem to practice withdrawal of love.[15] Mothers who express

[11] Maccoby, *op. cit.*, based on work by Martin L. Hoffman, p. 253.

[12] Aronfreed, *op. cit.*, pp. 44, 50, 309–310.

[13] Robert R. Sears, Lucy Rau, and Richard Alpert, *Identification and Child Rearing*, Stanford University Press, Stanford, 1965, pp. 5–7.

[14] Urie Bronfenbrenner, "Freudian Theories of Identification and Their Derivatives," in Celia Burns Stendler, ed., *Readings in Child Behavior and Development*, (2nd ed., Harcourt, Brace and World, New York, 1954, p. 105 citing R. R. Sears, Eleanor E. Maccoby, and H. Levin, *Patterns of Child Rearing*, Row, Peterson and Co., Evanston, Ill. and White Plains, N.Y., 1957. Also John W. M. Whiting and Irvin L. Child, *Child Training and Personality: A Cross-Cultural Study*, Yale University Press, New Haven, 1953, pp. 241–242, 254–255, 258.

[15] Roger Brown, *Social Psychology*, The Free Press, New York, 1965, p. 386.

positive affective concern are also more likely to have children who have internalized standards of excellence.[16]

Three kinds of discipline techniques have been tested for their relationship to the development of internalized orientations.[17] They are *power assertion*, where the authority figure capitalizes on power and authority; *love withdrawal*, where authority figures make direct but nonphysical expressions of anger and disapproval; and *induction*, where authority figures focus on the consequences of an act for others. An attempt was made to test whether internal orientation is based on fear of external detection derived from the use of power-assertive techniques of discipline, or whether it is independent of external sanctions and is based rather on guilt [shame] derived from non-power-assertive discipline techniques. It was found that power assertion is the least effective technique for the development of internalized standards, because it generates intense hostility. It is probable that children see both love withdrawal and induction as involving loss of love, but love withdrawal, when used separately, was found to relate infrequently to moral development. Induction, however, enlists both the child's need for love and his empathy, and was found to be most strongly related to moral development. Unmentioned but crucially important is the fact that induction, to be effective, relies heavily on cognitive and evaluative development, especially with regard to an understanding of roles and role behavior.

In the three sections that follow we shall attempt very briefly to describe and analyze the learning environment of Chinese children and, to a lesser extent, of American children, as it is experienced at several role levels. We shall first examine primary-level learning within the home. Second, we shall examine the schools, in which systematic efforts are made to train children in secondary-level role behavior. Lastly, an analysis will be made of training in secondary-level role behavior at the interaction level of a social milieu wherein most fellow participants are

[16] George De Vos, *Achievement and Innovation in Culture and Personality*, Japanese and Korean Series, Reprint 291, Center for Japanese and Korean Studies, Institute of International Studies, University of California, in Edward Norbeck, Douglass Price-Williams, William M. McCord, eds., *The Study of Personality*, Holt, Rinehart, and Winston, New York, 1968.

[17] Martin L. Hoffmann and Herbert D. Saltzstein, "Parent Discipline and the Child's Moral Development," *Journal of Personality and Social Psychology*, vol. 5, no. 1, January 1967, pp. 45–57.

unknown. We term this the social or polity level. While examining these levels we shall be attempting to assess why internalized behavioral controls may develop in varying degrees depending both on the particular social system and on the role level. We shall also examine how shame anxiety may be manipulated during socialization to motivate the development of a distinctive repertoire of behavior.

Our analyses derive from several years of systematic observation of interaction patterns within a wide variety of Chinese and American contexts. Our data has been abbreviated here and interwoven with findings of other researchers. Readers who are interested in a fuller and more descriptive explication of the socialization process in one of our societies, Taiwan, are referred to an earlier work by the author.[18] It is *not* our purpose here to set forth a complete analysis of both the process and content of learning nor to replicate our own or other findings concerning socialization generally, but rather to discuss sparingly those aspects of the learning environment which we feel help to make understandable social and age-related differences in "moral" learning.

SECTION ONE.   PRIMARY-LEVEL ROLE LEARNING—THE FAMILY

Research on primary groups varies in focus. Emphasis shifts from the primary group as a whole, to its location in some larger social category such as class, to the problems associated with various positions within the group. Regardless of the focus, much effort is usually expended on analysis of norms and social and situational factors that influence behavior. For any given child there are clearly a wide variety of primary-group influences, beginning with parental idiosyncrasies and extending to those influences associated with locale, class, sex, sibling position, etc.

The development of behavior patterns and attitude complexes is a stochastic process involving an interaction between environmental stimuli and appropriate, gradually developed response patterns by the self. Ultimately, attitudes become attached to anchoring values such that attitudinal change past the point where the values themselves must

---

[18] Richard W. Wilson, *Learning to be Chinese: The Political Socialization of Children in Taiwan*, Massachusetts Institute of Technology Press, Cambridge, Mass., 1970.

change may require uniquely radical and reinforcing methods.[19]

A powerful parent who both rewards and punishes provides more effective control of a child's actions than one who uses only unconditional love.[20] But the ability to punish is not the same as the ability to influence. Influence is related more to mild threats than to severe ones, and mild threats are also more effective in inducing long-range internalized obedience. A powerful parent is also imitated more spontaneously than a powerless one and because of this need not use his power as often in order to elicit modeling. The characteristics of powerful agents tend to be adopted because the rewards and punishments of this agent are more impressive, the motivation to imitation is higher, and the necessity for predicting the agent's behavior is more important.[21]

It may be that extremes of either affection or discipline are both deleterious to the learning process. A minimum level of nurturance is required for internalized control, but beyond that minimal level it has not been verified that internalization is a continuous function of nurturance. The minimum level is necessary in order that positive and negative values may be associated with socializing influences.[22] Bandura and Walters feel that internalized control is related to early and severe socialization pressures reflecting the extent of rewards for conformity with parental standards and punishments for deviance. Lack of self-control manifested by aggression appears related to a lack of nurturance and a punitive attitude by one or both parents, and to inconsistency in disciplinary techniques.[23]

The reinforcement of shame anxiety in socialization appears related to parental warmth, to use of induction techniques of discipline, and to parental establishment of high goals of performance. A parent does not constantly have to show contempt or disapprobrium for a shame orientation to develop, but needs only do so at critical times, when there

[19] William J. McGuire, "The Nature of Attitudes and Attitude Change," in Gardner Lindzey and Elliot Aronson, eds., *The Handbook of Social Psychology*, 2nd ed., vol. 3, Addison-Wesley Publishing Co.. Reading, Mass., 1969, pp. 169, 173.

[20] Leonard Berkowitz, "Social Motivation," in Lindzey and Aronson, *op. cit.*, p. 77.

[21] Orville G. Brim, Jr., "Family Structure and Sex Role Learning by Children: A Further Analysis of Helen Koch's Data," *Sociometry*, vol. 21, 1958, p. 3.

[22] Justin Aronfreed, "The Concept of Internalization," in Goslin, *op. cit.*, pp. 304–306.

[23] Bandura and Walters, *op. cit.*, pp. 29–30.

is a confrontation of wills. Otherwise the parent may be quite mild. But the child knows that ultimately he or she will always "lose," and the cumulative effect of this may prove irresistible, producing a kind of serenity at the cost of immobility and conformity. A heightening of the importance of shame anxiety is reinforced by parents who humiliate a child, requiring confessions of unworthiness and promises to reform. The impact may be further developed by a parent who shows that he himself is deeply ashamed by the child's behavior.[24]

Socializing agents may reward or punish in front of others in the hope that positive and negative reinforcement will affect the future behavior of the witnesses. Publicizing rewards and punishments in order to modify the behavior of the group by the example of a few is a frequently employed technique of social influence, which, in the case of punishment, may be deeply humiliating to the victim. In all these instances the technique is usually that of "prosocial aggression," which includes verbal and physical actions indicating disapproval for antisocial attitudes or actions. Such practices are a peculiarly adult form of aggression and are related to parental warmth, high demands, parental modeling of good behavior, and love-oriented techniques of discipline.[25]

There are few societies more difficult to assess regarding childhood training within the family than the United States. Not only is there broad diversity among ethnic groups, but patterns appear to change rapidly and there is considerable lack of consensus among authorities on the subject. Lipset has noted how foreign observers of America in the nineteenth century commented on conformism and other-directed traits, which, according to scholars like David Riesman, reflect more recent American value orientations.[26] Others have seen an appreciable change from rigidity and strictness to greater permissiveness, more freedom of expression of affect, and increasing reliance on psychological techniques of discipline.[27] Still others have seen a movement away from increasing

[24] Silvan S. Tomkins, *Affect Imagery Consciousness*, vol. 2. *The Negative Affects*, Springer Publishing Co., New York, 1963, pp. 358–360, 416–417.

[25] Sears, Rau, and Alpert, *op. cit.*, p. 113.

[26] Seymour M. Lipset, "A Changing American Character?" in Seymour M. Lipset and Leo Lowenthal, eds., *Culture and Social Character: The Work of David Riesman Reviewed*, The Free Press, New York, 1961, pp. 142–145, 168.

[27] Urie Bronfenbrenner, "The Changing American Child—A Speculative Analysis," in Neil J. Smelser and William T. Smelser, *Personality and Social Systems*, John Wiley and Sons, New York, 1963, pp. 347–348.

permissiveness toward more restrictive forms of socialization.[28] Within a class-analysis framework, Becker has found the American middle class to be characterized by permissive training techniques and the working class by more restrictive training techniques; Kohn, on the other hand, testing fifth graders, found no appreciable difference between the middle and working classes in terms of the relative role of the mother or father in decision making, their relative role in setting limits on the child's freedom of movement, and the frequency with which either resort to physical punishment.[29]

By the 1950s, comparative cross-cultural analyses of child-training techniques indicated that American practices of that time were unusual by world standards.[30] For instance, the American middle class was found to be characterized by very low oral indulgence, extreme anal training, and severe sexual training. Aggression training and dependency training were about average, except that whereas independence was fostered within the home there was an unusually long period of dependency for activities outside the family. Generally, American society is characterized by low general indulgence; in an average ranking of 47 societies American society ranked in second place with respect to intensity of severity of socialization. Whereas most societies tended to be initially most indulgent concerning dependence and least so concerning aggression, and overall most severe concerning aggression and dependence in that order, American middle-class society showed the greatest initial indulgence to dependence and aggression but overall the greatest severity toward anal training and aggression in that order, while dependency was the least severely socialized. Although these patterns may well have shown some significant changes since the 1950s, it is probably still fair to characterize American socialization as relatively severe overall, as relatively low in severity concerning dependency training, and as initially relatively indulgent concerning aggression.

Two other factors in American primary-group socialization which are of some interest are the degree of family orientation and the decline

[28] John A. Clausen, "Family Structure, Socialization, and Personality," in Lois W. Hoffman and Martin L. Hoffman, eds., Review of Child Development Research, Vol. 2, Russell Sage Foundation, New York, 1966, p. 18.

[29] Wesley C. Becker, "Consequences of Different Kinds of Parental Discipline," in Hoffman and Hoffman, op. cit., vol. 1, p. 171; and Melvin L. Kohn, "Social Class and the Exercise of Parental Authority," in Smelser and Smelser, op. cit., p. 300.

[30] The data that follows is drawn from Whiting and Child, op. cit., pp. 70–115.

of the father as a strong figure. Solomon has presented data showing that on one attitudinal indicator concerning relative commitment to family or nation Americans tend to be more family-oriented than Chinese; in his own analysis Solomon tended to qualify this finding and concluded that it indicated only that Americans and Chinese are not poles apart.[31] There appear to be additional reasons, however, for questioning the validity of a strong American family orientation.

Tomkins has noted a critical change in American socialization, whereby mothers have become both love object and punisher and fathers have become emasculated. Beginning about 1950, he noted that about a third of his undergraduates were introducing the theme of a weak father into TAT stories. Previously this had not happened.[32] If Tomkins's assessment of the change in the role of the American father is correct, then a substantial new element has been added into American socialization practices. As late as 1952 Tasch was reporting considerable support for the traditional concept of the American father as head of the house, lawgiver, arbiter, and disciplinarian; the person in whom family authority resides.[33] Although working-class fathers might resort to physical punishment more frequently than middle-class fathers, both were conceived of as punishers. Fathers, for instance, were more likely than mothers to physically punish sons for fighting with siblings.[34] In terms of goals, middle-class fathers wanted their girls to be nice, sweet, pretty, affectionate, and well-liked; the characteristics least desired for sons were disobedience, lack of responsibility and initiative, inadequate performance in schools, passivity, athletic inadequacy, overconformism, excitability, tearfulness, homosexuality, and childishness. All children were trained to believe that withdrawal from competitive situations was shameful.[35]

While the conception of the father's role was still relatively "traditional" in the fifties, there is some indication that change had already

[31] Richard H. Solomon, "Mao's Effort to Reintegrate the Chinese Polity: Problems of Authority and Conflict in Chinese Social Processes," in A. Doak Barnett, ed., *Chinese Communist Politics in Action*, University of Washington Press, Seattle, 1969, pp. 276–277.

[32] Tomkins, *op. cit.*, pp. 552–553.

[33] Ruth J. Tasch, "The Role of the Father in the Family," *Journal of Experimental Education*, vol. 20, no. 4, June 1952, p. 350.

[34] Kohn, *op. cit.*, p. 310.

[35] Bernard Barber, *Social Stratification*, Harcourt, Brace and World, New York, 1957, pp. 270–271, 279

proceeded quite far. The responsibility for discipline between mothers and fathers was acknowledged to be fluid. In terms of participation in everyday activities, fathers themselves did not mention rules, skills, or family organization as their primary areas of responsibility but rather "going places," or other activities concerned with developing social standards, conduct, and control. Only 39% of Tasch's sample of 85 fathers mentioned "moral and spiritual development."[36] In discussing methods of discipline with children, 62 fathers mentioned physical punishment, 44 verbal punishment (shaming, warning, reasoning, suggesting, etc.), and 30 the withholding of pleasures or attention (isolating, ignoring, and depriving).[37] The last two categories, which most fathers reported using, are largely psychological punishments. In terms of self-conception of paternal influence, the top four categories (of thirteen) were, in order, guide and teacher, economic provider, authority, and influencer of personal characteristics and habits.[38] Authority and leadership, then, were components of the role behavior and self-conception of fathers two decades ago, but the drift since then has been toward partnership, the use of psychological punishments, and a self-conception as guide and provider rather than as leader and disciplinarian.

Mothers, of course, have always been disciplinarians, even though the image of them held by their children may not be as such. But discipline is only one of the important aspects of a mother's behavior, and it is often colored by her role as love object, by her permissiveness in dealing with others, and by her temperamental qualities as a woman. By a process as yet only partially understood, children very early begin to imitate their mothers along a broad spectrum of behavioral ranges, including role play, morals learning, aggression training, appropriate sex behavior, etc. In all such areas the learning of appropriate behavior is paralleled by the development of standards of right and wrong with regard to that behavior. The channeling, reduction, and, at times, redirecting of primary drives is the foundation of socialization and is largely carried out by the mother. Hence Peck and Havighurst emphasize the "profound and influential" effect of the mother on the child's character and personality development.[39] It is the mother who not only

[36] Tasch, *op. cit.*, p. 323 (Table I).

[37] *Ibid.*, p. 337 (Table VII).

[38] *Ibid.*, p. 347 (Table X).

[39] Robert F. Peck with Robert J. Havighurst, *The Psychology of Character Development*, John Wiley and Sons (Science Editions), New York, 1960, pp. 118, 175–177.

cares for the bodily needs of her infant but in addition establishes early in the child's life the generalized goal of pleasing the mother, so that subsequent interaction with significant others is sought not just for organic reasons but to obtain and hold the love of another as well. This critical development underlies much of socialization and is the foundation for the development of the personality.[40]

There are two major categories of maternal behavior. The first involves love-oriented techniques, wherein praise is used as a reward and isolation and withdrawal of love are used as punishments, and the second involves object-oriented techniques, wherein tangible incentives are used as rewards and deprivation of privileges and physical means are used as punishments.[41] Love-oriented punishment "signifies to the child that his mother at the moment does not love him. The thought can be more painful than a dozen blows."[42] Love-oriented techniques seem often to involve a lack of response rather than a positive action, and *mothers are very reluctant to acknowledge use of these techniques*, because they cannot see themselves telling a child they do not love him.[43] For the development of conscience and self-control, love-oriented techniques must, as we have partially discussed, occur in conjunction with parental warmth and reasoning, the former to give meaning to the manipulation of the affective relationship and the latter to give the child the cognitive structure for self-evaluation of his own and other's responses.

The data for American mothers shows that regardless of social class they are not prone to use physical punishment.[44] Scoldings or admonishments are used more frequently for almost all types of offenses and for both boys and girls, although boys are allowed some leeway and independence while girls must both not do what is forbidden and do what is required. Working-class mothers are more prone to punish for violations of negative injunctions than for not doing something one was supposed to do. When working-class mothers punish for wild play it is frequently because reputability and rules of propriety have been

[40] Talcott Parsons, "Social Structure and the Development of Personality: Freud's Contribution to the Integration of Psychology and Sociology," in Smelser and Smelser, *op. cit.*, pp. 39–41. (Originally published in *Psychiatry*, vol. 21, 1958, pp. 321–340.)

[41] Robert R. Sears, Eleanor E. Maccoby, and Harry Levin, *Patterns of Child Rearing*, Row, Peterson and Co., Evanston, Ill. and White Plains, N.Y., 1951, p. 478.

[42] *Ibid.*, p. 334.

[43] *Ibid.*, p. 341. Italics added.

[44] The data that follows is largely drawn from Kohn, *op. cit.*, pp. 303–313.

violated; middle-class mothers, who also punish for wild play, seem particularly concerned with self-control and find losses of temper—especially by sons—intolerable. Regardless of social class, fighting with siblings in a physical way or losing one's temper in a violent or aggressive way are very heavily negatively sanctioned by mothers.

With the decline of the father as overt disciplinarian the disciplinary techniques of the mother become more salient to the child, and her image as nurturant figure is clouded by the necessity to acknowledge her role as punisher. In effect the mother's role, like the father's has become ambiguous, and there are no clear-cut objects for the child for feelings of affection, competitiveness, or resentment. In reaction to their own loss of role definition many mothers turn to permissiveness, but it is a stance which must be repeatedly violated by the necessity to punish, making the position of the mother vis-à-vis her children not less but even more ambiguous. The major point is that in modern American society the limits of maternal behavior have become undefined, and parental roles generally have lost structure and meaning.

If American family practices are difficult to describe except in general terms, the same must also be said for the Chinese. Nevertheless some general patterns do emerge and are apparently both widespread and persistent (especially, for instance, if statements of psychologists in Hong Kong that mainland refugee family patterns are virtually identical with those of ordinary lower-class Hong Kong families can be believed). Many obesrvers feel that the severity of socialization in Chinese societies is considerably less than in American families, but this should not imply a lack of interest or of capability in the control of children. This apparent lack of severity is by no means a modern phenomenon, as Arthur H. Smith pointed out in his observations of late nineteenth-century China.

> That Chinese children have no proper discipline, that they are not taught to obey their parents, and that as a rule they have no idea of prompt obedience as we understand it, is a most indubitable fact attested by wide experience. But that the later years of these ungoverned or half-governed children generally do not exhibit such results as we should have expected, appears to be not less a truth.[45]

45 Arthur H. Smith, *Chinese Characteristics*, Fleming H. Revell Co., New York, 1894, p. 173.

Perhaps part of the explanation for this comparative lack of "order" lies in a different pattern of family organization and integration. Many Chinese families seem rarely to be together. For the upper classes in Hong Kong and Taiwan there may be a certain avoidance among family members due to heavy social obligations, while for the lower classes, where both parents work, children are often sent out of the house to play with peers or siblings. At mealtimes people join or leave as they wish, whereas in American society this time is usually set aside as a set and defined period of interaction. As in some descriptions of medieval Europe, in a Chinese home, however large, the rooms may have several different functions, such as sleeping and working, some going on at the same time.[46]

In public places, such as on buses, children can be seen determinedly pushing adults out of the way to get where they wish to go. A number of Westerners report little discipline within the home, weak restrictions against aggression, weak internalization of values regarding self-control in the expression of personal wants and needs, and a general tendency on the part of parents to feel that it is the school's job to train children in self-control. Such observations seem to reflect the biases of the observers concerning appropriate techniques of discipline as much as they do actual outcomes. Certainly there is very powerful evidence that rather rigorous training goes on within the Chinese home, although clearly in different ways and with different phases than in the United States.

Modesty training, for instance, begins very early for Chinese children. By four years of age children will spontaneously cover their genitals with their hands during physical examinations. At the Yaumati Medical Centre in Hong Kong Dr. F. Baber reported that Chinese children seemed to fear taking off their clothes more than European children and that their mothers were often reluctant to have them do so. Several male university students in Taiwan emphasized during an interview that even if alone in a bedroom they would feel uncomfortable without some clothes on. Children, they noted, are admonished that it is impolite and immodest not to be at least partially dressed. Similarly, the open expression of affection between mothers and fathers is considered both bad for the child and in bad taste.[47] Mothers express affection by

[46] Philippe Aries, *Centuries of Childhood: A Social History of Family Life*, Random House, Vintage Books, New York, 1962, pp. 390–415.

[47] Margery Wolf, "Child Training and the Chinese Family," in Maurice Freedman,

cooking good food, by giving privileges, and by listening to a child talk, and these object-oriented techniques of interaction become so heavily infused with affective content that their manipulation is in effect a category of love-oriented training.

Although children may at times appear rambunctious and ill-behaved, at other times there is a seeming passivity in the face of authority. Dr. F. Baber has noted how when Chinese children four years of age or younger were measured or undressed they did not resist or show displeasure to the doctor as much as European children, but rather whimpered and complied. Many adult Chinese have a tendency to expect conflict in family relations and to have little expectation of co-operation.[48] For the child the appropriate response in such a situation is one of withdrawal and not of reactive aggression, a form of behavior which he has been severely trained to suppress. In a family, where fulfillment of obligations receives heavy positive sanction, emotional withdrawal is one of the few permissible outlets in cases of conflict. The seeming alternations in restrictiveness and looseness in Chinese family interaction may be a response to the needs of members on the one hand for solidarity and the fulfillment of obligations and on the other hand for latitude in terms of intensity and frequency of interaction.

Techniques of disciplining children cover an extremely broad range. In Hong Kong, spanking begins at about one year of age. Beatings or threats of beatings, often administered with the hand but sometimes with a bamboo rod or leather strap, are not at all uncommon. In some cases children may be threatened with the fate that will befall them in a Buddhist hell for disloyalty to parents or for lack of obedience. Far more common, however, are verbal scolding; deprivation of something desired, like dinner; invective, such as calling someone stupid; or, more severely, threatening a child with being sold to another family.[49] This ultimate threat of abandonment is powerfully buttressed by developing a fear of strangers and foreigners that in many children is quite pronounced.

Negative sanctions are only one aspect of the interaction process with authority figures. There is a great deal of tactile intimacy between

ed., *Family and Kinship in Chinese Society*, Stanford University Press, Stanford, 1970, pp. 43–45.

[48] Solomon, *op. cit.*, p. 292.

[49] Bernard Gallin, *Hsin Hsing, Taiwan: A Chinese Village in Change*, University of California Press, Berkeley and Los Angeles, 1966, p. 195.

mothers and children and between older siblings and younger ones. Children are carried on the backs of mothers and older children, and often walk arm in arm as well. While voice inflection in speaking to a child may be flat or meaning relatively nonexpressive affectively (as saying "behave yourself, be good" when a child hurts himself), there may be an accompanying amount of fondling which is highly affective in content. Older siblings usually take great care of younger ones, dispensing nurturance but also being compensated for their responsibility with authority. At the same time the older children are informally teaching the younger ones about the family group and the responsibilities within it.

Respect and loyalty for parents and older siblings are taught by example and also by stories, plays, and movies which constantly stress these themes. In many if not most plots there is little attempt to disguise the moral content. Good and bad people are highly stereotyped. The basic theme is that lack of unity, loyalty, and respect for the group and its leaders never pays in the end. Moreover, children are taught that it is never too late to turn over a new leaf and begin to behave properly. At times the degree of "filiality" required appears to demand the utmost from those involved, yet there is no suggestion that the requirements are not just and necessary. Children on Taiwan, for instance, can purchase a popularly sold book called *Twenty-Four Stories of Filial Devotion*, in which, in one story, a daughter keeps her toothless mother-in-law alive for years by suckling her from her own breast. In another story children read of a son who became an official and whose father became ill. The doctor informed the official that the father could be cured if his feces tasted bitter but not if they tasted sweet. Loyally, therefore the good son tasted his father's feces (regrettably sweet).[50] These are, of course, ideal examples but doubtless few American children would feel even in theory that their obligation to authority extended to such a limit.

In traditional China kinship was of overwhelming importance, and despite the notable Chinese Communist attempt to reduce this importance kinship remains a potent force even on the mainland. It should be kept in mind that the family group of which we speak is virtually always the nuclear family. The joint family is a statistically rare phenomenon, although Cohen has presented some evidence that the joint family,

[50] *Twenty-Four Stories of Filial Devotion* (*Er-Shih-Sz Hsiao-de Ku-shih*), Wu Chin-fu, publisher, Taipei, Taiwan, 1970. Book 1, Story 10, and Book 2, Story 2.

while rare, still remains as an ideal.[51] Family roles and self-conceptions concerning roles are no doubt influenced by this fact.

In traditional times, so folk and much scholastic lore have it, sons unquestioningly obeyed their fathers, for by the very fact of fatherhood one achieved power legally, ideally, and actually over subordinate members of the household. In theory a son could humbly correct his father if he felt the father was in error, but if the father should decide to beat his son as a consequence there was nothing the son could do about it. This is the legend, and no doubt it was sufficiently true in a large enough number of cases to have inspired considerable fear and reticence in many sons and to have been the basis ultimately of an ideal of unquestioning loyalty and obedience. Nothing is usually said, however, of the countless adjustments families must have made, especially in the lowest classes, to conform in actual practice to this ideal, nor of the fact that mortality was sufficiently high that many sons never reached adulthood and those that did often did not have to worry for long about the domination of their aging fathers.

Many Chinese attest and field observation amply confirms that at least until school age fathers treat little children with loving care, holding and speaking to them without great restraint. With age, however, and especially with the start of school, many fathers begin to emphasize in their relations with their children a sense of responsibility for the child's "moral" development and an implicit belief that it is through the father's own example that these lessons can best be learned. From a loving authority the father becomes a model of rectitude and obedience from whom overt manifestation of feeling is increasingly suppressed, and relations become aloof and formal with an emphasis on modeling after the father's proper behavior. Even in the People's Republic of China a strict father is a pronounced aspect of literature.[52]

Despite the fact that strictness and aloofness increasingly come to characterize a father's relations with his children, it should not be assumed that in practice he is universally feared and that conflictual feelings come to predominate in the father-child relationship. In the first place the traditional ideal was always more of a gentry pattern than

[51] Myron L. Cohen, "Developmental Process in the Chinese Domestic Group," and John C. Pelzel, "Japanese Kinship: A Comparison," in Freedman, *op. cit.*, pp. 25–26, 229.

[52] Ai-Li S. Chin, "Family Relations in Modern Chinese Fiction," in Freedman, *op. cit.*, pp. 108–109.

an established fact for all Chinese, and in the second place changes in Chinese family organization, especially in urban areas, have tended to change the roles of both the father and mother. Many fathers today do not—and could not—maintain the rigid strictness and aloofness of the past. Older children and especially girls are able to talk about reciprocation of tenderness and care and to interact with the father in a familiar manner. A small example of this comes from a book called *Dialogue of Family Education*, printed in Hong Kong, in which there is a discussion about children hitting and speaking back to their fathers, behavior which is at complete variance with the traditional ideal:

> Since father loves the child he will let him hit his face and will be over-joyed to hear him scold. Father may pretend to stop this perverted humor of the child with severe words but in his heart he is overjoyed. Sometimes he will even ask the child to hit and scold the mother and the child does as suggested. This happens in many families. But in China, educated families never ask their children to hit or use harsh words against their parents for fun.[53]

Despite these changes in family patterns our observations indicate that fathers are still generally looked upon as the head of the house, the final authority, and the person from whom punishment is most to be dreaded. That he may in fact be none of these things still does not detract from this conception of him held by his children. And finally, although the father may be considered "old-fashioned" by his children it is still expected that he will set a proper example of what is correct behavior in order that those who emulate him may be respected and credit reflected upon the entire family.

Chinese socialization has been described as one of "authority-dependence," in which relationships are highly structured hierarchically and the subordinate is excessively dependent on those above in the hierarchic chain. The prototype for this social phenomenon, which exists in modified form in modern China, is presumed to be the father-son relationship. Dependency itself is manifested by overt conformism and a general suppression of hostility, especially against authority, and is maintained by various sanctioning devices, not the least of which is shaming.

[53] Hui Ching-chao, ed., *Dialogue of Family Education* (*Chia-ting Chiao-yü Chiang-hua*), 2nd ed., Nam Yang Book Co., Hong Kong, 1968, p. 156.

Here we will attempt to make a brief assessment of the origins of dependency itself. This analysis, admittedly brief and somewhat speculative, relates to techniques of child rearing within the home and to the maximization of shame anxiety in socialization. There is reason to believe that the actual dynamics of the origins of dependency are somewhat different from what is normally posited.

Identification with family norms, ideas, and values and gratification from emotional dependence do not necessarily imply conformism or excessive need for nurturance. Dependency is by no means a simple trait but is a generalization concerning a variety of behavioral modes and affective and cognitive stances and arises from a complex training process. In some formulations dependency arises from permissive and child-centered notions of child training and from an equality of the mother and father, wherein neither one serves as an effective model of independence.[54] Dependency may also be fostered by a value system in which depending and presuming on another's love and indulgence are expected and highly valued attributes of child-parental (especially child-mother) relationships and, to a less intense degree, of other relationships as well.[55] A certain amount of dependency is essential for learning, for without it authority figures cannot serve adequately as models.

Contrary to popular notions in Chinese studies that the father-son interaction leads to dependency, the evidence points conclusively to the overpowering influence of the mother; it is this factor which underlies continuing observations of dependency in many areas of Chinese behavior. Bandura and Walters say flatly that mothers who indulge children and reward dependency have highly dependent children.[56] Palmer notes that dependency is directly related to the degree of auditory, visual, kinesthetic, and tactile contact with the mother.[57] Physical punishment is not related to dependency except when the punishment is against aggressive acts directed at parents.[58] Although the cause-effect

[54] Diana Baumrind, "Effects of Authoritative Parental Control on Child Behavior," *Child Development*, vol. 37, no. 4, December 1966, pp. 888–891. Also Urie Bronfenbrenner, "The Changing American Child," in Smelser and Smelser, *op. cit.*, p. 353.

[55] L. Takeo Doi, "Giri-Ninjō: An Interpretation," in R. P. Dore, ed., *Aspects of Social Change in Modern Japan*, Princeton University Press, Princeton, N.J., 1967, pp. 327–329.

[56] Albert Bandura and Richard H. Walters, *Social Learning and Personality Development*, Holt, Rinehart, and Winston, New York, 1963, p. 141.

[57] Francis H. Palmer, "Inferences to the Socialization of the Child from Animal Studies: A View from the Bridge," in Goslin, *op. cit.*, p. 34.

[58] Sears, Maccoby, and Levin, *op. cit.*, p. 171.

relationship between dependency and training has not been determined, there appear to be two factors which must both be present for dependency to develop: (1) openly expressed maternal affection and (2) repeated use of love withdrawal as a discipline and punitiveness against aggression directed at parents.[59] It is the withholding of positive reinforcers in love withdrawal rather than the giving of negative ones which intensifies dependence toward the socializing agent. To the extent that Chinese mothers use love withdrawal as a disciplinary technique with their sons and to the extent that they are themselves models for dependent behavior (although the widening of role opportunities for women has clearly lessened this), there will be an impetus for the development of dependency in the son quite unrelated to the father's behavior as such. For "when the parent of the opposite sex rewards dependency, the child develops behavior qualities characteristic of that sex."[60]

Association with mothers, nurturance from parents, and low punishment appear related to responsiveness to adult pressure and to the strong development of internalized standards. Although the relationship between the development of "conscience" and the use of love-oriented discipline techniques is small, there is a positive correlation between conscience and both maternal warmth and acceptance and love-oriented discipline techniques and a negative correlation between conscience and use of object rewards, deprivation of privilege, and physical punishment.[61]

On Taiwan and in Hong Kong the father's position as head of the house, his role as exemplar of proper behavior, and the authority which in theory and frequently in fact has been his to wield as he thought best in the interests of his family, although reduced from traditional times, have all tended to be highly visible and to focus attention on the father–son relationship as the area where the greatest amount of psychic interpersonal tension must presumably lie. This emphasis has completely obscured the fact that the mother's relationship with her children was and is the major dynamic in the socialization process and is the anxiety source which limits and charges all other relationships, providing the impetus for behavioral and attitudinal development. Indeed, if the father–child relationship has had any importance in transitional or

[59] *Ibid.*, p. 175.
[60] Sears, Rau, and Alpert, *op. cit.*, p. 255. Italics in original.
[61] *Ibid.*, pp. 224–225.

modern times it is basically because fathers can no longer claim, in theory or in actuality, the capacity to unambiguously model appropriate behavior despite the fact that this role function is still the expected one for fathers. This leaves the child with impaired primary-level guidance for appropriate behavior (no doubt partially substituted for by political authority) with which to allay the anxiety concerning correct behavior arising from the mother–child relationship.

An old proverb says "Strict Father, Kind Mother," and this image of the dichotomy in parental treatment of children has persisted despite all the qualifications concerning this image which must be made to accord with reality. Indeed, to admit otherwise concerning one's father would be tantamount to an admission that he was deviant from the ideal of what the good and proper father was expected to be. For fathers, above all, are ideally expected to set a proper example of behavior and, by doing so, to exhibit the qualities of their family. In like manner, mothers in Chinese society carry the stereotype of all-loving and affectionate beings who counterbalance the strictness and aloofness of fathers. In a chapter called "Love That Will Never Be Forgotten," the care of a mother during an illness is remembered as follows: "Recalling the past events at the present time, I feel that my mother is the kindest, most amiable and tenderest one in the world."[62] Or again, in a poem entitled "The Song of a Wandering Son," the mother is depicted as endlessly loving: "Who can say that the son's love, though considerate and sincere, can repay that warm bright sunlight of the kind mother's love?"[63] Mothers are said to appreciate and remember the love given them, as is shown in the words of a mother to a child on Mother's Day on hearing that the child could not afford a present: "A precious gift can be worn out and lost. But your love for mama will be treasured in my heart. I will remember it always and it will forever be the same."[64]

Between mothers and children there is a great deal of fondling and physical intimacy. Although many Chinese say the practice is declining, observation indicates that the carrying of children on the mother's back

[62] Hoi Fung, ed., *Model Essays for Students* (*Hsueh-sheng Tso-wen Shih-p'ien*), Wui Tung Book Co., Hong Kong, 1968, p. 71.

[63] Mang Chao, "The Song of a Wandering Son," in Nam Ya Publishing Society, ed. and publisher, *Selected Poems for Primary Schools* (*Hsiao-hsueh Shih-tz'u Hsuan-i*), Hong Kong, 1970, p. 34.

[64] Law Koon-Kiu, ed., *The Children's Paradise* (*Erh-t'ung Lo-yuan*), The Children's Paradise Bi-weekly Publishing Co., Series No. 416, May 1, 1970, pp. 12–13.

is still extremely widespread. It is also the practice for a child to sleep with its mother until ten years of age or so unless displaced earlier by a younger sibling. Mothers are extremely protective. The calling of children in from the street can be as a game, catching and hugging the little ones as they are marched home. The giving of food is considered of great importance. In Hong Kong this is particularly important, as children are taken off milk at about six months of age and then given rice, which colloquially (but erroneously) is believed to be very healthful. In fact, nutrition is virtually unknown, and for many children the following year is one of actual malnutrition, manifested by crying and crankiness on the part of the child. The mother's response is feeding and the rewarding of the child for good behavior with food. This giving, however, is heavily invested with love and attention. In this way the nurturant and loving role of the mother is elicited and reinforced, although at least partly from causes of which she is unaware.

The image of mothers as loving and nurturant persists despite the disciplinary role which they play (there are reports of fathers so aloof that they delegated discipline to the mother). In cases where the grandmother may live with the family it is frequently the grandmother who appears as the real disciplinarian, folklore about spoiling grandparents notwithstanding. In public places Chinese mothers often seem less demonstratively affectionate toward their children than Europeans. Beyond the age of about two children are not bounced on their mother's knees, perhaps because "proper appearances" are violated by such displays. The showing and giving of affection are increasingly channeled into culturally appropriate forms such as giving of food and protective concern for "proper" development. Although mothers may be initially indulgent in many aspects of training, there is no hesitation about spanking the young child as a method of punishment or even slapping the face in order to eliminate some type of behavior. An idealized notion of how to combine this strictness with warmth is summed up in a chapter entitled "Maternal Teaching is More Important than Maternal Love" in a book on home education sold on Taiwan. After noting that love is the basis for the environment which a mother provides, the text continues:

> ... amiability must go hand in hand with strictness. These two characteristics seem contradictory but actually they supplement each other.

Amiability should be applied to breeding while strictness is applied to teaching. While in most cases the children are undisciplined, teaching should be conducted with strictness so as to train them to behave properly. It has been evidenced by illustrious mothers of history who succeeded in teaching their children that strictness is necessary in maternal teaching. When applying strictness, the mother should behave herself squarely and uprightly. With sincerity of mind and uprightness of behavior, a mother can set a model for her children to follow which will be more effective than teaching by lecture. Only through maternal teaching comprising amiability and strictness can children be expected to behave squarely and elegantly.[65]

Although physical punishment is observed in the dealings of Chinese mothers with their children, techniques of love withdrawal (strictness) combined with warmth and induction training are by far the most common forms of maternal behavior. A not uncommon injunction to children is the phrase "If you do that, mama will not love you." This direct manipulation of the affective relationship is mirrored in other ways. One Hong Kong mother, for instance, reported that her favorite method for getting things done by her children is to ask who can do it first in a way that explicitly conveys that prompt performance will best earn her love. Such examples from our observations are more numerous than it is possible to record. The ultimate result of such training practices, we feel, is the development of anxieties with regard to interpersonal relations in which fear of abandonment is accentuated and in which there is a consequent high internalization of values related to standards of behavior. These techniques operate powerfully to keep the child directed toward the securing of parental and especially maternal love. The consequences of one's behavior for others become a matter of acute concern, while the behavior of others is subjected to continuing scrutiny in order to ascertain the overt and covert meanings which may be associated with a given act.

Aronfreed has accurately summed up the way in which anxiety concerning love withdrawal arising from techniques of induction training can become overwhelmingly important.

There is in fact no reason to suppose that physical or direct forms of

[65] Yin Yun-hua, *Home Education* (*Chia-t'ing Chiao-yu*), Hu Yung-chi'ng, publisher, Taichung, Taiwan, 1970, pp. 182–185.

punishment are more painful or aversive in magnitude to the child than are the forms of punishment which have been placed here in the category of induction discipline. It is quite possible, on the contrary, that withdrawal of affection, which parents often make the focus of induction discipline, may be the most aversive component in the child's experience of any kind of punishment.[66]

From the extensive literature on the subject Becker has noted the extreme importance for behavioral dispositions of the mother's training techniques.[67] Maximum rule enforcement and conformity both occur when the mother is both warm and restrictive. Where this combination exists children are likely to misbehave at home but be good in school and to exhibit the behavioral characteristics of submissiveness, dependency, politeness, neatness, obedience, minimal aggression, maximum rule enforcement (boys), non-friendliness, non-creativeness, and maximum compliance. Warm and permissive mothers, on the other hand, tend to rear children who are active, socially outgoing, creative, successfully aggressive, minimally rule enforcing (boys), independent, friendly and creative and exhibit low projective hostility. Our observations clearly reveal that Chinese mothers are generally warm with children but are neither all-restrictive nor all-permissive. Socialization is not initially severe, but restrictions are increasingly applied, especially in the development of unquestioning loyalty to the group and its leaders,which for the child initially means the family and the parents. With heavy emphasis on induction training involving love withdrawal these pressures increase and become embodied in behavioral manifestations of conformity to explicit parental example, dependency, and extreme reluctance to express hostility, especially toward authority, unless legitimized by specific violations of codes of behavior by others.

SECTION TWO.   SECONDARY-LEVEL ROLE LEARNING—THE SCHOOLS

By the time children arrive in third grade they are at an age of maximum suggestibility.[68] For many children this is their fourth year of systematic

66 Aronfreed, "The Concept of Internalization," p. 311.

67 Becker, *op. cit.*, pp. 196–198.

68 McGuire, *op. cit.*, p. 248.

schooling and their ninth year of exposure to family socialization. Many theorists posit a relationship between attitudes toward political or economic authority, as they may be learned in places like the school, and attitudes toward family authority. Yet while we would not assert an autonomy of attitudes in the economic or political realm, it is also true that a direct linkage with family-related attitudes is neither necessary nor always probable. There is some reason to question theories which maintain that it is within the family that attitudes and behavior patterns relevant to all social levels are transmitted and acquired. Rapid and extensive shifts in normative behavior within a single generation make such formulations improbable and suggest that changes in family interactions, even when they occur, may be relatively unimportant as an explanation for such shifts. Rather there may be a more complex process in which attitudinal and behavioral learning is continuous among several learning levels, with families providing general guidelines but not the complex cultural training that takes place at a different social level.[69] The critical location of such training in modern societies is the formal school system. Here children are gathered together away from the family for a relatively long and set number of hours per day in a group setting in which the high-intensity affective bonds that characterize the family are muted. Attitudes concerning role behavior are frequently phrased in terms of negative or positive values relating to "the group" rather than to particular others such as mothers or fathers. There develops a highly powerful reference group bound by norms of interpersonal behavior, many of which are unrelated to specific individuals.

The learning of skills requires conformity to set steps and procedures—a process of acquisition of knowledge. This learning process is closely related to attitudinal learning, which takes place within the same group context. Small groups such as classes are focal points for the development of attitudes, habits, and values. Here the pressure to conformity is a function of the affective tie of the individual to the group, the degree of public commitment to group goals that has been required or spontaneously obtained, the degree of agreement among group members, and the length of time one has belonged to this particular group. Modern schools make extensive efforts to maximize each of the above

[69] Albert Bandura, "Social-Learning Theory of Identificatory Processsses," in Goslin, *op. cit.*, pp. 250, 255.

conditions. They also tend to encourage a show of group participation in attitudinal decisions, a learning technique which has been found to develop adult-oriented moral orientations in children and which increases commitment by tying new beliefs or attitude orientations to issues or areas of commitment which are already valued. Thus when a child learns about the "Mother Country" or the "Fatherland" there is expected to be a linkage between affective patterns toward parents and the new group concept of nation.

Schools vary in philosophy of education, educational style, and organizational structure. In many educational systems there is an emphasis on rigidity, hierarchy, formalism, and separation of the sexes. Teachers stress formal learning; children in their contacts with authority are expected to be both passive and deferential. In other societies educators self-consciously attempt to reject this style of interaction between teacher and student.

Social systems which emphasize the authority of the teacher often place great emphasis, too, on group activities. Bronfenbrenner has shown how schools in the Soviet Union stress shared and joint activity in which comparing and competing in classroom activities and the giving of rewards and punishments are done on a group basis as standard practices.[70] Collective discipline and altruism are positively reinforced through a constant and heavy emphasis on morals. For deviant behavior withdrawal of affection is the most common form of punishment. The emphasis on the group and on morals appears to develop a high sense of appropriate behavioral standards, a fierce group loyalty, and a suspicion, approaching xenophobia, concerning outsiders.[71]

For Americans the intrinsic worth of the individual is one of the basic values governing all relationships, and is closely linked with values concerning equality of opportunity and government by consent.[72] Such values are quite different from traditional and current Chinese notions of the intrinsic and basic value of the group, the paramount necessity for loyalty, and the notion that opportunity is directly related to some social criterion of individual worth (being a degree candidate in

[70] Urie Bronfenbrenner, *Two Worlds of Childhood*, pp. 9–14, 21, 49–55, 57–69. Also Joseph M. Notterman, (citing Bronfenbrenner, *Behavior: A Systematic Approach*, Random House, New York, 1970, pp. 338–339.

[71] See Wilson, *op. cit.*

[72] Grace Graham, *The Public School in the American Community*, Harper and Row, New York, 1963, p. 39.

traditional China or being classified as of poor peasant background in modern China are two examples). In traditional China there was great emphasis on "morality" as acquired through the rote emulation of book precepts or specific models and fulfilled by careful attention to social obligations. One should copy the goodness of others and, regardless of station in life, behave in such a way that others would follow this example. Loyalty and faith in what was socially sanctioned as good were virtues that should not be violated even when experience suggested the falsity of the model. Superior morality was thought to bring victory, a precept which appears to be deeply rooted in China's tradition and which is still a widespread lesson in many Chinese communities today.[73]

In the People's Republic of China some of these patterns have taken on a new and vibrant identity. Textbook content is reported to be serious and moral, carrying the injunction that pleasure is found in hard work and helping others and that cooperation makes for happy children.[74] Teacher education stresses the importance of moral-political training, and moral-political education, in turn, is the central component of education, much of it outside the formal curriculum.[75] Individuality is strongly frowned upon as self-interest or selfishness, and in its place socialist morality and proletarian solidarity are stressed. Loyalty to Mao Tse-tung is heavily emphasized, especially in the sense that one is loyal to those who deserve emulation and Mao's personal life and writings are praised as entirely appropriate guides for behavior. Lesser models lower in the hierarchy are also extensively utilized. Both negative and positive examples of appropriate behavior are constant features of the learning environment. Thus, the emphasis on loyalty, group unity, identity through the group, and morals has persisted from traditional times even while the content of these concepts has changed greatly.

Many of the educational patterns on Taiwan have been set forth in previous research.[76] General educational doctrine stresses that the school will be a transition from the family environment to citizenship in a wider society. In order for education to achieve this shift the family

[73] Wolfram Eberhard, "The Cultural Baggage of Chinese Emigrants," *Asian Survey*, vol. 11, no. 5, May 1971, pp. 460–462.

[74] R. F. Price, *Education in Communist China*, Routledge and Kegan Paul, London, 1970, p. 122.

[75] *Ibid.*, pp. 134–135, 229, 263.

[76] Wilson, *op. cit.*

and school are expected to have congruent goals and to coordinate their separate influences. Parents are exhorted to take an interest in their child's education in terms of both "moral" development and academic achievement, the two being closely associated as means and effect. In many people's minds a teacher is felt to have a more profound influence on a child than the parents, for the teacher is supposed to be both teacher and parent while the child is at school. Ideally a teacher is supposed to be a model of good conduct and to have the explicit responsibility of imparting behavioral standards to children.

Primary-group socialization stresses the value of obedience, respect, and loyalty within the context of highly particularistic relationships. In school education on Taiwan a considerable effort is made to intensify the value commitment underlying these behavior patterns but to wean these values away from particularistic relationships and stress them as universal codes applicable to all levels of role behavior. On Taiwan this is a consciously directed process in which both length and intensity of education are seen as of great importance in achieving this goal. Compulsory education (now through ninth grade) and absolute central control of the curriculum are deemed essential.

After noting that morality is developed solely from the influence of the social environment and only after prolonged training, a recent text on child psychology in Taiwan states succinctly the goal of school education as perceived by educational authorities:

> The most desirable behavior is that based on standards of morality not influenced or affected by other's opinions. Through education and experience in the school and family we come to accept others' sympathy and constructive advice, to admire virtue and condemn vice. . . . We would conscientiously feel self-condemnation if we failed to behave properly. This is what we call moral sentiments, with which we form our personality. . . . it is possible for the average child, through family and school education, to behave by certain rules such as obedience to parents and teachers, love of group and country, and observing orders. At first these rules only have an indirect and slight effect and are observed solely for the sake of social practice. However, these rules will gradually be observed habitually. Through development this moral sentiment finally constitutes the foundation of personality.[77]

[77] Huang I, ed., *Childhood Psychology* (*Erh-t'ung Hsin-li-hsueh*), Li Chieh, publisher, Taipei, Taiwan, 1969, pp. 125–126.

The school training of children on Taiwan emphasizes a morality in which loyalty to the group and the leader are paramount virtues. The learning environment involves the use of shaming, emulation of appropriate models, and induction training. The stories that children read are often highly and straightforwardly moral in content, and these lessons are reinforced in an ever more direct way by a multitude of signs and injunctions. Wall slogans include such pithy expressions as "Strictly Guard Order," "Keep Silent," and "Mutually Cooperate," and, pointed out to me as the most important of all, "Politeness, Righteousness, Frugality, and To Know Shame." Within the classrooms, regulations are posted which further delineate appropriate behavior. Seventh-grade boys learn: (1) To lovingly protect the school is to keep the school's regulations; (2) To enthusiastically do things for the group is to grasp the highest honor; and (3) To be a good student in spirit and body is to be a good Chinese. The first four regulations in a fifth-grade girl's class state: (1) Loving the Country. I love the Country and love its people; (2) Obey the Laws. I obey the regulations and follow the guidance of the teacher; (3) Cooperation. My classmates and I are mutually friendly and affectionate; and (4) Group Togetherness. I wish to cooperate with everyone.

As occurs in any school system, the quality of teaching and leadership provided by teachers on Taiwan varies. Generally speaking, however, teachers are considered by the children to be authority figures worthy of great respect. Most children and adults noted in interviews their feeling of discomfort in openly questioning an authority figure, particularly if this person was accorded high status, as a teacher is. Children stand and bow on the teacher's entrance and departure, or when meeting the teacher in the hallway or returning a paper in class. In many cases the bearing and mannerisms of teachers reinforce their authority. Students are ordered to stand up or sit down at the beginning and end of a response; the other students are sometimes ordered to handclap their approval for a correct response. A small but typical example of the reinforcement of the teacher's role is that children, beginning in third grade, are taught that when writing a letter to the teacher one should write the characters for "to send above" after one's signature. This should be done because the letter is addressed to a teacher, who by definition is a member of the elder generation and thus of higher status as far as children are concerned. (Despite this reinforcement of authority, however, it would be highly inaccurate to portray teachers as always and unbendingly formal. As late as seventh grade in a boys' class, one can observe instances when a formal class will end and the boys surround the male teacher, some of them even hanging onto his back with arms around him.)

The teacher operates within the class context to inculcate attitudes concerning "appropriate" role behavior within a "group" context, but the size of the "group" and the quality of its membership are often vague for the child, except that he knows he is expected to apply in all situations the behavior patterns he has learned in a particularistic primary context. Moreover, although the relationships expand well beyond face-to-face ones it is expected that loyalty to the group will be maintained and also that the group will be retained at least ideally as a reference for appropriate behavior.

Group identity and a sense of group responsibility are fostered by a variety of techniques. There are row contests in classrooms; games and stories emphasize group themes; and the teacher may attempt to foster solidarity by group punishments for individual deviations. Peer groups are scrutinized for the effect the members will have on each other. In competition children are expected to learn that the group's performance reflects on oneself and that therefore personal sacrifice and inconvenience are appropriate if necessary for the group's goals to be achieved.

Physical punishment is used in the schools by the principal and by the teachers. Teachers can be observed slapping the behinds of little children who are late for recess on the playground. In a seventh-grade girls' biology class nearly half the class failed a pre-final exam. One by one those children who failed were called to the head of the class, scolded, and then struck across the hand once or twice with a bamboo switch. When told to return to their seats they were ordered to stand until the punishment for everyone had been meted out. Later the children remarked that this type of punishment occurred more frequently in elementary school. What was noted with particular intensity, however, was that the physical punishment was relatively easy to bear while the shame of being rebuked before one's classmates was excruciating.

Shaming, in fact, is a most persistent, observable, and increasing feature of the learning environment on Taiwan. The few examples given here can only begin to indicate the prevalence of this technique. On the aversive side, children are required to stand exposed to their peers for behavioral (including intellectual) failures. Having to stand at one's seat for missing an answer is a common practice. Students who are fearful or have eccentric habits may be openly criticized or ridiculed. Those who do not have the proper uniform, have dirty fingernails or ears, or do not have handkerchiefs are requested to stand and give their names. On the positive side, correct responses may be warmly applauded. The group that wins a class row competition may be singled out as especially worthy. Children are reminded over and over that it is through their group participation that they may attain worth as individuals. In all injunctions, either negative or positive, values such as cooperativeness, unselfishness, unity, and loyalty are stressed as appropriate goals of role behavior, whatever the context the child may be in. The fulfillment of or failure to fulfill moral precepts is increasingly emphasized as the basis for reward or grounds for punishment. As the children grow older, moral injunctions are both reinforced and increasingly linked into a comprehensive, interlocking set of precepts.

There are both major differences and major similarities between the educational systems of Taiwan and Hong Kong. Perhaps the major difference is that education in Hong Kong is not compulsory (although it is widespread through the elementary years), nor is there in Hong Kong a comparable control of the educational system by the government. Syllabus and textbook preparation by subcommittees within the Education Department provides what are considered to be appropriate guidelines to publishers as well as suggested book lists for teachers who may wish to select material from a reviewed and approved list. In theory each school, and indeed each teacher, can choose the textbooks they wish. Both implicitly and explicitly there is a similar emphasis by educational authorities on coordination between home and school education. School, it is said, should be regarded as a "second home," where a "noble morality" will be learned.[78] Time will mold casual behavior into unbreakable habits that will apply in any circumstance, but for this to happen parents and teachers must be alert to correct the smallest misbehavior.[79] As one is filial to parents and does not fail to live up to their expectations, so it is expected that children will obey

[78] Tu Chia-chung, ed., *Economic and Public Affairs* (*Ching-chi Chi Kung-kung Shih-wu*), Book One, Grade 7, Wen Fung Book Co., Hong Kong, 1969, p. 11.
[79] *Ibid.*, p. 42.

school regulations in order to become good citizens. The purpose of these regulations is to develop as far as possible the attributes of respect for teachers, befriending of classmates, protection of public property, attention to order and cleanliness, observation of communal obligation, sincerity and honesty toward others, and humbleness and politeness in speech and manners.[80]

Children are taught that morality is the basis of good character and that family morality emphasizing mutual respect, filiality toward parents, and harmony among brothers and sisters is the model for social relations.[81] Yet morality in education is stressed much less heavily than on Taiwan despite the fact that the British educational authorities are concerned about character building and social training, both of which are considered to be as important as academic success. In the schools, a principal may use approximately half an hour of one morning each week to call the students together and lecture them concerning good conduct, right morals, etc.; on Taiwan, weather permitting, these lectures are held every morning.

Exams in Chinese language are heavily based on traditional proverbs with moral content, and many textbook-lesson stories stress moral themes such as loyalty or honesty. However, moral precepts and slogans are not generally a feature of classroom walls, and where they are they are likely to be very different from those observed in Taiwan. For little children, poster models may be of Donald Duck or Mickey Mouse or of figures such as the postman or doctor. In one class the signs under pictures on the wall exhorted the children in the following way: (1) Please see how happy we are; (2) We practice doing homework; (3) We are enjoying our reading very much; (4) The great painters of the future; (5) Do you like to be a doctor or a nurse?; and (6) This is an opportunity to train our thinking.

Politeness and respect for teachers are considered of paramount importance. As Hong Kong seventh graders learn:

> Teachers impart knowledge to us before we know how to reason properly. Therefore we should respect our teachers. To respect teachers is to respect the character and knowledge of teachers and to accept their instruction sincerely without an iota of hypocrisy.[82]

[80] *Ibid.*, pp. 63–65.
[81] *Ibid.*, pp. 4–8.
[82] *Ibid.*, p. 12.

For the child the status of the teacher is extremely high, equal to that of the parent. In dealing with such authority figures "good manners" are highly emphasized, including standing at the appropriate time, obedience, the maintenance of "discipline" at prescribed times such as going to and from class, and bowing. To be impolite is frequently noted as the worst thing children can do. In dealing with "impoliteness" teachers are often brisk in the maintenance of order; an older child will be requested to stand and will then be spoken to. Silence in the presence of teachers is expected. When class begins or ends the children will stand as they do on Taiwan and bow to the teacher together. While bowing to the teachers or the principal in the corridors is not as prevalent as on Taiwan it does occur.

Although teachers in Hong Kong are told to be firm in imparting good behavior and knowledge to children, it is not expected that they will be authoritarian, and observation indicates that in most instances they are not. The stress in learning about leadership is on the spirit of service, fairness, kindness, and politeness as the attributes of the good class prefect. In addition, of course, the good class leader, like the teacher, is expected to be a good example to others and to obey the school regulations.[83]

Inculcating a sense of group order and discipline is also a goal of the educational environment in Hong Kong. As a second-grade reading primer puts it, "The school is a big family and many schoolmates are together. You help me and I'll help you and everybody will be very harmonious. The school is a small society. Life in school has many good points. Together we study and together we work. All of us have discipline."[84] As on Taiwan the children wear uniforms. In about 70% of the schools, before classes begin or after recess the children line up in a large open hall by classes. Even in nurseries—ages two to five—there is much supervision and practice concerning getting into line and marching. At the beginning of a new school year the smallest children practice

[83] "Letter to Young Friends: On the Responsibility of a Class Prefect," in *Children's Garden, Overseas Chinese Daily (Erh-t'ung T'ien-ti, Hua-ch'iao Jih-pao)*, Jan. 6, 1971; and Editorial Board of the Modern Educational Research Society, ed., "The Election of a Monitor," in *Elementary School Reader (Hsiao-hsueh Kuo-yu)*, Second Term, Grade 2, Modern Educational Research Society, Hong Kong, 1969, pp. 11–12.

[84] Editorial Board of the Modern Educational Research Society, ed., "The School is a Big Family," in *Elementary School Reader, op. cit.*, First Term, Grade 2, Lesson One.

marching in two lines up and down stairs, partly as a safety measure but also as group training in discipline.

In the classrooms children sit in rows, two by two, as on Taiwan. There are row games and competitions, while at other times class responses will be made in unison. At one school, when the bell to signal the end of recess sounded the children instantly stopped their activities, the smallest ones "frozen" as in a game. Many were at attention and there was complete silence. "Move," said a voice; then "stop," then "move;" and the children lined up at attention by class ready to return to work.

Desirable behavior patterns are reinforced by praise and a variety of rewards, including the singling out of those whose behavior is especially exemplary. Failure, however, is punished by physical punishment and by shaming techniques. One observer in a New Territories government-aided primary school made the following observation indicative of the prevalence of physical punishment for small children. "One interesting thing. When they were caught doing something wrong, or could not answer the questions asked, they would very naturally and without any hesitation or being asked, raise up their hand to be slapped by the teacher."[85]

The most prevalent form of punishment is shaming. For pre-school children at day centers the worst technique of punishment is to make the child stand in a corner facing out and to publicly point out what he has done and that he is a naughty child. The punishment is ended by words such as "You can now rejoin the group." In one elementary school, when the senior master was asked what teachers do if a child misbehaves in class he responded that they make the child stand and talk to him. "They do not punish," he said, completely unaware of the aversive aspects of this form of treatment, "but put emphasis on good conduct." In one school (approximately 700 students), the children were lined up in a large open hall to leave and one boy was being disciplined by being made to stand in front on a platform facing his schoolmates. He remained standing there while the others left and did not leave until all were gone. Then a teacher spoke with him and permitted him to go.

In all such shaming punishments there is a component of ridicule, but the component of ostracism or separation from the group appears even more strongly. The dread of shaming punishments plus the

[85] Siu-tong Kwok, in personal correspondence.

emphasis on group discipline and on respect and loyalty toward leaders by children result in an aversion to being in situations where shaming punishments can be incurred and the development of strong supportive feelings concerning group unity and conformist behavior. On the negative side, conformism appears to generate considerable fear and concern by the teachers as to whether the children are "active" enough (i.e., whether they are too dependent).

For children in Chinatown, New York City, and New Jersey, compulsory education takes place within locally governed school systems in which curriculum is controlled within widely varying limits. The variations among school systems are sufficiently large that it is possible here only to speak generally about the average American educational process. For both groups of children a large portion of the day is spent in attendance at an English language public school. In Chinatown, however, there is further attendance for approximately two hours per day for some children at an "after-school school," where the Chinese language as well as the history and culture of China are taught. The school exists specifically to meet the need of parents who do not wish their children to grow up without any systematic exposure to Chinese cultural patterns that are of great importance to the parents.

The Chinese school in Chinatown is similar in many respects to schools in both Taiwan and Hong Kong. The children stand when the teacher enters or leaves the classroom and they also stand when responding. The textbook materials come from either Taiwan or Hong Kong and contain the same moral precepts and lessons which are learned in those two areas. Classes are conducted in Chinese and every effort is made to approximate as closely as possible the "Chinese" learning environment. For discipline the children are sent into the hallway and told to stand quietly in a row, the smallest first, facing a large gilt bust of Sun Yat-sen. Presumably the moral example of Sun's life will inspire young miscreants to better behavior.

It is extremely difficult to make an accurate assessment of the differences in the learning environment between the Chinese school in New York City and the public school systems in Hong Kong and Taiwan, because the differences in outward style are so slight. When asked about the difference between Hong Kong and Chinese-American children, a Hong Kong teacher who had recently returned from teaching at a Chinese school in Los Angeles replied, "Very little, if any."

Perhaps one of the clearest distinctions is captured in the fact that the children in New York City do not wear uniforms. For the observer there is a sense that the degree of group unity existing in Taiwan and Hong Kong schools is missing, that the degree of respect for authority is less, and that the sense of group discipline is lower, despite the great effort made to achieve these goals. An observer feels that the Chinese school is an episode rather than a basic experience, and that a more powerful socialization experience for these children is occurring elsewhere. The feeling is not that this educational episode is irrelevant but that the strenuous efforts to create a particular style of secondary-level role behavior have been co-opted elsewhere and that the Chinese school is more an extension of the family and its environment than a dynamic interface between the family and the social system.

For the "average" American child ages three to sixteen, about one-sixth of the normal day is spent watching television.[86] The extent of the influence of television is variable and thus injects an element into the socialization of American children that is currently debated in terms of effect, intensity, and direction. There is also a considerable diversity of ethnic background, which in terms of family training has a decreasing but still noticeable effect. One of the unifying forces in American sociali-zation is the educational system, despite the fact that even here severe qualifications must be made. Nevertheless both state and federal govern-mental influence and the professionalization of teacher and administra-tor training in terms of generally common standards have tended to impose a degree of uniformity on "American" education. This uniformity is now sufficiently widespread that Americans moving from one area to another are able to carry with them a general set of expecta-tions concerning both the style and content of their children's education.

Since the late nineteenth century, overt moralizing in American schools has been increasingly in disfavor. Classroom prayers, common a decade ago, have been abolished, and the elimination of prayers is merely symbolic of a deeper and longer lasting trend. It should not be assumed, however, because of the tendency away from moralizing in terms of some specific creed, that the teaching of values is not an aspect of the American classroom. It is reported, for instance, that some of the major values that permeate the educational system are those of com-

---

[86] Eleanor E. Maccoby, "Effects of the Mass Media," in Hoffman and Hoffman, op. cit., vol. 1, p. 329,

petitive success, conformity to group standards, emphasis on "democratic" values and "democratic" relationships, and the development of patriotic values and beliefs.[87] The value systems of American boys and girls stress the importance of intelligence, sociability, likableness, dependability, reliability, interpersonal courage, independence, self-reliance, and maturity. Girls put more stress on being liked and on interpersonal harmony and success and boys put more stress on motoric values, physical courage, and interpersonal control or dominance. Both sexes heavily stress likeable attributes.[88]

Stories stressing the moral values of George Washington or Abraham Lincoln are still used in schools, but more prevalent are less personalized stories of animals, trains, cars, or everyday people who succeed in tasks, learn to cooperate, and win the approval of their neighbors. Social approval, particularly in middle-class America, is contingent on achievement striving, and on learning how to keep this striving from having socially harmful consequences. The desire for approval is reflected on the emphasis given to the development of likable qualities; it is by no means a recent phenomenon. Over twenty years ago Riesman asked some sixty young people what they wanted most: money, fame, or the respect of their community. The overwhelming majority chose respect of the community.[89]

In American socialization approval for many children means first of all approval by their peers. To a great extent American socialization patterns exhibit a high degree of age-segregation, and this development is not checked by any systematic effort in the schools to instill a sense of membership in a larger, multiple-age group. There is little or no stress on the responsibilities that children owe to a broader social grouping, a deficiency which in some sense reflects the emphasis on independence and individualism. To an extent the whole process of maturing in any society involves some shift in frame of reference from rigid adherence to adult rules to an awareness and concern for the opinion of peers. Americans, however, are particularly peer- and peer-group oriented, and this orientation is most heavily directed toward groupings in which face-to-face relationships predominate. McClelland found that Ameri-

[87] Graham, op. cit., p. 23 citing Robin M. Williams, Jr., American Society: A Sociological Interpretation, Knopf, 1960, p. 296.

[88] Morris Rosenberg, Society and the Adolescent Self-Image, Princeton University Press, Princeton, N.J., 1965, pp. 254–256.

[89] David Riesman, The Lonely Crowd, Yale University Press, New Haven, 1950, p. 120.

can high-school boys listed an average of five group activities whereas German boys listed only one. Americans were also much more likely than Britons or Austrians to agree to items which stress guidance by or conformity with the views of others.[90]

American peer groups have sets of norms and sanctions whereby conformity is rewarded and deviance punished. These norms are highly variable among groupings and are not necessarily a reflection of the larger social system. Within these groups children learn to cooperate and to adjust to the expectations of others, although much of the activity also stresses self-development virtues. Competitive striving with an emphasis on achievement and independence takes place within a framework of autonomous peer groups that in many respects replaces the family as the primary focus of the emotional support that is required if competitive achievement is not to be too disorganizing to the personality.[91]

Peer groups may stress autonomy and achievement orientation or they may stress opposite values. The capacity of a peer group to impose its own value orientations—which in some cases may be at variance with larger social norms—is a function of the level and intensity of association by its members. Resistance to peer pressure has been found to be strongest where association with parents is high. For Americans this is especially so with respect to interaction with the mother,[92] a factor which again emphasizes the reduced saliency of the American father in primary-level socialization. For many American children, however, family control decreases markedly with age and is replaced by peer orientation. The need for peer approval is sufficiently strong that American children, unlike Soviet children, are more rather than less inclined to break adult norms if they know their peers are aware of their actions.[93] The autonomy of American peer groups competes with the priorities of the larger social grouping and imparts to the learning and practice of secondary-level role behavior a highly particularistic flavor.

[90] David C. McClelland, *The Achieving Society*, D. Van Nostrand Co., Princeton, N.J., 1961, p. 197.

[91] Talcott Parsons and Winston White, "The Link Between Character and Society," in Lipset and Lowenthal, *op. cit.*, pp. 121–127.

[92] Edward C. Devereux, "The Role of Peer Group Experience in Moral Development," in John P. Hill, ed., *Minnesota Symposia on Child Psychology*, vol. 4, University of Minnesota Press, Minneapolis, 1970, p. 111.

[93] Bronfenbrenner, *Two Worlds of Childhood*, p. 78.

Pupil-teacher relations place the teacher in an adult authority role outside of the peer group, as an authority figure who directs and whose role is distinct and separate from the peer group. This placement, however, does not imply emotional distance, for relations with teachers are usually friendly and are not surrounded by overt forms of respect for authority such as bowing, standing when spoken to, etc. The relationship is one of trust and the teacher's function is less that of an authoritative source of knowledge and behavioral norms and more that of an integrative, permissive, and cooperative guide. Teachers do not pose as the embodiment of knowledge. Rather than vigorously applying highly articulated moral judgments to events they tend to shy away even from noncontroversial opinions and to discourage the critical and open evaluation of events and institutions unless there is a known public sanction for doing so.[94]

American teachers are not expected to be surrogate parents, nor are they expected to be punishers in the traditional sense that fathers were. Despite the fact that male teachers were in the majority at the high-school level by 1960 the evidence suggests that they have not made teaching more "masculine" but in fact play "feminine" roles.[95] In any case, teachers in the United States do not tend to be powerful authority figures or models such as they are in China and Japan. In answer to the question who can make you follow a rule, only in Japan (of six countries; the test did not include China) was the teacher ranked higher than the parents. Everywhere else, including America, the position of the teacher followed that of the parents, who were in first place.[96]

Physical punishments are forbidden in New Jersey schools, and while an occasional shaking or ear pinching may take place such punishments can and have earned the reprimand or expulsion of the teacher involved. Within the classroom scolding involving shaming may be employed, but the teacher does not normally make such an instance the cause of a lecture on a moral precept, since doing so would reflect on the moral worth of the student involved and is thus considered too degrading or humiliating a punishment. If classroom misbehavior is too severe the child may be asked to stand in the hall or be sent to the principal's

[94] Harmon Zeigler, *The Political Life of American Teachers*, Prentice-Hall, Englewood Cliffs, N.J., 1967, pp. 97–98, 119.

[95] *Ibid.*, pp. 9, 12.

[96] June L. Tapp, "A Child's Garden of Law and Order," *Psychology Today*, vol. 4, no. 7, December 1970, p. 64.

office. Frequently a special counselor is on the staff whose function is to "adjust" the difficulties involved. In extreme cases parents may be called to the school to consult with the principal or teacher concerning the child or the child may be suspended or expelled from the school. Beyond a classroom rebuke, perhaps the most common form of punishment is to require the child to speak with the teacher after the class or after school, when an individual scolding is administered, extra work may be assigned, and play or recess time may be withheld. Punishment is usually an individual matter between the student and the teacher and does not involve the overt invocation of group standards or group censure.

For children from New Jersey, Chinatown, Taiwan, and Hong Kong, some of the most important lessons in secondary-level role training involve learning about leadership position and group membership. Three questions which dealt with these problems from the standpoint of spatial organization were asked of children from our samples. These questions were as follows (see Appendix for complete questionnaire):

13. Here is a group of people. Who is the leader? Put an X on the one you think is the leader:

The circles were drawn of unequal size in order to draw the children's attention to the larger ones. The assumption was that children would tend to select either the large circle outside the group to the left or the large circle within the group. Using an analysis of variance technique, the response patterns for "leader outside the group" and "leader inside the group" were analyzed separately for group (Taiwan, Hong Kong, Chinatown and America), sex, grade level (3, 5, and 7), and interaction effects. Significance was set at the 0.5 level. For the "leader outside the group" responses there were no significant differences among groups or between sexes. There was a significant interaction effect between group and sex. For the "leader within the group" responses there were significant differences only among groups and among grade levels.

20. Here are two groups. Which group would you like to be leader of?
    Draw a big circle all around the group you pick:

The response patterns for this question also establish whether the leader is seen as "within" the relevant group context or "without," and here the children are also asked what their *own* preferences would be in a leadership position. Again these responses were tested separately for "leader within" or "leader without" the group. For the "leader within" group situation there was a significant difference among groups but not between sexes or among grade levels, nor were there significant interaction effects. For the "leader without" group situation there was a significant difference among groups and a significant interaction effect between group and sex. There were no other significant differences or significant interaction effects.

29. Here are four groups of people. Which of these groups would you like to be a member of? Draw a big circle all around the group you pick.

The purpose of this question was to examine the desirability of "closeness" in a group context. Responses 1 and 3 were grouped together as representing a "close" group context, and responses 2 and 4 were grouped together as representing a "loose" group context. For the "close" group context there was a significant difference among groups, between sexes, and among grade levels and a significant interaction between group and grade level. For the "loose" group context there was a significant difference among groups, between sexes, and among grade levels but no significant interaction effects.

Graphs representing a portion of this data will be presented. Our assumption is that certain types of training techniques tend to emphasize highly cohesive groups in which leadership is seen as "within" and the function of leadership is to create and maintain a sense of inclusiveness, cohesiveness, and hierarchy. Other types of training techniques tend to favor loosely organized groups with leadership essentially outside the group and interacting with the group as a whole rather than, through internal hierarchic channels, with all subordinate group members. In analyzing the responses from these three questions the responses for each question that fall under the "close group/leadership within" pattern will be presented first, followed by data for "loose group/leadership without" responses. Data will be presented only for group and grade-level differences. Other differences were not sufficiently pronounced in significance or in pattern to warrant presentation.[97]

When the four groups were compared for the case of "close group/ leadership within," the response pattern was as shown in Graph 1. Among groups the average of the mean percentage values gives Taiwan

[97] For the "close group leadership within" responses there was a significant difference between sexes and a significant interaction effect between group and grade level on question 29. For males the mean percentage value was 71%, while for females it was 80%. The figures for the interaction effect between group and grade level were as follows:

QUESTION 29

	Grade 3	Grade 5	Grade 7
America	58%	83%	67%
Chinatown	61%	91%	85%
Taiwan	62%	84%	90%
Hong Kong	66%	70%	88%

For the "loose group leadership without" responses there was also a significant difference between the sexes on question 29; males were 27% and females 17%. There were significant interactions between group and sex on questions 13 and 20. This data is as follows:

QUESTION 13

	Male	Female
America	56%	58%
Chinatown	44%	69%
Taiwan	60%	50%
Hong Kong	59%	60%

QUESTION 20

America	67%	62%
Chinatown	51%	78%
Taiwan	51%	77%
Hong Kong	51%	44%

54%, Hong Kong 53%, America 46% and Chinatown 43%. The average rank orders are Taiwan 1.7, Hong Kong 2.0, Chinatown 3.0, and America 3.3.* Among grade levels the average of the mean percentage values gives seventh grade 58%, ahead of fifth grade with 50% and third grade with 40%. The average rank orders are seventh grade 1.0, fifth

GRAPH 1   *Comparison among Groups of "Close Group/Leadership Within" Responses, Percent*

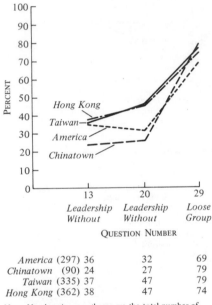

America (297)	36	32	69
Chinatown (90)	24	27	79
Taiwan (335)	37	47	79
Hong Kong (362)	38	47	74

Note: Numbers in parentheses are the total number of respondents in that category.

Question 13: F = 7.25
Question 20: F = 8.43
Question 29: F = 7.30

* Since there are four groups, if one group had been in first place on all questions its average rank order would have been 1.0, while if it had been lowest on all questions its average rank order would have been 4.0.

GRAPH 2   *Comparison among Grade Levels of "Close Group/Leadership Within" Responses, Percent*

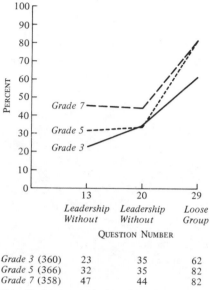

Grade 3 (360)	23	35	62
Grade 5 (366)	32	35	82
Grade 7 (358)	47	44	82

Note: Numbers in parentheses are the total number of respondents in that category

Question 13: F = 33.05
Question 20: F = n.s.
Question 29: F = 62.96
n.s. − not significant

grade 2.3, and third grade 2.7. When grade levels are compared, the response pattern is as shown in Graph 2.

For the case of "loose group/leadership without" the response pattern among groups was as indicated in Graph 3. Among groups the average of the mean percentage values gives America the highest "loose group/leadership without" response rate with 50%, ahead of Chinatown with 45%, Hong Kong with 43%, and Taiwan with 41%. The average rank orders are American 1.3, Hong Kong 2.0, Chinatown 3.0, and Taiwan 3.7. Among grade levels the average of the mean percentage values gives third grade 54%, fifth grade 44%, and seventh grade 37%, with average rank orders of 1.0, 2.3, and 2.7, respectively. A comparison among grade levels is shown in Graph 4.

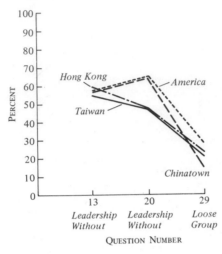

GRAPH 3 *Comparison among Groups of* "*Loose Group/Leadership Without*" *Responses, Percent*

	13 Leadership Without	20 Leadership Without	29 Loose Group
America (297)	57	65	29
Chinatown (90)	56	64	15
Taiwan (335)	55	47	21
Hong Kong (362)	59	48	23

QUESTION NUMBER

Note: Numbers in parentheses are the total number of respondents in that category.

Question 13: F = n.s.
Question 20: F = 10.67
Question 29: F = 8.56
n.s. — not significant

Questions 13 and 20 relate specifically to leadership "within" or "without" the group, while question 29 relates specifically to the "closeness" or "looseness" of group organization. While the data presented here is not conclusive in itself, it suggests that genuine differences do exist between American children and children of Chinese

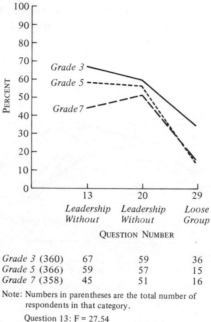

GRAPH 4   *Comparison among Grade Levels of "Loose Group/Leadership Without" Responses, Percent*

	13 Leadership Without	20 Leadership Without	29 Loose Group
Grade 3 (360)	67	59	36
Grade 5 (366)	59	57	15
Grade 7 (358)	45	51	16

Note: Numbers in parentheses are the total number of respondents in that category.

Question 13: F = 27.54
Question 20: F = n.s.
Question 29: F = 48.37
n.s.–not significant

background and also between different age levels of children in general.

On the whole, the children from the America and Chinatown samples placed less emphasis on leadership being within a group than did the children from Taiwan and Hong Kong. All children, although the percentage decreases markedly with age, tended to see leadership as somewhat "without," but this was more marked for the America and Chinatown groups than for the Taiwan and Hong Kong samples. The children from all four groups and children generally with age tended to prefer membership in close-knit groups. This was more the case, how-ever, for children from Chinatown, Taiwan, and Hong Kong than it was for children from New Jersey. Although the differences were not great, there seem to be pressures within Chinese societies for close, inclusive social relationships, pressures which are reflected in statements concerning the need for unity, cooperation, and suppression of hostility. When one connects this pattern of more highly valued group closeness with a greater tendency to see leadership as "within," there emerges the pattern of a highly unitary group structure with a leadership that maintains cohesion through relationships with members that are conceived of at least partially as direct vertical links between the members and the leader rather than as vertical links between the group as a whole and the leader.

SECTION THREE.   SECONDARY-LEVEL ROLE BEHAVIOR—THE POLITY

It is generally in school that children in societies with universal educational systems first begin to learn in a systematic way the structural components and roles of the social system in which they live. School, of course, is not the only area of learning concerning secondary-level roles and secondary-level organizations. It is the area, however, where children are most consistently taught and encouraged to develop attitude and behavior patterns that increasingly mirror the type of attitudes and behavior they will be expected to exhibit in secondary-level situations. Thus, as an example, classroom activity may emphasize achievement or impersonal honesty, and it is expected that these attributes will characterize later behavior and be standards against which the behavior of others will be measured.

Despite the fact that the school appears to be a consistent force in socializing children to secondary-level behavior, it should not be assumed that this learning process is an orderly one. Certain roles, such as the Presidency, may early be highly salient, while other roles that are structurally closer to the child, such as the mayor, may be much less well known. The ways in which children evaluate role behavior are initially diffuse. The good person is the good citizen, in whom goodness is associated with those attributes which the child has already learned will be rewarding in terms of primary-level participation. Early conceptions about the goodness of primary-level leaders and a general lack of knowledge of structural organization appear to have some relationship to the generally favorable orientations that most children by third grade have toward secondary-level leaders and to the groups which these leaders head, however dimly understood in structural terms they may be. Only with time are sets of behavioral standards learned that are abstractions governing behavior generally.

Children learn secondary-level behavior through direct education, by anticipation of future role occupancy, by modeling, by experience, and by exposure to a myriad number of offhand remarks, the meaning of which may be only partly understood at the time they are heard. Regardless of the mode of learning, a critical factor for firmly obtaining appropriate secondary-level attitudes and behavior patterns is the perceived possibility and probability of actually needing a particular role attribute. If what is learned—even dimly—is not conceived of as "necessary," it is likely to be only latent in terms of one's attitudinal and behavioral dispositions.

Modeling is a ubiquitous aspect of learning. The most successful models are those that have attributes which impress the learner as desirable or worthy of respect. That parents, teachers, and leaders in all societies are able to some extent to manipulate the conditions which make them desirable models (as, for instance, by appearing to have greater intelligence and knowledge through access to a greater number of cues than are available to followers) only points up one of the most powerful ways in which authority figures direct the socialization process in terms of ends they themselves deem to be desirable. Conformity to a set of goals is achieved in a number of ways: by compliance, if the authority figure's power is based on means-control; by identification, if power is based on attractiveness; and through internalization, if power is based on credibility.[98] Authority figures usually have all of these resources available in varying degrees and are thus effective as models along several dimensions.

In many social systems political leaders have a special place in the pantheon of models. Work on American political socialization indicates that the President is a primary model and an ego-ideal source for little

[98] Herbert C. Kelman, "Compliance, Identification, and Internalization: Three Processes of Attitude Change," *Journal of Conflict Resolution*, vol. 2, no. 1, 1958, p. 54.

children. For them he is first on the question of "who would you most like to be?" and outranked only by father and teacher for the question "who do you like the best?"[99] For young children the President is not perceived as likely to do any wrong. He is one of the earliest symbols of political authority for children but is also highly personalized. It is this characteristic which helps the child bridge the gap from relationships which are personalized at the primary level to impersonal ones at the secondary level. The ideal attributes of a leader may vary. American children tend to emphasize benevolence and honesty more than competence, although the first two attributes decline in salience with age and the last increases. In Japan competence is overall the most highly stressed leadership attribute, whereas honesty and benevolence as attributes decline precipitously in comparison by age thirteen.[100] The notions that people have of themselves and their leaders have complex origins that relate both to conceptions of group organization and to the roles of members and leaders within that group context.

Scholars of traditional China have frequently remarked on the relative lack of spontaneous "cause-oriented" groupings above the primary level and the way in which those groups that were formed used pseudo kinship notations in order to legitimize roles and provide a basis for group cohesion. Fulfilment of primary-group goals was considered so basic to the individual's own sense of worth that even sacrifice of the self or family for the society was treated as an instance of honor for the family. Violation of group norms at any level was "unthinkable." Different roles and their status ranking were clearly defined, and the obligations and perquisites pertaining to status and role were often minutely delineated. Although abstract qualities such as benevolence or respect were used to define role behavior, they were always attached with varying degrees of explicitness to particular roles in such a way that they functioned particularistically rather than as general qualities defining all role behavior.

Modern Chinese educational systems vary in the extent of which universalistic criteria are stressed as the basis for role behavior generally. Such an emphasis appears to characterize education in the People's

[99] David Easton and Jack Dennis, *Children in the Political System: Origins of Political Legitimacy*, McGraw-Hill Book Co., New York, 1969, pp. 145–146.

[100] Robert D. Hess, "The Socialization of Attitudes Toward Political Authority: Some Cross-National Comparisons," *International Social Science Journal*, vol. 15, no. 4, 1963, pp. 555–559.

Republic of China, although we have not collected any extensive data on this subject. There, as Tillman Durdin so pithily observed, "A new generation has appeared, and though much of the old China is too indelible to erase as yet, a new China with ways quite different from the old is in existence."[101] Politics reigns in the People's Republic, and it is a politics unabashedly infused with moral fervor and universal moral injunctions. Han Suyin, talking about the feelings of duty of young children, summed up this orientation with the comment, "There is no hiatus between morality and politics. Morality is politics."[102]

In this context the traditional small-group discussion has been utilized as an important means of social transformation. Here general behavior patterns are discussed, and the individuals evaluated in terms of both his understanding of the general applicability of these standards and his capacity to utilize such standards in his relations with others in a variety of contexts. As aids in the development of politico-moral attitudes and behavior patterns, modeling of and learning from leaders are heavily stressed. These models may be brave schoolchildren, semi-legendary People's Liberation Army heroes, or top political leaders themselves. The adulation of Chairman Mao Tse-tung is well known, but is only a particularly striking example of the generally held belief that authority figures must embody correct behavioral attitudes and attributes, must point out correct orientations, and must ensure that negative examples are exposed and controlled. The ultimate purpose of such activity is to ensure a general political orientation at the macro level by inculcating appropriate attitudes and behavior patterns at the individual level and by requiring that those involved be cognizant of the relationship.

On Taiwan also, aspects of traditional China coexist with a new and emergent social system. Especially in the educational system, a massive attempt has been made to transfer prime loyalties from the family to the state and to change the value basis of behavior patterns from particularistic to universalistic. Education is avowedly for the state's and society's interest. Children are constantly told that their lives are to be devoted to the society and that if conflict with the family should arise it is the family which must give way. Slogans within and outside the

[101] Tillman Durdin, "China Transformed by Elimination of 'Four Olds,' " *New York Times*, May 19, 1971, p. 14.

[102] Han Suyin, "China's Generation Gap," *New York Times*, Oct. 12, 1970, p. 37.

schools call for diligence, honesty, and hard work in a context of loyalty to the group and for respect for teachers, parents, elders, and above all the leaders of society. The development of appropriate and universal standards of behavior is considered to be not a random affair but a matter that requires assiduous attention.[103]

On Taiwan learning secondary-level role behavior begins with the knowledge that one is a member of a larger societal grouping and that there are definite obligations associated with this membership. The sense of being part of a larger entity than the primary group, one that is entitled to one's highest loyalty, is an important one, for it validates and makes meaningful the attitudes and behavior patterns that are being learned.

The protection of the group and its unity and effectiveness are often cited on Taiwan as basic goals and are used as justifications for much behavior. Two-thirds of the students Appleton tested felt that "A man ought not to be allowed to speak if he doesn't know what he's talking about."[104] These sentiments are similar to the comments of children from our sample that speaking out in a group against a leader is necessary if the leader says something that is felt to be wrong, because it is one's duty to air problems which may have a harmful effect upon the group. Such criticism protects group interests and proves one's worth as a good group member.

Despite the fact that ideally children on Taiwan learn that group interests are paramount, in practice disrespect to leaders at any level is negatively sanctioned. The leader's face must be regarded, for in many ways the leader is felt to represent the group to outsiders. Respect and loyalty are stressed as appropriate attitudes toward leaders at any level of social generalization, because they reflect the loyalty and respect owed to the particular group of which both leader and follower are common members. Since secondary-level membership in community and society is stressed in education on Taiwan, the value attributes of leader-follower behavior at that level are generalized to cover many situations and ultimately become the criteria for relations even at the primary level.

Chiang Kai-shek and Sun Yat-sen are considered to be the outstanding models for secondary-level behavior. Posters and stories use

---

[103] Wilson, *op. cit.*, pp. 19–49, 69–87, 153–173.

[104] Sheldon Appleton, "Taiwanese and Mainlanders on Taiwan: A Survey of Student Attitudes," *China Quarterly*, no. 44, Oct.–Dec. 1970, p. 57.

Chiang and Sun in a variety of ways to stress desirable behavioral attributes such as bravery, perseverence, loyalty, and diligence. The role of both men as models is constantly reinforced by demands for respect. In the schools even the mention of Chiang or Sun's name or title is likely to result spontaneously in attention in one's seat and silence.[105] In an isolated but interesting example a group of seventh-grade girls were asked who the best person in the world was; without hesitation the common reply was President Chiang. No, I said, not a person of the present time. Equally quickly the response was Sun Yat-sen. The girls were then asked to think of all world history and pick out the one greatest person. With greater hesitation the response was Confucius, coupled with individual questions concerning how well Americans really know Confucius. Certain respected models then, are widely shared and have relatively high salience in the learning process.

The effort to develop an unambiguous sense of large-group membership and loyalty to that group has not been without difficulty in Hong Kong, a British Crown Colony. Traditionally, social structure in the Hong Kong area was atomized. Villages, under the control of strong and often arbitrary leaders, were the largest focal point of effective identification.[106] To the observer, there still often seems to be little cooperative behavior with unfamiliar others when the threat of compliance is missing and self-interest is not clearly manifest. This was verified in our repeated observations at playgrounds, club centers, and in street activity. A typical and mundane example occurred at the Jordan Road playground, where a group of young men were playing soccer. Spectators or other park visitors who wished to get to the other side of the well-defined soccer field calmly walked across the field, often in the middle, and did not quicken their pace even when the play was near them, or, in one case, even when the soccer ball struck the intruder. The players did not object; there was mutual indifference. The crossers and others at the park might not have been known to exist for the players except that the latter's shirts were piled in the center of the field from fear that they would otherwise be stolen.

Just as intense and explicit moralizing is absent from Hong Kong classrooms, so also, for the most part, are political symbols, which can

---

[105] Wilson, *op. cit.*, pp. 77–98.

[106] Hugh D. R. Baker, *A Chinese Lineage Village: Sheung Shui*, Frank Cass and Co., London, 1968, p. 134.

serve at appropriate moments to focus a student's attention on this membership in a larger entity. The British flag may be displayed in front of schools and in the principal's office there is likely to be a photograph of Queen Elizabeth and the Duke of Edinburgh and/or Prince Charles; these are generally the only overt political signs, and for both children and teachers these symbols do not appear to be of high salience. One principal explained the presence of the Queen's photograph as "to satisfy the government," while another noted that children recognize and respect Elizabeth as Queen of England "because they know that in China's past there was also a monarch." Within both the Communist and the Nationalist schools in Hong Kong explicit reference to alternate political models and symbols is made, but in the vast majority of schools under the Hong Kong Education Department political moralizing is less prominent than in the People's Republic or on Taiwan and political models and symbols are most notable for their lack of salience.

The lessons that Hong Kong children learn in school concerning civics and their own future role in society are almost totally informational in content and the stress is on the subject nature of the citizen. For older children there is factual data about Hong Kong as a whole and instruction in virtues that characterize the good citizen, such as honesty, loyalty, unselfishness, and cooperation, but there is far more space allocated to such items as water and food supply, the airport, road safety, industry, housing, trade, marketing, the Stock Exchange, population, etc. Government is discussed in terms of the constitution of Hong Kong, the Executive and Legislative Councils, the role of the Governor, and political parties, with most emphasis placed on the Civil Service, revenue and expenditures, the law courts, and the Labour Department. In a fifth-grade social studies text the roles of government and citizen are set forth in this way:

> In what way will a government be good? A good government watches out for the people, protects their lives and property, and plans improvements in their living such as by imposing country security, police arrangement, and other items of law. In addition, the spread of education, the development of industry and commerce, and the like are all aimed at promoting the people's standard of living. These are also the people's immediate rights. A government that makes the people enjoy their rights to the fullest extent is a good government.
>
> Then, in what way will citizens be good? Passively, a good citizen sees

that he observes the law and order of society. Actively he can help the government to execute its orders, developing public-mindedness and avoiding corruption. There are also the immediate duties of citizens. Those who see that they fulfill their immediate duties are good citizens.[107]

Children are taught their "rights and freedoms," including freedom of religion, speech, and association and rights of equality, petition, and participation, in addition to the right to receive an education.[108] These are balanced by injunctions on the importance of maintaining social order and observing regulations. Secondary-level role learning in this area stresses passivity and compliance; there is no emphasis on membership or participation at this level of social organization, or on the ways in which appropriate secondary-level role behavior can define one's worth in a valued group context. About the most pressing demands are the large signs in the middle of downtown Nathan Road which read "Public Health is the Most Important . . . "

There is a reluctance in Hong Kong to become involved with the government or its organs. People prefer to solve their problems by other means. The government, the press, and individuals generally report a distant, uninvolved attitude toward the police on the part of most citizens. In Hong Kong there are countless ways of reminding the Chinese who live there that they are Chinese, but this knowledge is not fostered in the schools in order to develop secondary-level citizen behavior. Even among those whose families have been several generations or more in Hong Kong there is little sense of special citizenship. People do not identify with Hong Kong as such but rather say that they are Chinese who live in Hong Kong for a variety of reasons, mostly commercial or political or because they were born there. In a very traditional sense people are apolitical, and with some exceptions— notably the Communists—they orient their lives within the context of family, peers, and co-workers without reference to broader secondary-level membership and the role behavior required for social participation at that level.

In the United States, "Who are you?" appears to be one of the major problems facing Chinese Americans. For many Americans of

[107] Editorial Board of the Modern Educational Research Society, *Social Studies* (*She-hui*), First term, Grade 5, Modern Educational Research Society, Hong Kong, 1968, pp. 13–14.

[108] Tu Chia-chung, *op. cit.*, p. 30.

Chinese ancestry there is a perplexing problem of living in two cultures. In many families and in America's "Chinatowns" older patterns of interpersonal relations and control still exist, but these patterns coexist and compete with the majority values of white America, in a context in which racial discrimination has been largely eliminated and the consequent barriers to acceptance of those values lowered. The compulsory public educational experience, moreover, introduces these values to the young, as do TV and other media.

New York City's Chinatown is probably the most cohesive community left in the city. Nevertheless it is experiencing increasing social turmoil, manifested by rising crime statistics. Part of the reason for this change is that over one-quarter of the 45,000 people who live in the community arrived in the last five years, mainly from Hong Kong. Turmoil in Chinatown has deeper roots than either the cultural conflict arising from the intensification of support for "Chinese" culture represented by the new immigrants, or the low socio-economic conditions of many in the community, or the spillover from a generally tumultuous American society, important though these factors are. We know that when individuals are socialized into two different normative systems conflict is likely to develop. A perception that "Chinese" values and goals are not respected by groups in the society who are respected and whose esteem is valued may be conducive to abandonment of traditional ways. The result, however, is likely to be intergenerational tension within the highly affectively oriented primary group, the family, leading to a certain amount of disorganization of family relationships in which traditional patterns begin to break down but new patterns are not yet completely established.[109]

There is a sign in a Chinatown meat store which reads "Do What You Are Supposed To . . . Not What You Want To." This appeal implicitly recognizes both the existence of new values and the strictures of traditional patterns. In practice, compliance with this injunction is achieved by many young people in Chinatown through a selective rejection of their Chinese past combined with a search for identity through a secondary-level Chinese-American group membership which

[109] Roberta Sigel, "Assumptions about the Learning of Political Values," in Rieselbach and Balch, *op. cit.*, p. 87; Robert A. LeVine, *Dreams and Deeds: Achievement Motivation in Nigeria*, University of Chicago Press, Chicago, 1966, p. 87; Wilbert E. Moore, *Social Change*, Prentice-Hall, Englewood Cliffs, N.J., 1963, p. 102.

affirms their Asian heritage. There is for many a heightened sense of awareness of and loyalty to an ethnic minority group seen as embedded in a larger and still somewhat alien American context. It is our hypothesis that secondary-level role learning for many Chinese Americans involves both a diffuse attachment to the larger American entity and a more intense awareness of membership in a Chinese-American community in which the norms governing relationships are in a process of definition.

In an interview, an eight-year-old Chinese American boy was asked about his feelings toward Chinese and American groups. His reply is interesting and illustrative of how early an awareness of group membership is acquired. He said, "Well I don't know which group I'd join. It's hard to decide. I'd join the Americans but if one were Chinese I'd join them. But I'd join the Americans first because I was born here." This ambivalence, this question of who you are, continues with age. Some statements by Chinese-American students are given below. They sum up the search for unity, the need for new models, and the conflict between the past and the present.

> We are like bananas, yellow on the outside, white on the inside.
>
> The time has come for us to distinguish our white minds from our yellow skins, and arrest this self-contempt and shame many of us hold for ourselves and our people.
>
> ... the American establishment [viewed] the Chinese and other Asian-Americans as the "ideal colored minority group" because they were hard-working, non-complaining people who were content and happy with what they had. Such a honey-sweet image of what is really filth, deprivation, and oppression was created by the "Confucian moralists" of the Chinese communities who contrary to moralism of any sort, Confucian or otherwise, obtain the privilege and ease of being "Confucians" by exploiting their own people. [From an untitled pamphlet distributed at Rutgers, The State University of New Jersey.]

American political socialization has been more intensively studied than that of any other society. The findings indicate considerable differences in orientations and cognitions by age, sex, family background, intelligence quotient, and social status.[110] At a higher level of generaliza-

[110] Robert D. Hess and Judith V. Torney, *The Development of Political Attitudes in Children*, Aldine Publishing Co., Chicago, 1967, pp. 105, 183, 223–224. Also Kenneth P.

tion, scholars have assessed a number of attitudinal orientations common to Americans generally. Generally speaking, American children between the ages of nine and sixteen score high on political efficacy and on support for a competitive party system and have low *overall* levels of anti-democratic feeling. However, American children score less high on items concerning freedom to criticize the government and tolerance of minority dissent. When compared with fifth-grade children from Britain, Italy, and Germany, American children are the most anti-democratic.[111] In a sample of 2,040 high-school seniors questioned as to the characteristics of the good citizen, 39% said an active, participative political orientation; 31% said loyalty and a passive political orientation; and 10% mentioned community activism and concern.[112] The overall emphasis in secondary-level political behavior is on participation and concern, but a sizable portion of children do indicate uncritical loyalty and passivity as prime political attributes.

Research findings reported in the 1960's indicated that, compared to adults, seniors in high school still have a trusting image of the government, particularly at the national level and least so at the local level. Cynicism appears to develop after high school and to be more prevalent among the less well educated.[113] This sense of trust in government, reported by high school students, presumably has its origins in earlier childhood feelings concerning authority figures. Children indicate a moderately high and stable trust in and respect for the police; when asked what they would do if they thought a policeman was wrong the most popular response changes from "Do what he tells you but tell your father" (45.5%) in grade 2 to "Do what he tells you but ask the policeman why" (58.4%) in grade 8.[114]

The trust of Americans often seems highly personalized, for once adulthood has been reached and the security of the peer group and the

Langton, *Political Socialization*, Oxford University Press, London, 1969, pp. 63–70; Easton and Dennis, *op. cit.*, pp. 251–252.

111 Jack Dennis, Leon Lindberg, Donald McCrone, and Rodney Stiefbold, "Political Socialization to Democratic Orientations in Four Western Systems," *Comparative Political Studies*, vol. 1, no. 1, April 1968, p. 86 (Table 4) and p. 95.

112 M. Kent Jennings and Richard G. Niemi, "Patterns of Political Learning," *Harvard Educational Review*, vol. 38, no. 3, 1968, p. 460 (Table 5).

113 *Ibid.*, pp. 462–465. Also Robert E. Agger, Marshall N. Goldstein, and Stanley A. Pearl, "Political Cynicism: Measurement and Meaning," *Journal of Politics*, vol. 23, no. 3, August 1961, pp. 484, 487.

114 Hess and Torney, *op. cit.*, pp. 56–57.

initial primary group has diminished, there is a marked turning away from faith in the goodness of others to a feeling that some others must be restrained. According to Hess and Torney, the percentage who agree with the statement "If most agree the rest should go along" hardly varies in school from 29.9% in grade 2 to 27.6% in grade 8, but contrasts sharply with the 67.6% given by teachers.[115] A nationwide poll of 1,136 people indicated that about 75% would prevent extremist groups from demonstrating against the government even if there were no clear danger of violence and over half would not allow anyone to criticize the government if the criticism were thought to be damaging to the national interest.[116] Clearly, many adults have a strong feeling that there are others in the social community who do not share their own attitude and behavior orientations and who may, in fact, be dangerous. This lack of trust and sense of division indicates a lack of uniformity in secondary-level role learning and indicates the ambivalence and diffuseness with which many Americans regard their membership and participation at the secondary level. Patriotism or loyalty to the larger social grouping is tempered by a fear of and lack of trust in fellow participants at that level.

In school, some form of political and social education occupies almost 46% of American school time from grades 5 to 12 (whereas in the USSR the time spent on these areas is just short of 38%).[117] Political attachment and compliance are learned in a school environment that theoretically is outside the political arena itself, thus allowing, presumably, for certain basic attitudes to be learned independent of partisan interpretation. Until approximately grade 3, many children confuse God and country, which allows religious sentiments—and these are not always uniform—to undergird support of the polity. The development of "critical evaluation" as a component of political and social education is often minimized, partly because teachers feel that it is not right to express political opinions and therefore avoid controversial positions and partly because many teachers are relatively conservative and hence discuss politics and social conditions in terms of the status

---

[115] *Ibid.*, p. 66 (Table 13).

[116] James Reston, "Washington: Repeal the Bill of Rights?" *New York Times*, April 19, 1970 (The Week in Review), p. 16.

[117] Easton and Dennis, *op. cit.*, p. 406, citing G. Z. F. Bereday and B. B. Stretch, "Political Education in the U.S.A. and the U.S.S.R.," *Comparative Education*, 7, 1963, pp. 9–16.

quo.[118] Although political news is often emphasized in the media, such as television, to which children are exposed, role models are frequently nonpolitical and the stress is frequently on youth and attractiveness rather than on the model's orientations toward social issues. In fact, some recent evidence indicates that there has been a shift in role models to entertainment figures and away from moralizers and political leaders. The percentage of children naming George Washington as an examplar, is reported to have declined from 29.2 in 1902 to 3.2 in 1958.[119]

The most salient political dimension covered in civics textbooks is democratic creed (52%), followed by descriptive references (23%) and emphasis on political activity, citizen's duty, and efficacy (12%).[120] By high school civics courses have ceased to be of real influence, as the major socialization impact has occurred in the pre–high school period. Much of the material that young children read does stress the "democratic creed" but does so with little if any explicit reference to role modeling or national consciousness and has, rather, a high degree of emphasis on exaggerated and idealized individualism. In one of the fifth-grade classes sampled in this study, the children read the following concerning the President and the Congress:

"Mother," asked Tom, "is the Congress the same as the government?"

"No," said Mother. "Congress is only one part of the national government. It is the part which decides on new laws. It is also the part which decides how much money we should pay in taxes."

"If Congress decides all that," said Tom, "it must be the boss of the whole country."

Mother laughed. "It's a good thing that you aren't a Congressman, Tom," she said. "Any Congressman who thought he was the boss of the United States would soon find himself out of a job. In this country, the people are the boss. A Congressman tries to do what the people who voted for him want him to do. If he doesn't, they won't elect him again. . . .

"I may be just a housewife [says Mother] but my vote is just as important

[118] Zeigler, op. cit., pp. 96–98, 119.

[119] Fred I. Greenstein, "New Light on Changing American Values: A Forgotten Body of Survey Data," Social Forces, vol. 42, no. 4, May 1964, pp. 445 (Table 1).

[120] Richard E. Dawson and Kenneth Prewitt, Political Socialization, Little, Brown and Co., Boston, 1969, p. 150 (Table IX. 1), citing 1335 paragraphs analyzed and reported in Edgar Litt, ed., The Political Imagination, Scott, Foresman, Glenview, Ill., 1966, p. 489.

as Daddy's. It is as important as a Congressman's vote. The boss of this country, the real boss, is the voter. . . ."

"The people of the United States let you decide many things, Mr. President, but they do not let you decide who the next President will be. They decide that."

"That's a fine house you live in, Mr. President. The people of the United States want you to live in a fine house. But it is not your house, Mr. President. That house belongs to the people of the United States."[121]

In a new Social Studies Curriculum Guide used in New Brunswick, N.J., in Kindergarten through Grade 7, there is considerable stress on diversity and on the fact that there is no "right" answer for many of the issues the children may be exposed to. In the teaching of "patriotism" the idea of belonging to a larger group is noted without stress on inclusiveness or the need for exclusive loyalty. The "basic ideas" concerning patriotism for grades one and six are set forth as follows; patriotism is not included at all for grade 7.

GRADE 1

"One's country is a larger group to which one belongs; a concern for one's country is appropriate to this sense of belonging; patriotism is something which people of all nationalities possess."

GRADE 6

"Contributions of each civilization to the total human experience may be sources of national pride for different countries and their citizens; the United States world role requires evaluation."[122]

These examples are, of course, an extremely small sample, and are intended to be provocative rather than definitive. They serve, we hope, to highlight our contention that the intensity of loyalty has diminished, and the sense of belonging to a larger national grouping become more diffuse, for the majority of Americans, and that these changes are reflected in a comparable increase in ethnic identification. As an inclusive

---

121 Paul R. Hanna and Clyde F. Kohn, "The Congress" and "Mr. President," *Cross Country: Geography for Children*, Scott, Foresman and Co., Chicago, 1950, pp. 139–140.

122 *New Brunswick Schools Social Studies Curriculum Guide, Grades K-7*, New Brunswick, N.J., 1970, pp. 13, 28, 73.

observation this statement would need severe qualification, but we believe it does hold true for large segments of the population especially in the urban and suburban conglomerates where a large portion of the American people now live.

Secondary-role learning for Americans does not involve intensive training in the need to conform in attitudes and behavior patterns. The historical American normative order is still highly intact, but the groups with which Americans identify and toward whom normative criteria apply have shifted both up from the family and down from an inclusive stereotype of "Americanism." Americans still learn moral values, albeit less explicitly than in the past. Their current anxieties with regard to moral violation are less often about sex or aggression and more often about failure. Achievement—and fear of failure—is heavily emphasized, but in the context of peer relations or occupational roles. With a highly urbanized population engaged in a multitude of occupations, there are now many identities to choose from.[123] Secondary-role behavior attributes are phrased in universalistic terms but are learned with less stress on shared identity in a larger unit and in practice are largely fulfilled in social contexts where concern for particularistic criteria is heavily stressed. There is a sense of differences, of the relativity of moral imperatives, and of the "legitimate" and varying needs of individuals and groups.

SUMMARY

In American society it is not the later permissiveness in primary group socialization alone that favors peer orientation but rather a combination of this factor and the relative severity of early socialization practices. An increasing conception of a weak and impotent father and initial indulgence of aggression contribute to the sense that authority can be opposed, while, at the same time, both the severity of socialization and the changed role of the mother, which now includes the "punisher" role, foster a feeling that affect cannot be focused on an unambiguous love object within the family. This in turn, we feel, heightens the desire to establish friendships among peers and to perceive of friendliness as a fundamental requirement in group interaction.

Shaming is an aspect of primary-group training for both American

[123] Tomkins, op. cit., pp. 402–403; Parsons and White, op. cit., pp. 103, 105, 106.

and Chinese children. For Chinese children, however, there appears to be a greater manipulation of abandonment anxiety and a consequent heightened concern for behavioral conformity. While the role of the father is changing, he remains a symbol of authority and with older children is apt to be aloof and severe in his demands. As with American fathers, his function as a model for behavior has been reduced in scope and importance and increasingly preempted by others outside the family. Two heavily stressed models for Chinese children are teachers and representatives of political authority. Unlike the father, the mother is conceived of as warm, emotionally nurturant, and an effective source of affection within the family. Both parents may show considerable initial indulgence in socialization, but with age there is heightened restrictiveness with regard to the necessity for suppressing hostility within the group, especially toward authority, and the need for conformity to behavioral codes. In these areas the mother may be relatively strict. Her predominant influence, however, is not due to a conception of her as a rule enforcer but derives from her capacity to manipulate her affective relationship with the child in such a way that great anxiety develops concerning failure to approximate correct behavior.

The data for secondary-level role learning indicates that children from Taiwan and to a lesser extent from Hong Kong tend more than America or Chinatown children to see leaders as within the group. Children from Chinatown, Taiwan, and Hong Kong are also significantly more likely than those from America to choose a close-group context as an ideal. The desirability of close-group relations appears to be a highly persistent aspect of Chinese socialization generally. Within this structural context, however, there appears to be considerable variability concerning the learning of "rules" governing group behavior. Explicit morals training is the most salient feature of education on Taiwan and morals training is an implicit aspect of much of the education in Hong Kong. For America and Chinatown children, overt morals training as an aspect of the school curriculum is discouraged, and teachers in the American school system also tend to shy away from controversial subjects about which a moral judgment might be required. We feel the evidence strongly suggests that overt morals training as such is perhaps a crucial factor in the strong development of internalized control. For maximum effectiveness this training should be relevant to primary-role learning, so that a consistent set of value orientations can legitimize behavior at both the primary and secondary levels. Where this is not the case, as with the children from Chinatown, there may well be a persistent search for meaningful value guides once the incongruity between the patterns of attitudes and behavior in the family and in school is comprehended.

The strong development of internalized control is related not only to morals training but also, it appears, to shaming punishments, where shaming and morals training are closely linked. Anxiety about group censure and the possibility of nonconformity, and the fear of expressing hostility, especially to authority, are relieved by the careful learning of norms of behavior. For these norms to become impersonal guides and legitimizors of behavior there must be schooling apart from the primary group and this schooling must be long, intensive, and without competition from alternate and valued norm sources. This appears especially to be the case for children from Taiwan. There develops for these children a set of ideals that legitimizes behavior within a close, overarching group context. Generally speaking, peer groups are not sufficiently autonomous in Taiwan to contradict the labeling of students by teachers as either shamefully deviant or appropriately conformist. Loyalty and the suppression of hostility toward teachers become critical for anxiety reduction.

For children from America, peer orientations are powerful focuses of conformity and loyalty demands. These groups exist in a context separate from both the family and the school. The normative criteria for behavior may vary by group; adult leadership is seen as outside the peer group, which exists as a protective buffer against a challengeable adult authority; and morals training is not overtly stressed. Shaming in terms of an adult criterion or in terms of a school-defined group context is minimized. There is a stress on likableness in relationships. Secondary-level role learning has a high degree of personalized content.

Children between grades three and seven increasingly learn that important aspects of their lives concern their membership in secondary-level groups. School systems attempt to impart both a sense of membership and belonging in these groups and appropriate attitude and behavior patterns for the roles one will occupy. To a greater or lesser extent the child is presented with opportunities for the practice of these patterns. However, the extent to which these patterns come to define behavior in general depends on the degree of identification with secondary-level membership and the consequent degree of importance of the role attributes being learned.

On Taiwan there is great stress in the learning process on appropriate secondary-level attitudes and behavior patterns. These are presented explicitly in the form of "morals" of stories, slogans, plays, etc. In daily activities a failure to conform to positively sanctioned norms of behavior is cause for a variety of punishments, the most prevalent and severe of which is shaming. Great effort is expended on developing a firm sense of membership in a Chinese national community and the necessity for loyalty to that community.

In Hong Kong, training in the schools in secondary-level attitudes and behavior contains considerable "moral" content but is less explicit than on Taiwan and less heavily emphasized. Nevertheless, failure to live up to expected norms of behavior receives negative sanction, sometimes through the use of physical punishment but more frequently by shaming in front of schoolmates. While the learning process does stress development of cognitive awareness of Hong Kong as a secondary-level unit, there is much less emphasis on affective attachment to this grouping and on the development of an unambiguous sense of membership in this group. The importance of secondary-level membership appears attenuated; the notion of "Chineseness" persists but, for many, in an apolitical sense. Family and subgroup identification remains strong, and the more particularistic patterns of these primary groupings challenge the development of generalized secondary-level attitude and behavior patterns.

In Chinatown, New York City, one of the primary questions facing children is "who am I?" Trained in American public schools for most of the day, many children in this community receive after-school training with morals content in "Chinese" schools. The learning of secondary-level attitude and behavior patterns is dichotomous. Those patterns learned in the Chinese school and applicable for Chinese groupings are often less stressed or inapplicable in American public school training. Identification with and attachment to a national secondary group are diffused by an awareness of and attachment to a subnational ethnic minority membership.

For American children generally, there is considerable emphasis in the schools on developing an awareness of the secondary level, its structure, and its symbols of loyalty. There is also an attempt to develop affective attachment to this grouping and to stress the importance of acquiring secondary-level attitude and behavior patterns. Nevertheless a uniformly shared sense of membership in a common group does not exist, nor is there an equal intensity of loyalty toward that group. Some of the reasons for this appear to be a hesitancy within the schools to face issues on which consensus does not exist and a reluctance to apply a relatively unvarying set of "moral" criteria in the discussion, analysis, and solution of these issues. There is also a reluctance to employ group sanctions within the schools, partly because these punishments appear too harsh and partly because no uniform normative standards are felt to exist. Identification at a national level is diffuse. For most American children a national focus of identity is not challenged by the family as a locus of loyalty, as it still is in Chinese communities. Instead peer groupings have become one of the major areas for the development and practice of secondary-level behavior, and occupational roles—largely undefined in school—are among the primary sources of identity at the secondary level. The peer group as a training area infuses the learning of secondary-level attitudes and behavior patterns with particularistic criteria, placing stress on the personal nature of both positive and negative sanctions.

PART III ATTITUDE LEARNING IN CHINESE AND AMERICAN SOCIETIES

CHAPTER 4 Attitudes and

Behavior

Shame is an anxiety activated by a fundamental fear of abandonment, and becomes manifest whenever the actuality of behavior fails to approximate a learned set of ideals that has positive valence in the individual's value hierarchy. This set of ideals is acquired through direct and indirect training in role behavior and is elaborated with cognitive development.

Shame incorporates both consciousness of transgression and the fear of mutilation, which have usually been assigned as characteristics of guilt. The ideals against which behavior is compared may be a coherent set of codes and taboos or may be more diffuse and generalized. The type of behavioral output associated with shame anxiety varies with cognitive development, with the individual's physiological state, and in accordance with cultural norms governing appropriate behavioral expression. In general, a range of probable responses to various levels of experience of shame anxiety can be articulated, from mild embarrassment to intense self-hate or dislike of others.

In order to understand the development of internalized evaluative structures, a wide range of role-learning influences, including types of punishment, permissible areas for the expression of hostility, and conformity and reciprocity training, must be examined. All such influences act upon the process of identity formation, during which the child progressively attempts to behave in certain prescribed ways. The patterns that are ultimately established become highly self-rewarding in them-

121

selves and are thus not attenuated either by their successful achievement or if they go unrewarded by others.

Among the common attributes of humans is the capacity to screen reality or cognize, usually by late childhood involving contemplative operations but also including in a subordinate way sensorimotor operations and simple perceptivity. There is also the generally recognized capacity to express feelings (affect), and to relate the self to others (identification).[1] Concepts which relate to the ability to cognize not only have reference points in reality but also have emotional valences. Even the simplest statements are "bands" made of two concepts, subject and object, associated by a relationship, a verb, which can imply or state with the addition of adjectives and adverbs a positive or negative valence between the two concepts. "He likes her" is an example of two directly related concepts with positive valence, while "He ate the dinner reluctantly" is a more indirect statement with possible negative valence.[2]

Values have been perceived as "a succession of provisional hypotheses" that develops initially as a set of guidelines for anticipating or explaining rewards and punishments and that can be dropped if disconfirmed or inconsistent.[3] Only later, after constant repetition and experience, do these hypotheses begin to approximate an interrelated set of dispositions having a "moral" character. In conceptual terms, some theorists posit a continuum of opinion, attitude, interest, and value; while others see values as parts of attitudes. For those in the latter category, attitudes toward some person or condition are composites of the negative and positive valences of all the values which relate to that person or condition.[4] An attitude is a composite of concepts formed into a relationship in which it is possible to recognize (1) a cognitive component: how the concepts are perceived and with what degree of stereotyping, (2) an affective component: feelings toward and relating the concepts, and (3) a conative component: behavioral propensity

[1] Fred I. Greenstein, *Personality and Politics: Problems of Evidence, Inference, and Conceptualization*, Markham Publishing Co., Chicago, 1969, p. 3.

[2] Robert E. Lane, *Political Thinking and Consciousness: The Private Life of the Political Mind*, Markham Publishing Co., Chicago, 1969, p. 74.

[3] William Bezdek and Fred L. Strodtbeck, "Sex-Role and Pragmatic Action," *American Sociological Review*, vol. 35, no. 3, June 1970, p. 501.

[4] William J. McGuire, "The Nature of Attitudes and Attitude Change," in Gardner Lindzey and Elliot Aronson, eds., *The Handbook of Social Psychology*, 2nd edition, vol 3, Addison-Wesley Publishing Co., Reading, Mass., 1969, p. 151.

toward the concepts.[5] These components of attitudes are highly inter-correlated and can be further defined and given dimension through the following properties of attitudes: direction (favorable or unfavorable, positive or negative feelings), intensity (strength of feeling), ambivalence, salience (prominence), cognitive complexity (richness of ideational content), overtness, embeddedness (degree of connection with other beliefs, values, and attitudes), flexibility (degree to which the attitude can be modified), and consciousness.[6] While the list of attributes of attitudes is an impressive one and is complex in terms of the learning involved, it is nevertheless true that attitudes serve the function of simplifying the problem of devising response patterns in any given situation by providing cognitive, affective, and behavioral guidelines for an appropriate response. Attitudes thus serve to "dispose" people toward selecting a way to achieve a desired goal, and they also serve as handy rationalizations for explaining both consciously and unconsciously motivated behavior.

In socialization research the value content and orientations of individuals and populations are most frequently ascertained through attitude questionnaires or by studies of behavior at least some of which is presumed to be attitudinally motivated. Attitudinal dispositions are important as explanatory intervening variables because they are important in situations where the stimuli appear to be the same but behavioral output varies or where behavior is the same but the stimuli are different.[7] By subsuming cognitive, affective, and conative components, attitudes help explain the understanding, affective orientation, and motivation of individuals with regard to a given circumstance. They are thus parsimonious explanatory variables concerning possible response patterns in what may be complex social situations.

If values are provisional hypotheses acting as guidelines for role behavior in anticipation of reward or punishment, then attitudes, at a more general level, include these evaluative guidelines as components. Attitudinal standards develop not simply from personal experience but also as the result of receiving "guideline" information from others.

[5] *Ibid.*, pp. 155–156.

[6] William S. Scott, "Attitude Measurement," in Lindzey and Aronson, *op. cit.*, vol. 2, pp. 206–208.

[7] Kenneth P. Langton, *Political Socialization*, Oxford University Press, London, 1969, p. 13, citing Lewis A. Froman, Jr., "Personality and Political Socialization," *Journal of Politics*, 23, May 1961.

Information may be transmitted in many modes and may occasionally be contradictory in nature, but the assumption is that over a long period of time certain messages will emerge with a relatively standard cognitive content and affective valence. There is no assumption of complete uniformity between the attitude complex of a given individual and that which characterizes the groups to which he belongs. Individual differences and discontinuities in terms of sex, sibling position, social class, etc., preclude such standardization. Recognizing these dissimilarities, however, we can still define groups as having certain shared attitude dispositions. In fact, it is the proximate relationship of individual members to a statistically shared set of dispositions which helps define a collection of individuals as a group. In the last analysis, however, emphasis must be placed on the word "shared," for even the most apparently cohesive group is statistically a pattern of variations around a central tendency. Furthermore, attitude sets must be judged not merely in terms of similarity of content but also in terms of the pattern of salience felt by the individuals involved. When we speak therefore of the modal Chinese or American we refer only to a pattern of shared dispositions and not to the behavior or attitudes of some specific individual. We must also remember that role learning and behavior vary with the age of the individual and among generations. We cannot, therefore, assume an absolute linkage for any given individual between childhood and adult attitudes. Nor can we or should we make any naive assumptions that what any given generation learns is a replica of the social system as a whole.

It may be that in order to understand some operations of a social system emphasis must be put upon the congruence or similarity of attitudinal dispositions and behavioral patterns. This emphasis, however, must never be allowed to obscure the fact that a social science construction in which we talk of ideal character types or of ideal relationship patterns is not an accurate reflection of either the individual or of the social system. In terms of an ideal character type a person may be one way in some roles (as husband, for instance) and quite different in others (as diplomat, for instance), and relationship patterns which are presumed to characterize a given social unit may also vary markedly according to which roles are paired in a relationship (as husband with wife or doctor with patient).[8]

[8] Marion J. Levy, Jr., *Modernization and the Structure of Societies*, vol. 1, Princeton University Press, Princeton, N.J., 1966, esp. p. 164.

There is good evidence that many attitudinal patterns are not culturally idiosyncratic. Tagiuri has noted evidence of both universality and particularity across cultures.[9] Clausen has found that " . . . a substantial degree of autonomy in a variety of situations is probably required of the adult in all societies."[10] In a comparative examination of social systems, therefore, we must not necessarily expect to find that the variation of the categories under analysis will tend toward bipolarity in terms of the populations being analyzed. Rather we may well find that in many significant areas social units differ not in kind but only in degree. That differences in degree may be highly significant we do not, of course, deny. What we do wish to caution against is any simplistic belief that extreme differences along one dimension—say, extent of industrialization—must unfailingly imply equal differences along other dimensions—say, attitudinal dispositions. Such an inference is neither logical nor, as it turns out, correct.

Although it is generally assumed that attitudinal dispositions are the most important sources of control over behavior, there is evidence of frequent discrepancy between a verbal expression concerning action and the action itself.[11] In fact, we can only be sure that the behavior we observe—conformity to norms, no apparent shame, atonement, etc.—is related to a coherent set of learned standards if we can be sure that the situation wherein we have observed or tested for these standards is free from fear, including the desire to avoid the disapproval or obtain the approval of others.[12] Since most formal testing situations have some element of fear involved, it is imperative that the results obtained be verified as far as practicable by observation, interviews, or other testing mechanisms. Furthermore, one must be able both to link the attitudes which are expressed to significant aspects of the social learning environment and to understand and account for the most significant needs and anxieties (such as shame) motivating the person in terms of the particular set of attitudes in question. As Fleron and Kelly have so aptly put it:

[9] Renato Tagiuri, "Person Perception," in Lindzey and Aronson, op. cit., vol. 3, p. 403.

[10] John A. Clausen, "Family Structure, Socialization, and Personality," in Lois W. Hoffman and Martin L. Hoffman, eds., Review of Child Development Research, vol. 2, Russell Sage Foundation, New York, 1966, p. 6.

[11] Justin Aronfreed, "The Concept of Internalization," in David A. Goslin, ed., Handbook of Socialization Theory and Research, Rand McNally and Co., Chicago, 1969, p. 269.

[12] Daniel R. Miller and Guy E. Swanson, Inner Conflict and Defense, Henry Holt and Co., New York, 1960, p. 142.

Psychologists have known for a long time that neither words nor actions are invariably accurate reflections of underlying beliefs, attitudes or goals. A person's beliefs and attitudes prejudice an issue by determining his *set*, i.e., his way of reacting to new facts and experiences. They become *mental habits* which, *if aroused*, determine actions. But since attitudes are intervening variables and must be determined indirectly, to assert that a particular attitude regarding a goal, object or belief motivated a person, one must be able to link that attitude with antecedent conditions and consequent behavior. It is not sufficient to study just the verbal statements of attitudes or just the consequent behavior. One must analyze all of the above plus the need level and drives of the individual or of the individuals that compose a group.[13]

Given our current state of knowledge of the socialization process, it is likely that any theory which attempts to relate parsimoniously a number of variables suffers both from researcher bias and from problems of adequate testing. Within these virtually unavoidable limitations, however, it is our task to construct a design that meets the requirements of falsifiability, parsimony, and logical structure. We have begun this process, therefore, with a theoretical exposition concerning shame and moral development and some brief comments concerning the learning environments of Chinese and American children. We shall now continue with an outline of our research procedures and rationale, and finally introduce the specific hypotheses we will be testing.

First, it is not our intention to study purely psychological processes and development patterns in terms of specific individuals. Rather, we will examine the relationship of the learning process to grossly held attitudinal dispositions which we assume to be the result of role learning mediated by a commonly held psychological attribute of shame anxiety. This psychological attribute, however, can be intensified or modified by the learning process itself in such a way that it acts upon the dimensions of attitudinal dispositions, affecting their intensity, salience, overtness, flexibility, etc. In turn, therefore, there is a feedback of progressively characterized dispositions into the learning process, which act to give that process itself a progressively characteristic set of attributes. Overall we view the learning situation (the social variable) and commonly held shame anxiety (the psychological variable) as independent variables,

[13] Frederick J. Fleron, Jr., and Rita Mae Kelly, "Personality, Behavior and Communist Ideology," *Soviet Studies*, vol. 21, no. 3, January 1970, p. 308 Italics in original.

although we recognize a degree of interaction between them. Our dependent variable is role behavior as we actually observe it. The intervening variables are the attitudinal dispositions concerning role behavior, which shall be assessed through questionnaires and interviews.

We shall divide attitude dispositions into two distinct types, which shall be referred to as *autocentric* and *heterocentric*. The fundamental difference between these two dimensions is the source cited as the authority for specific actions or cognitions.

AUTOCENTRIC

Where particular others are *not* cited as the authority for behavior: orientation to rules or principles.

HETEROCENTRIC

Where particular others are cited as the authority for behavior: orientation to others.

The terms *"autocentric"* and *"heterocentric"* have a clear generic relationship to Piaget's concepts of autonomy and heteronomy. Piaget's terms have not been used here because the meanings attached to *"autocentric"* and *"heterocentric"* vary in certain significant ways from autonomy and heteronomy. In the first place, the concepts we shall employ have no inherent notion of continuity (stages) between them. Rather we assume them to represent *types* of attitude disposition that coexist within each individual and within cultures. We do expect that the relative weight of attitude type will vary, on the average, among social systems, but this variation is not on a stage basis and has no bias or implication as between less developed and developed societies. Secondly, *"autocentrism"* and *"heterocentrism"* are not associated with guilt and shame, respectively, as these distinctions have normally been used in the past. For both *autocentrism* and *heterocentrism* shame is operative; the self is central in both cases and the distinction posed is whether actual behavior is measured against an internalized set of *learned dispositions invested with value orientations* (*autocentrism*) or whether others provide the cues for expected ideal behavior (*heterocentrism*).

Norms and values are aspects of attitude dispositions. In the learning process, values are conceived of as components of attitudes that legitimize or condemn the acquisition and later expression of particular behavioral patterns. Someone's values help tell us why he does something; they are good or bad components of particular acts. The reference component of values can be defined on a continuum usually expressed in social theory as universalistic/particularistic.

UNIVERSALISM

Where the standards of desirability with regard to behavior primarily reference general principles of applicability to everyone.

PARTICULARISM

Where the standards of desirability with regard to behavior primarily reference specific relationships.

While we cannot prove a strict causal connection between universalism and autocentrism or between particularism and heterocentrism, we do feel there is a high correlation. In both pairings the components are linked by role learning. Within any given relationship the definition of appropriate behavior is normally always more the prerogative of the superordinate. When values are particularistic and implicitly or explicitly reference the hierarchical positions, there will be a pronounced tendency for the superordinate to define the quality and nature of follower behavior and a greater tendency for the subordinate to seek out and rely on such definitions. When values related to role behavior are universalistic, we assume there will be less reference by followers to the superordinate himself.

The power and prestige of the parent vis-à-vis the child is such that in all societies heterocentric attitudes will govern early family interactions. Small children, by and large, indicate considerable heterocentrism. Where secondary-level role learning is heavily emphasized and where congruity is expected between primary and secondary-level role behavior, we will find increasing autocentric attitude dispositions with age.

With these criteria as background, we may set forth the following six interrelated hypotheses with regard to autocentric and heterocentric attitude dispositions:

HYPOTHESIS 1:

Depending upon which type of values is most heavily emphasized overall in role learning, we expect to find attitudes as predominantly heterocentric or predominantly autocentric. The development of generalized autocentrism is related critically to heavy emphasis on learning involving universalistic values. Conversely, where role learning involving particularistic values is emphasized, we expect attitudes toward role behavior in general to be predominantly heterocentric.

HYPOTHESIS 2:

Attitudes cannot be viewed in isolation from the learning process (methods of punishment, reward, etc.), in which interpersonal reaction is involved. Punishments, especially by authority figures, act to check deviance from accepted attitudes. For a heterocentric attitude disposition we would expect the most prevalent and severe punishments to be phrased in terms of particularistic criteria. For an autocentric attitude disposition we would expect to find the most prevalent and severe punishments phrased in terms of universalistic criteria.

HYPOTHESIS 3:

Punishments may elicit hostility. With predominantly heterocentric attitude dispositions, hostility in terms of particular others in a positively sanctioned relationship receives heavy negative sanction. However, toward those with whom no specific relationship exists, there may be hostility or aggression according to the situation or context with weak negative sanction. With predominantly autocentric attitude dispositions, although hostility and aggression are generally also negatively sanctioned where specific inter personal relations exist, these reactions may be permissible in situations where universalistic values are violated, regardless of the interpersonal relationship.

HYPOTHESIS 4:

With heterocentric attitude dispositions we expect to find the expression of opposition to authority inversely related to the strength of the interpersonal tie. With autocentric attitude dispositions we expect to find opposition to authority directly related to the extent of deviance by authority figures from positively sanctioned universalistic criteria.

HYPOTHESIS 5:

With either heterocentric or autocentric attitude dispositions conformist behavior will be observed. With heterocentric attitude dispositions conformity to group patterns is legitimized by institutionalized group leaders (parents, teachers, etc.). Conformity to leader behavior by followers is positively sanctioned. Nonconformity to specific legitimized leaders receives heavy negative sanction. With autocentric attitude dispositions conformity to group patterns may also be legitimized by institutionalized group leaders. However, nonconformist behavior in terms of transcending universalistic values may be permissible.

HYPOTHESIS 6:

Reciprocity between authority and nonauthority figures differs with attitude disposition. With heterocentric attitude disposition mutual obligation receives the heaviest positive sanctions regardless of any contradictory universalistic values. With an autocentric attitude disposition we would not expect to find reciprocity defined solely in terms related to the interpersonal relationship itself. Rather, we would expect to find reciprocity also defined in terms of universalistic values.

A questionnaire was designed and pretested to examine these six hypotheses with regard to third-, fifth-, and seventh-grade boys and girls from Taiwan, Hong Kong, Chinatown (New York City), and Princeton and New Brunswick, New Jersey. The data will be presented in four sections, hypotheses one and two being treated independently and hypotheses three–four and five–six treated as units. On the questionnaire each question had five possible responses (including a "don't know" response), with two of the responses categorized as autocentric and two as heterocentric. (Additional questions, similarly constructed, assessed universalistic and particularistic value orientations.) For each question the responses categorized as autocentric or heterocentric (universalistic or particularistic) were separated and the answers within each response category combined to obtain a mean percentage value for autocentrism or heterocentrism (universalism or particularism) in terms of group (America, Chinatown, Taiwan, and Hong Kong), sex, and grade level (third, fifth, and seventh). An analysis of variance technique was then applied to test differences in autocentrism or heterocentrism in terms of each control category and to test the interaction effects among these categories (group, sex, and grade level). The usual significance level of .05 was chosen.

We label our four groups as America, Chinatown, Taiwan, and Hong Kong while fully recognizing that our samples have limitations with regard to representativeness and that the Chinatown sample is as much "American" as the group we have arbitrarily labeled America. Where appropriate in the text, we will note where significant differences or interaction effects occur or where the distribution appears to have important characteristics. A description of the methodology and sample selection procedures employed can be found in the Appendix.

In the sections that follow we shall analyze the distribution of autocentrism and heterocentrism for each hypothesis primarily in terms of overall group differences and overall grade level differences. A description of age-related differences within each group is presented in the conclusion of this chapter. For those less interested in the somewhat detailed information involved in the discussion of the six hypotheses, it is recommended that they read the summaries at the end of each section, the conclusion at the end of this chapter, and the discussion in chapter 5. The overall patterns which evolved from the data are presented in these summations.

SECTION ONE.   HYPOTHESIS 1

HYPOTHESIS 1:

Depending upon which type of values is most heavily emphasized overall in role learning, we expect to find attitudes as predominantly heterocentric or predominantly autocentric. The development of generalized autocentrism is related critically to heavy emphasis on learning involving universalistic values. Conversely, where role learning involving particularistic values is emphasized, we expect attitudes toward role behavior in general to be predominantly heterocentric.

The main testing instrument given to the four groups of children had twenty-three questions, randomly distributed. Of these five questions related to hypothesis 1, three questions each related to hypotheses two through six, and three questions related to group spatial perception. We shall deal in this section with the five questions related to hypothesis 1.

In order to assess the five questions related to hypothesis one, six additional questions were asked at the start of the test relating specifically to secondary and/or primary groups and designed to test universalistic or particularistic value orientations with regard to various types of behavioral situations. The children were cautioned verbally and in writing that these questions "ask what *should* happen. Choose the answer that is closest to what you think *ought to* happen." Before beginning our analysis of the questions relating to attitude dispositions, we shall first analyze the six "value" questions in order to determine which type of values is most heavily emphasized by the groups we have under consideration (see Appendix C, questions 1–6). In order to obtain a clearer conception of the ways in which universalistic and particularistic value orientations characterize a given group or grade level, graphs have been prepared on the basis of the percentage mean values for each group or grade level. As significant interaction effects between group

GRAPH 5 *Comparison among Groups of Universalistic Value Responses, Percent*

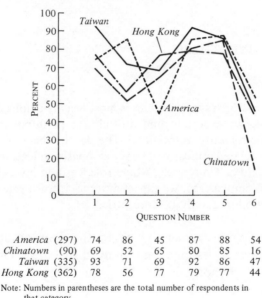

		Q.1	Q.2	Q.3	Q.4	Q.5	Q.6
America	(297)	74	86	45	87	88	54
Chinatown	(90)	69	52	65	80	85	16
Taiwan	(335)	93	71	69	92	86	47
Hong Kong	(362)	78	56	77	79	77	44

Note: Numbers in parentheses are the total number of respondents in that category.

Question 1: F = 10.85   Question 4: F = n.s.
Questoin 2: F = 12.16   Question 5: F = n.s.
Question 3: F = 22.83   Question 6: F = 14.32
n.s.—not significant

and grade level occur only in question 5, the graph of this effect has been omitted.

For the combined universalistic value responses there were significant differences among groups on four of the six questions (1, 2, 3, and 6). When the mean percentage values for all questions are plotted for each group the pattern emerges that is depicted in Graph 5. The data indicates that for all groups universalistic values tend to dominate in terms of ideal role attributes.

When the mean percentage values for each group are averaged, Taiwan overall has the most universalistic value response pattern with 76%, followed by America with 72%, Hong Kong with 69%, and Chinatown with 61%. With regard to all six questions, Taiwan has an average

GRAPH 6 *Comparison among Grade Levels of Universalistic Value Responses, Percent*

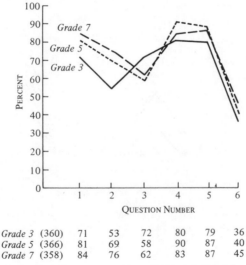

		1	2	3	4	5	6
Grade 3	(360)	71	53	72	80	79	36
Grade 5	(366)	81	69	58	90	87	40
Grade 7	(358)	84	76	62	83	87	45

Note: Numbers in parentheses are the total number of respondents in that category.

Question 1: $F = 6.42$ Question 4: F = n.s.
Question 2: $F = 9.16$ Question 5: F = n.s.
Question 3: $F = 7.88$ Question 6: F = n.s.
n.s. — not significant

rank order of 1.7, America 2.0, Hong Kong 2.8, and Chinatown 3.5. This means that the Taiwan children were on the average either first or second relative to the other groups in the expression of universalistic values, whereas, by comparison, the Chinatown group was on the average in third or fourth place relative to the others.

Among grade levels there was a significant difference in terms of universalistic value response patterns for questions 1, 2, and 3. For questions 4, 5, and 6 no statistically significant differences were reported. The universalistic value response patterns for grade levels are shown in Graph 6. For all children, universalistic value responses are at their lowest in third grade, the mean percentage values being 65% on the

GRAPH 7   *Comparison among Groups of Particularistic Value Responses, Percent*

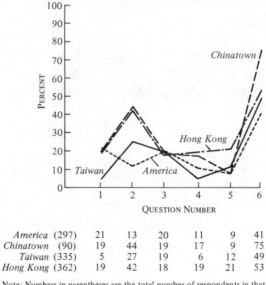

America (297)	21	13	20	11	9	41
Chinatown (90)	19	44	19	17	9	75
Taiwan (335)	5	27	19	6	12	49
Hong Kong (362)	19	42	18	19	21	53

Note: Numbers in parentheses are the total number of respondents in that category.

Question 1: F = 5.75   Question 4: F = 8.39
Question 2: F = 7.89   Question 5: F = 7.92
Question 3: F = n.s.   Question 6: F = 12.81
n.s. — not significant

GRAPH 8 *Comparison among Grade Levels of Particularistic Value Responses, Percent*

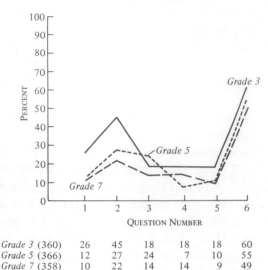

Grade 3 (360)	26	45	18	18	18	60
Grade 5 (366)	12	27	24	7	10	55
Grade 7 (358)	10	22	14	14	9	49

Note: Numbers in parentheses are the total number of respondents in that category.

Question 1: F = 10.92   Question 4: F = 9.10
Question 2: F = 7.33   Question 5: F = 7.61
Question 3: F = n.s.   Question 6: F = n.s.
n.s. — not significant

ssess the validity of the value distributions given above. It is
ly specific attempt to measure directly the relationship
ues and attitudes.

twenty randomly distributed attitudinal questions in the
heterocentric questionnaire, five relate specifically to
ne. All of the attitudinal questions were preceded by both
written instructions telling the children that the questions
what will happen. In each of these questions check the
st to what *you* think the people in the question will *really*
the time that the test was being taken this injunction was
eral times. We are aware that for many children the differ-
n what people ought to do and what people actually do is

average in comparison with 71 % in 5t
The average rank order is 1.5 for seven
2.7 for third grade. The spread among
the increase which does take place witl
pleted by fifth grade (approximately a

When we turn to the particularis
there were significant differences amo
the exception of question 3. The mean
plotted for each group are shown in
laristic values are generally secondary
By and large the patterns of response
amplitudes vary greatly.

When the mean percentage val
Chinatown overall has the highes
pattern with 31 %, ahead of Hong K
and America with 19 %. For all ques
have an average rank order of 2.2
We may thus pair Hong Kong an
likely to express particularistic valu
likely.

An analysis of particularistic
levels indicated significant differenc
significant differences were discover
ticularistic value response patterns
8. Again we note that while the patt
are similar, the amplitudes vary wi
less particularistic value orientation
in the expected direction. In cor
percentage values for the six questic
grade has an average response rat
23 % and seventh grade with 20 %.
grade, 2.0 for fifth grade, and 2.8

Since values are a critical co
that all attitudinal dispositions sho
value orientations. This relationsh
tion has been shifted in later secti
behavioral modes such as expres
first hypothesis, which is consid

attempt to a
also the o
between val

Of the
autocentric/
hypothesis
verbal and
"ask about
answer close
do." During
repeated sev
ence betwee

sometimes a nebulous one, but great care was taken to make the distinction as clear as possible.

The questions ask about role behavior, but the responses are not, of course, behavior itself but affective, cognitive, and conative choices or statements with regard to behavioral possibilities. The responses are therefore attitudes, one component of which is evaluative, concerning what people, including the respondents, actually do. It is not what people ought to do in a given situation, free from any constraints, but what they actually do. This "doing" clearly has an "oughtness" or value component but it also involves role behavior as it is actually perceived (or cognized) and carried out. We assume the value quality of an attitude to be an extremely important component but not the sole one. In some cases these attitude questions address the evaluative component rather directly but in other cases only in an indirect fashion. The questions relating to hypothesis one are questions 8, 11, 15, 22 and 26 (see Appendix C).

For these five questions as a whole there were two questions (8 and 26) where there were significant differences in autocentrism, and three questions (8, 15, and 26) where there were significant differences in heterocentrism, among groups. By grade levels there were two questions (8 and 22) which showed significant differences for both heterocentrism and autocentrism. Males and females were significantly different for three of the heterocentric responses (8, 15, and 26). Graphical representations of these patterns are given in Graphs 9–11.

Significant sex differences (question 26) and interaction between group and sex (question 26) occurred only once each for the autocentric responses. For the autocentric and heterocentric responses there were also two cases each of significant interactions between group and grade level. (For autocentrism 8 and 26 and for heterocentrism 8 and 11.) Graphs for these cases have been omitted.

For the autocentric responses the mean percentage values for each question plotted for each group are shown in Graph 9. Overall the pattern indicates considerable autocentrism for all groups with this characteristic most marked for the Taiwan and Hong Kong children. When the mean percentage values for each group are averaged, Taiwan is the highest with 79%, followed by Hong Kong with 74%, Chinatown with 72%, and America with 66%. For all questions the average rank order for Taiwan is 1.2, ahead of Chinatown at 2.0, Hong Kong at 3.2, and America at 3.6.

GRAPH 9   *Hypothesis 1. Comparison among Groups of Autocentric Responses, Percent*

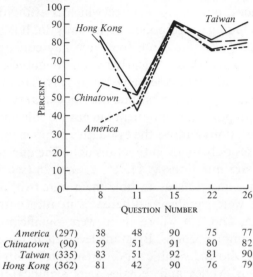

	8	11	15	22	26
America (297)	38	48	90	75	77
Chinatown (90)	59	51	91	80	82
Taiwan (335)	83	51	92	81	90
Hong Kong (362)	81	42	90	76	79

Note: Numbers in parentheses are the total number of respondents in that category.

Question 8: F = 90.73   Question 22: F = n.s.
Question 11: F = n.s.   Question 26: F = 10.16
Question 15: F = n.s.
n.s.—not significant

Among grade levels only two questions, 8 and 22, showed significant differences in autocentrism, in both cases with third grade the lowest, followed by fifth grade and seventh grade in ascending order. It is interesting to note that in both of these cases the differences are in the expected direction, toward increasing autocentrism with age. Table 1 sets forth the mean percentage values for all five questions by grade level. The average of the mean percentage values again indicates the increase in autocentrism with age, with third grade at 67%, fifth grade at 76%, and seventh grade at 75%. In terms of average rank order fifth grade is first at 1.4, seventh grade second at 1.8, and third grade last at 2.8.

TABLE 1   *Hypothesis 1. Autocentric Responses by Grade Level, Percent*

	GRADE LEVEL		
QUESTION NUMBER	3	5	7
8	56	69	71
11	45	51	48
15	91	94	88
22	63	84	87
26	79	85	82
Number Responding	*(360)*	*(366)*	*(358)*

Question 8: $F = 16.82$
Question 11: $F = $ n.s.
Question 15: $F = $ n.s.
Question 22: $F = 36.01$
Question 26: $F = $ n.s.

For the heterocentric responses there was a significant difference among groups on three of the five questions, questions 11 and 22 being the exceptions. The mean percentage values for each group for all questions are shown in Graph 10. Both the America and Chinatown groups have the same general configuration, although the America sample shows this pattern in a more pronounced way. The major difference between the America and Chinatown groups and the Taiwan and Hong Kong groups is the lower heterocentrism on question 8 for Taiwan and Hong Kong. In this question, which relates to a school situation, many America and Chinatown children express heterocentric attitudes. Heterocentrism is clearly pronounced for the Taiwan and Hong Kong groups only on the one question dealing with the family, question 11. An average of the mean percentage values for all questions indicates that the America sample had the highest average value of heterocentrism among groups with 28%, ahead of Hong Kong with 24%, Chinatown with 21%, and Taiwan with 18%.

The higher average value of heterocentrism for the America sample is clearly related to the high value for this group on question 8. On no other question is the America sample highest, being second on questions 15 and 26, third on question 11, and last on question 22. On question 26 the group and grade-level interaction data indicates that heterocentrism for the America sample decreases rapidly with age to the lowest position. The Hong Kong children, in fact, had the highest degree of heterocentrism on four of the five questions. For all responses Hong Kong had an

GRAPH 10 *Hypothesis 1. Comparison among Groups of Heterocentric Responses, Percent*

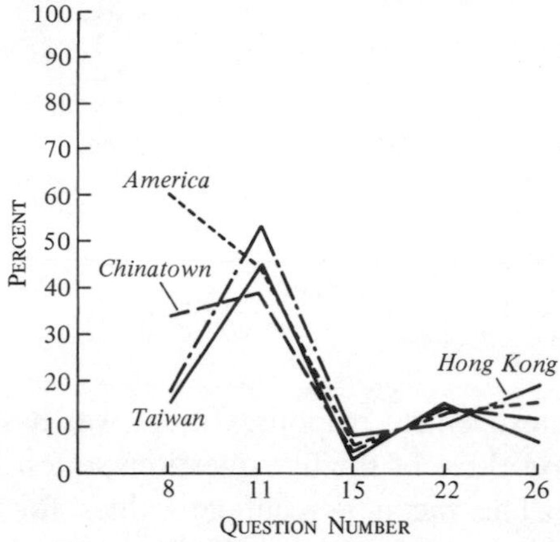

America (297)	60	45	8	13	16
Chinatown (90)	35	39	5	14	11
Taiwan (335)	16	46	4	17	7
Hong Kong (362)	18	55	9	20	19

Note: Numbers in parentheses are the total number of respondents in that category.

Question 8: $F = 133.74$ Question 22: $F =$ n.s.
Question 11: $F =$ n.s.   Question 26: $F = 4.97$
Question 15: $F = 4.93$

average rank order of 1.4, ahead of America at 2.4, Chinatown at 3.0, and Taiwan at 3.2.

There was a significant difference between the sexes on three questions, 8, 15, and 26, for the heterocentric case. The pattern of responses by sexes for hypothesis 1 for all 5 questions is given in Graph 11. An average of the mean percentage values indicates males at 23% and females at 22%. Although males are more heterocentric than females on three of the five questions (average rank order 1.4 versus 1.6 for females), the overall difference appears to be extremely minor despite reported significance on three of the questions.

Among grade levels there was a significant difference reported for

GRAPH 11   *Hypothesis 1. Heterocentric Responses by Sex, Percent*

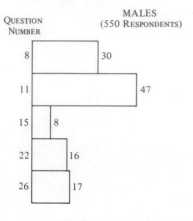

QUESTION
NUMBER

MALES
(550 RESPONDENTS)

8 — 30

11 — 47

15 — 8

22 — 16

26 — 17

FEMALES
(534 RESPONDENTS)

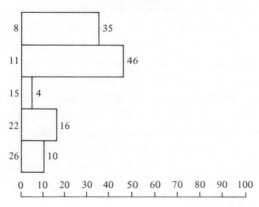

8 — 35

11 — 46

15 — 4

22 — 16

26 — 10

0   10   20   30   40   50   60   70   80   90   100

Question 8: F = 7.67
Question 11: F = n.s.
Question 15: F = 15.17
Question 22: F = n.s.
Question 26: F = 8.17
n.s.—not significant

questions 8 and 22. The heterocentric responses by grade levels are indicated in Table 2.

TABLE 2   *Hypothesis 1. Heterocentric Responses by Grade Level, Percent*

	GRADE LEVEL		
QUESTION NUMBER	3	5	7
8	43	28	26
11	53	42	44
15	7	5	7
22	34	10	5
26	16	11	13
Number Responding	*(360)*	*(366)*	*(358)*

Question 8: $F = 35.99$
Question 11: $F = $ n.s.
Question 15: $F = $ n.s.
Question 22: $F = 37.22$
Question 26: $F = $ n.s.

The general pattern among grades is relatively similar, but the average of the mean percentage values shows that third graders choose heterocentric responses 31% of the time, on the average, as compared with fifth and seventh graders both at 19%. The average rank order was 1.0 for third grade, 2.4 for seventh grade, and 2.6 for fifth grade.

Only approximately one fifth to one quarter of all children, on the average, chose a heterocentric attitudinal response as a guide to behavior, although this tendency is more pronounced for younger children and is very pronounced in situations where social interaction is clearly at the family level (Question 11). Boys are slightly more heterocentric than girls, but the difference is very small. Our data suggest that the Hong Kong group is the most heterocentric, followed closely by the America group (which is actually larger on an average mean percentage value basis). Taiwan would seem to be the least heterocentric, just slightly less so than Chinatown.

DISCUSSION AND SUMMARY

Hypothesis 1 posits a relationship between learning involving particularistic or universalistic values and the development, respectively, of generalized heterocentric or autocentric attitudes regarding behavior. Overall the children from all four groups tended to select universalistic value responses and also to reveal autocentric attitude dispositions. This pattern held true across groups and across grade levels. Among the groups the Taiwan children tended, on the whole, to express universalistic values more frequently than the other groups, with America and Hong Kong children in the middle and Chinatown children the least expressive of these values. In terms of autocentric attitudes, while Taiwan remained dominant, the America group moved to last place and the Hong Kong and Chinatown groups were located in the middle.

Among grade levels the expression of both universalistic values and autocentric attitudes increased with age. This is in the expected direction, and is in accordance with our assumption that, although universalistic values may be stressed in learning, only with the development of cognitive structure with age will universalism and autocentrism be in evidence.

None of the children in any of the groups emphasized particularistic values or heterocentric attitudes. Among groups the Chinatown and Hong Kong children emphasized particularistic values most frequently overall, while the Taiwan and America children expressed these values least frequently. In comparing these responses with the heterocentric attitude response pattern, Hong Kong and America tended to be highest in heterocentrism with Chinatown and Taiwan lowest. Among grade levels particularism and heterocentrism were both highest in third grade and declined with age. This pattern among grades was as expected.

The particularistic and heterocentric response patterns among groups showed generally the same pattern of congruence as was noted for universalism and autocentrism. The relatively higher particularism of the Hong Kong children was reflected in their higher heterocentrism and the relatively lower emphasis on particularism for the Taiwan group was reflected in their low heterocentric response pattern. However, the America sample expressed heterocentrism more frequently than their particularistic response pattern indicated and the Chinatown sample less frequently.

Overall there appears to be a generally good fit for the Taiwan and Hong Kong groups between the relationship of universalism to autocentrism and of particularism to heterocentrism, both in terms of magnitude and in terms of the relative position of the groups. This was not the case, however, for the America and Chinatown groups. America children seem relatively more prone to stress universalistic values with regard to ideal behavior but slightly less likely to stress autocentrism in actual practice. For children from Chinatown a reverse pattern appears. In both cases these differences, although minor, appear to reflect ambiguities or discontinuities in socialization which we have noted earlier (chapter 3). The actual patterns of behavior for children in both Chinatown and New Jersey appear to be organized somewhat differently than the ideal value structure relating to role behavior would indicate.

Although several questions—particularly with regard to the expression of heretocentric attitudes—reflected differences in response between the sexes, this distinction was not an important one. Research on this question to date has produced inconclusive evidence. Some analysts on political attitudes have found sex-related differences to be small and of no real consequence.[14] Others have found considerable differences in extent of knowledge.[15] It is generally recognized that boys and girls may differ across cultures in terms of ideals relating to role behavior and in terms of the fantasies they may report in dream themes, etc. The problem is a complicated one, however, and cannot be easily solved by any facile generalizations with regard to ideal feminine or masculine behavior.[16] In our data we have found no evidence to support notions about a difference between the sexes in levels or rates of learning of behavior and values associated with primary or secondary roles.

SECTION TWO.   HYPOTHESIS 2

HYPOTHESIS 2:

Attitudes cannot be viewed in isolation from the learning process (methods of punishment, reward, etc.), in which interpersonal reaction is involved. Punishments, especially by authority figures, act to check deviance from accepted attitudes. For a heterocentric attitude disposition

[14] David Easton and Jack Dennis, *Children in the Political System: Origins of Political Legitimacy*, McGraw-Hill Book Co., New York, 1969, pp. 341–342.

[15] Fred I. Greenstein, *Children and Politics*, Yale University Press, New Haven, 1965, p. 106.

[16] Orville G. Brim, Jr., "Family Structure and Sex Role Learning by Children: A Further Analysis of Helen Koch's Data," *Sociometry*, vol. 21, 1958, pp. 13–14.

we would expect the most prevalent and severe punishments to be phrased in terms of particularistic criteria. For an autocentric attitude disposition we would expect to find the most prevalent and severe punishments phrased in terms of universalistic criteria.

What punishment should be and what its probable effects are have been subjects of considerable attention by scholars, parents, and rulers alike. Recent work in this field, however, has begun to establish some definitive guidelines. For instance, within certain ranges of intensity the effectiveness of learning is often inversely related to the intensity of punishment.[17] In other words, although some restraints and some un-pleasantness may be necessary to obtain a consistency in behavior, the harsher these aversive stimuli are the greater will be the fear and anger evoked and the less likely the development of a positive motivation toward desired ends. Research has also warned us to avoid the notion that punishment consists only of such methods as beating, isolation, or severe disapproval. There are many minor stimuli transmitted by sociali-zation agents, such as change in voice tone or facial expression, with-drawing a reward, or disrupting some pleasurable activity, which, possibly due to prior association with harsher punishments, may serve to inhibit or suppress certain types of behavior.[18] Punishment covers a wide range of stimuli and degrees of intensity, and the more intense the punishment the more likelihood there is that several types of punish-ments will be associated.

Punishment may involve the withholding of some reward such as love or the pleasure of social community, or it may be a type of negative reinforcer such as physical or verbal abuse. Clearly these two types may be used together, although their relative intensity in any given situation is of some importance. Punishment of either type may develop an anxiety which becomes associated with the precipitating act. This anxiety later becomes a cue to stop performing a certain act, in which the reduction of anxiety that follows the cessation of the act serves as a reward for the alternate behavior.

Punishment usually directly follows the commission of an act, and terminates when the socializing agent feels that an "appropriate"

[17] Justin Aronfreed, *Conduct and Conscience: The Socialization of Internalized Control Over Behavior*, Academic Press, New York, 1968, p. 197.
[18] *Ibid.*, p. 166.

amount of aversive affect has been sustained by the child. The anxiety associated with this type of punishment is fear. Normally, the ending of punishment does not depend on the child making a self-punitive response. Rather, self-punitive responses such as self-criticism, apology, confession, and restitution have functional utility and are indulged in because they reinstate the affection and approval of the socializing agents.[19] Self-punitive responses, however, may become closely associated with certain types of punishments and, to be fully effective as a means of reinstating affection, require the ability on the part of the child to be cognizant of classes of behavior and to categorize the deviance in general terms. The development of this ability in turn appears related to certain styles of training, such as induction, where one is required to develop a sense of right and wrong based on an awareness of the results of behavior for others.

Induction training involves an intensive effort to have the child internalize standards of right and wrong (develop an ego-ideal) and develop an awareness of the consequences, in terms of these standards, of his acts for others. Self-punitive responses related to shame anxiety arise when these standards have been violated by one's behavior and one seeks to reduce the resultant anxiety by alternate behavior which will reinstate love and affection. Development of an orientation toward obtaining affection from authority figures appears related to techniques of discipline involving denial of love, threats of denial of reward, and threats of ostracism.

Type of punishment may vary according to the age, sex, social class, and culture of the child. There is no easy definition of the variance. In Taiwan and Japan, for instance, threats of denial of love are rather common in classrooms and in the home but slappings are also reported, more frequently in the home. In Japan one researcher reports changes in punishment style by age, with younger children receiving mild physical punishments and older children subjected to ridicule and ostracism.[20] In American society no clear difference in punishments among social classes has been found. For fifth graders the type and amount of punishment are the same across classes, while for adolescents the lower

[19] Albert Bandura and Richard H. Walters, *Social Learning and Personality Development*, Holt, Rinehart, and Winston, Inc., New York, 1963, pp. 186–187.

[20] Edward and Margaret Norbeck, "Child Training in a Japanese Fishing Community," in Douglas G. Haring, ed., *Personal Character and Cultural Milieu*, Syracuse University Press, Syracuse, N.Y., 1956, p. 673.

classes appear to be more permissive, contrary to popular notions. The main difference appears to be that the lower class punishes on the basis of the consequences of the child's disobedience, while the middle class punishes on the basis of perception of the child's intent.[21] Perception of intent and punishment on the basis of it assumes that the child has internalized an appropriate set of standards of right and wrong.

A complicating factor is that punishment style seems to be correlated with the extent of parental warmth, in that hostile parents tend to use physical punishment whereas warm parents use praise, reasoning, and induction training.[22] Here we have a socialization characteristic that is clearly not the sole attribute of some culture or social class, although it may be statistically dominant in some social units.

In this section we will not explore the actual training techniques employed with the children from our samples (see chapter 3), but will concern ourselves primarily with noting whether the correspondence we have noted between universalism and autocentrism and between particularism and heterocentrism applies in the area of punishments. We would expect that where internalization of universalistic values is most pronounced we will find attitudes concerning certain styles of punishment behavior to be more autocentric, reflecting the greater induction of universal values regarding interpersonal relations. Conversely, where internalization of universal values is less pronounced, we expect to find that attitudes regarding punishment behavior are more heterocentric. The questions relating to hypothesis 2 are 12, 14, and 27 (see Appendix C).

There were significant differences among groups in autocentrism and heterocentrism for two of the three questions (14 and 27). For the autocentric case there were two questions (12 and 27) where there was a significant difference among grade levels and for the heterocentric case one question (27) where there was a significant grade-level difference. A graphical representation of group differences is shown in Graphs 12 and 13; the one case of significant differences between sexes for the heterocentric case (question 27) and the significant interactions between

21 Edward Zigler and Irvin L. Child, "Socialization," in Lindzey and Aronson, *op. cit.*, vol. 3, p. 493.

22 Eleanor E. Maccoby, "The Development of Moral Values and Behavior in Childhood," in John A. Clausen, ed., *Socialization and Society*, Little, Brown and Co., Boston, 1968, pp. 248–249.

group and sex and group and grade level which occur for both the auto-centric and heterocentric cases on question 14 will not be presented in the text.

The mean percentage values for autocentrism for all questions plotted for each group are shown in Graph 12. Overall the pattern indicates considerable autocentrism for all groups, with this characteristic most marked for the Taiwan children. When the mean percentage values for each group are averaged, Taiwan is the highest with 77%, followed by Chinatown and America with 67% and Hong Kong with 66%. For all questions the average rank order for Taiwan is 1.7, ahead of Hong Kong and America both at 2.7, and Chinatown at 3.0. Auto-

GRAPH 12   *Hypothesis 2. Comparison among Groups of Autocentric Responses, Percent*

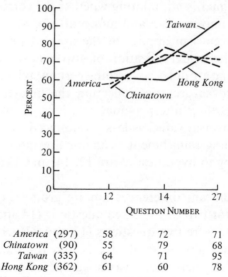

		12	14	27
America	(297)	58	72	71
Chinatown	(90)	55	79	68
Taiwan	(335)	64	71	95
Hong Kong	(362)	61	60	78

Note: Numbers in parentheses are the total number of respondents in that category.

Question 12: F = n.s.
Question 14: F = 6.31
Question 27: F = 45.02
n.s.—not significant

centric responses tend to be at a relatively high level for all groups. By and large the Taiwan children expressed the most autocentrism with regard to punishment behavior; the America, Chinatown, and Hong Kong children are lower and overall highly similar. Data for the interaction between group and grade level, however, suggests that autocentrism increases with age for the America children whereas it declines markedly from fifth to seventh grade for the children in the other groups (Taiwan, however, is still highest in autocentrism by seventh grade). With increasing age Chinese children retrograde toward more concern for particular others in the area of punishments.

For the heterocentric responses there were significant differences among groups for two of the three questions. Graph 13 gives the mean percentage values for heterocentrism for all questions for each group. In terms of averages of mean percentage values Hong Kong was highest overall in heterocentrism with 30%; America was next with 23%, followed by Chinatown with 21% and Taiwan with 19%. For all three questions the average rank order for Hong Kong was 1.7, for both America and Chinatown 2.7, and for Taiwan 3.0. Only in the responses of the Hong Kong children to a primary group situation (question 14) does the mean percentage value for heterocentrism approach 40%. Overall heterocentric responses for all groups were 25% or less. Hong Kong children tended to be the most heterocentric and Taiwan children, by a narrow margin, the least.

The pattern for grade levels is relatively unambiguous for the heterocentric responses, with third grade the highest. Question 27 was the only one where a significant difference among grade levels was reported. On that question third graders had a mean percentage value of 30%, decisively ahead of seventh and fifth graders both with 10%. This pattern was as expected. For the remaining two questions (12 and 14) third graders are also higher in heterocentrism than fifth and seventh graders, although the differences were not significant.

For the autocentric responses significant differences among grade levels were reported for two questions, 12 and 27. On question 12 seventh grade was lowest with 51%, below third grade at 62% and fifth grade at 65%. For question 27 third grade was lowest with 67%, below seventh grade at 83% and fifth grade 84%. Question 14 showed no significant differences among grade levels, with seventh grade falling below third grade and fifth grade in that order. Our assumption that

GRAPH 13   *Hypothesis 2.   Comparison among Groups of Heterocentric Responses, Percent*

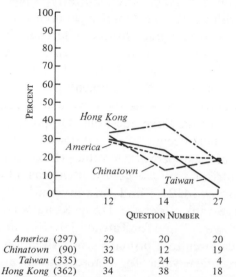

	12	14	27
America (297)	29	20	20
Chinatown (90)	32	12	19
Taiwan (335)	30	24	4
Hong Kong (362)	34	38	18

Note: Numbers in parentheses are the total number of respondents in that category.

Question 12: F = n.s.
Question 14: F = 30.34
Question 27: F = 11.50
n.s.—not significant

autocentrism should increase with age is not confirmed in the area of punishments. Heterocentrism, however, is more predominant among younger children.

Two other sources of data are available with regard to hypothesis 2. The first of these involves a visual test, in which the children were asked to evaluate two types of punishment situations shown pictorially. The two pictures used in this test were also partially used in interviewing. The pictorial-test evaluations and interview data serve to provide background data for a further assessment of our findings. The children tested were in all cases from the same classrooms where the multiple choice autocentrism/heterocentrism questionnaire was given, although due to various classroom activities the numbers involved in each test varied slightly.

The two posters concerning punishment (Exhibits A and B) were shown to the children and a question was asked of them, phrased in the following way, "Here are two situations. In one of them a father or older brother is talking to his son or younger brother. Let us suppose it is the father. In the picture the father looks like he is scolding his son and might even spank him. In the other picture it looks like a child may have done something wrong in the class. The teacher has asked the child to stand and is scolding him. Now, if you were in both of these pictures, which way do you think would be the *worse* way to be punished? Mark down which punishment you feel is *worse* and write down your reason for this."

The father–son picture reflects the possibility of physical punishment, which the teacher–pupil picture does not, and because it has been unambiguously described as a primary group situation, it contains

EXHIBIT A

EXHIBIT B

messages and an interaction content that we assume to be basically particularistic. The teacher–pupil scene, on the other hand, has an interaction context and style in which the message content is likely to be phrased in universalistic terms. Our major feeling was that the primary group physical punishment situation would be seen by the children as involving particularistic criteria while the classroom scene would be seen as involving universalistic criteria.

In the responses to this test there was a highly significant difference among groups and among grade levels but no significant difference between sexes nor any significant interaction effects. In all groups most children selected the schoolroom scene, the percentage of responses ranging from just over half for the Chinatown children to almost eighty percent for children from Hong Kong and Taiwan. By grade levels there was a significant difference, with older children selecting the classroom scene and younger children the father–son picture. The mean percentage values for the schoolroom scene and the

GRAPH 14 *Schoolroom and Father-Son Scenes: Responses by Group, Percent*

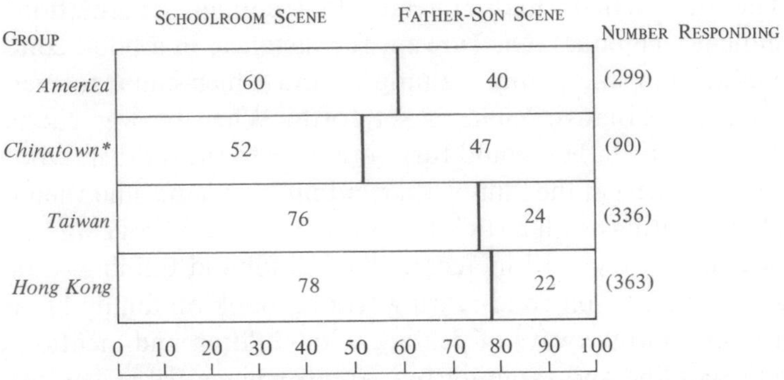

GROUP	SCHOOLROOM SCENE	FATHER-SON SCENE	NUMBER RESPONDING
America	60	40	(299)
Chinatown*	52	47	(90)
Taiwan	76	24	(336)
Hong Kong	78	22	(363)

0 10 20 30 40 50 60 70 80 90 100

*The Chinatown percentage does not equal 100.00 because there was one "don't know" in the Chinatown male seventh-grade responses.

Schoolroom Scene: F = 31.66   Father-Son Scene: F = 25.93

GRAPH 15 *Schoolroom and Father-Son Scenes: Responses by Grade Level, Percent*

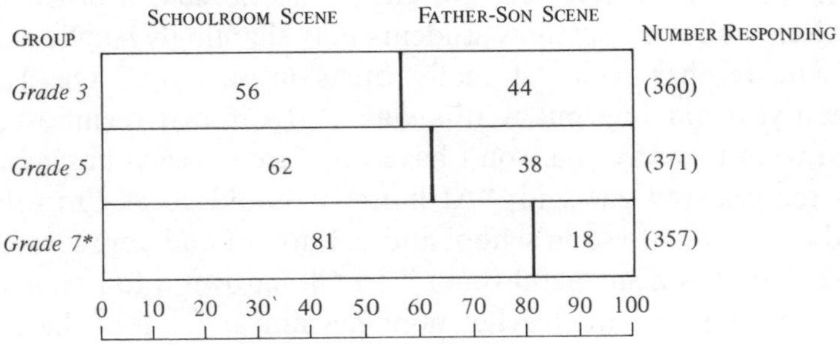

GROUP	SCHOOLROOM SCENE	FATHER-SON SCENE	NUMBER RESPONDING
Grade 3	56	44	(360)
Grade 5	62	38	(371)
Grade 7*	81	18	(357)

0 10 20 30 40 50 60 70 80 90 100

*The seventh grade percentage does not equal 100.00 because there was one "don't know" in the Chinatown male seventh-grade responses.

Schoolroom Scene: F = 42.57   Father-Son Scene: F = 39.08

father–son scene are set forth in Graph 14. The mean percentage values for both scenes in terms of grade levels are indicated in Graph 15.

The stories that children read often contain information about punishment techniques. On Taiwan, for instance, in a book concerning home education, the family training of Liu Chien-chun, former President of the Legislative Yuan, is set forth. When he was caught in a misdemeanor his father would turn him over to the mother, who would force him to kneel at the family altar, admit his blame, and then request how many beatings with a stick he should receive.[23] Flogging is, in fact, not infrequently reported in accounts of childhood training.[24] In Hong Kong, in a chapter on child-rearing from a book on family life there is criticism of contrary ways of dealing with children and mention of too frequent scolding and shouting by parents when quiet reasoning would be better.[25] It is still true, however, that much Chinese training in the school and home involves loss of love, injunctions concerning the general "moral" implications of bad behavior, and the mustering of group disapproval. It is experience with this training procedure that presumably made a fourteen-year-old girl from Hong Kong respond in the following way concerning her choice of the schoolroom scene as the worse form of punishment: "Because to be punished in front of others is very shameful; compared to any other punishment this is the hardest to bear"; another twelve-year-old girl said, "Because if others can see, then when school is out fellow students may shamingly laugh; moreover, when the teacher scolds it really hurts intolerably." On Taiwan a fourteen-year-old boy put it this way: "Because it seems that to be spoken to in this way you won't have any face to see your classmates"; and a ten-year-old girl said, "At home I should do as I'm told and I should even more do so in school and if I do not and am scolded by the teacher then it is a shameful thing." In Chinatown a fourteen-year-old girl wrote, "Because the teacher punishes him in front of the class and all the children could see who the teacher is punishing and they will laugh at him," while a ten-year-old boy responded, "Because the teacher will give me extra homework and in class it will make me embarrassed."

[23] Yin Yun-hua, *Home Education* (*Chia-t'ing Chiao-yu*), Hu Yung-ch'ing, publisher, Taiwan, 1970, p. 191.

[24] Chiang Chu-shan, publishers, *The Way of Happiness for Men and Women* (*Nan Nü Hsing-fu Chih Lu*), Taiwan, 1960, pp. 41–42.

[25] Yeh Hou-chung, *On Family Life* (*Chia-ting Sheng-huo Man-t'an*), Tai Dei Publishing Society, Hong Kong, 1957, p. 111.,

A twelve-year-old girl from New Brunswick said, "Because getting punished in front of a group of people would be embarrassing. But when alone you and the person punishing would only [sic] know." A nine-year-old boy from Princeton wrote concerning his choice, "The one in school because everybody would be watching and I would be *a little* embarrassed (a little, because I'm an extrovert)."

In contrast to these reports on being punished in class, children's comments on being punished by a parent are usually shorter and more reflecting of physical fear. For instance, a ten-year-old boy on Taiwan said, "Because I most fear my father hitting me." An eleven-year-old boy in Chinatown wrote, "At school the teacher can't hit me [but] at home your father can hit you." A nine-year-old Princeton girl wrote, "A daddy can hit but a teacher cannot," and a nine-year-old Princeton boy said, "Because scolding doesn't hurt like spankings." In all of these cases the anxiety reported is one of fear that seems to stem directly from the fact of physical punishment itself.

DISCUSSION AND SUMMARY

Given two situations, one involving punishment by a father and one involving punishment by a teacher before a class, most children feel the classroom punishment is more severe, and this feeling increases with grade level. Children from Taiwan and Hong Kong are more apt to feel this way than are children from the Chinatown and American samples. In giving reasons for why they feel the classroom scene is more fearful as a punishment, the children put emphasis on shame and embarrassment and *implicitly* note the threat of ostracism involved.

The relationship between style of punishment and value or attitude orientation is not a fixed one. Shaming punishments reference both specific others and failure to live up to an internalized ideal. In some contexts (schools, for instance) this may lead to an intensified internalization of certain universalistic standards; it is also clear that a shaming interaction can reference particularistic criteria and can occur at either the primary or secondary level. Indeed, we would expect that for shaming to be highly anxiety-provoking it would occur in both primary and secondary settings and be associated with both particularistic and universalistic value orientations. Similarly, physical punishment may result from a violation of either universalistic or particularistic values, although it is rarely administered, particularly in a family context, without the intrusion of some particularistic criteria. General autocentric or heterocentric attitude orientations toward punishment can therefore be related to similar styles of punishment. In addition, both individuals and groups can vary in terms of whether punishments primarily reference universal standards or whether they primarily reference specific relationship patterns with others.

The data indicates that the Taiwan group was highest in autocentrism and the Hong Kong group highest in heterocentrism, with both groups decidedly more anxious than the Chinatown or America children concerning punishment by group sanction. It would appear that shaming punishment, used initially at the primary level and involving violation of particularistic criteria, is powerfully and increasingly reinforced in Taiwan and Hong Kong by its use in school for the violation of universalistic criteria. In Hong Kong, however, shame arousal appears on a comparative basis to be related more to particularistic criteria (heterocentrism), whereas in Taiwan shame arousal has been more decisively transferred to violation of certain universalistic values (autocentrism). In both cases our field observations indicate that shame anxiety when generated is high, making cognition of both the criteria and the reference groups involved in punishment very important for the child.

SECTION THREE.   HYPOTHESES 3 AND 4

HYPOTHESIS 3:

Punishments may elicit hostility. With predominantly heterocentric attitude dispositions hostility in terms of particular others in a positively sanctioned relationship receives heavy negative sanction. However, toward those with whom no specific relationship exists, there may be hostility or aggression according to the situation or context with weak negative sanction. With predominantly autocentric attitude dispositions, although hostility and aggression are generally also negatively sanctioned where specific interpersonal relations exist, these reactions may be permissible in situations where universalistic values are violated, regardless of the interpersonal relationship.

Hostility is an attitude toward something, someone, or some set of events that has as one component a negative evaluative dimension. While no doubt a relationship exists between the intensity of feelings of hostility and behavioral manifestations, the relationship is not a fixed one, and other factors, such as the circumstances under which this particular feeling of hostility was aroused, individual personality characteristics, and cultural influences, must all be considered. Among a broad range of possibilities, hostility may be manifested as sullenness, joking, sarcasm, cynicism, or overt aggression. Hostility may be projected outward against others or turned inward against the self. In interpersonal relations hostility may be highly destructive of social bonds or, due to the catharsis of release, may strengthen these bonds. It may lead to the commission of acts highly dangerous to one's social grouping, or it may strengthen a sense of ingroup solidarity by focusing hostility against others and by sharpening awareness of the accepted mores of ingroup life.

The expression of hostility is usually modified, to some degree, by cultural patterns that help define both acceptable targets for hostility and legitimate reasons for its expression. Work on stereotyping has noted how social groupings have a tendency to select certain groups or certain clusters of attributes as particularly deserving of hostility, and how these clusters may vary markedly even among subunits of the same social system. Even body types—fat, thin, short, tall, etc.—have been found to evoke generalized concepts of favor or disfavor.[26] Stereotyping is enhanced both by contact and competition with other groups holding different values and in situations where social change and its concomitant disorganization and decreased predictability in interpersonal relations leave hostility relatively unfocused. The probability of overt expression of hostility toward outgroups will increase to the extent that the social system lacks vulnerable minorities and a multiplicity of minor cleavages.[27]

The commonest interpretation of hostility and resultant aggression or violence is that the individual has in some way been frustrated in the attainment of some goal or the fulfillment of some motivated act. In

[26] J. Robert Staffieri, "A Study of Social Stereotype of Body Image in Children," *Journal of Personality and Social Psychology*, vol. 7, no. 1, Sept. 1967, pp. 101–104.

[27] Wilbert E. Moore, *Social Change*, Prentice-Hall Foundations of Modern Sociology Series, Prentice-Hall, Englewood Cliffs, N.J., 1963, pp. 63–65.

social terms this is frequently conceptualized as a felt sense of "relative deprivation," particularly with regard to the unequal distribution of values or rights when that unequal distribution is not considered legitimate.[28] Legitimacy concerning the distribution of power and authority and other rewards is thus a key intervening variable. Whether the expression of hostile feelings about the distribution of rewards will be in terms of particularistic criteria or within the framework of a more or less structured ideology of universalistic values will depend upon the learning process within that social system.

Any disciplinary activity against a child will cause a certain amount of hostility by preventing the child from completing or repeating some act which he wished to perform.[29] Frustration may be only one of the factors causing overt expression of hostility, however; it may, in fact, be absent or relatively unimportant in certain situations. Modeling after the aggressive behavior of authority figures or reinforcement by authority figures of aggressive behavior may at times be more important than frustration as explanations for the overt expression of hostility.

The anxiety generated during punishment provides the underlying motivation for modifying behavior. It serves to suppress certain modes of behavior, so that alternate modes desired by the socializing agent can be initiated. By being highly anxiety-provoking, punishment sets the "affective stage" for the good feelings that result from the performance of "proper" behavior. As such, punishment may aid in internalization of evaluative standards with regard to certain modes of behavior.[30]

Physical punishment may lead to self-control and can prevent the occurrence of disapproved behavior, but it may also result in frustration, hostility, and retardation of learning of appropriate standards. These less desired ends occur because the child begins to concentrate more upon the risks of punishment than on the development of internal controls. It has been found, in fact, that the use of physical punishment is correlated with aggressive behavior at certain ages for both boys and

[28] Ted R. Gurr, *Why Men Rebel*, Princeton University Press, Princeton, N.J., 1970, p. 110; Lewis A. Coser, *The Functions of Social Conflict*, The Free Press, New York, 1956 (paperback), p. 37; Lucian W. Pye, "Hostility and Authority in Chinese Politics," *Problems of Communism*, vol. 17, no. 3, May–June 1968, pp. 12–15.

[29] Martin L. Hoffman and Herbert D. Saltzstein, "Parent Discipline and the Child's Moral Development," *Journal of Personality and Social Psychology*, vol. 5, no. 1, January 1967, p. 54.

[30] Aronfreed, *Conduct and Conscience*, p. 60.

girls, with variations in terms of intensity and locale of action.[31] The greatest expression of overt hostility seems to occur in learning environments where there is a tolerant attitude toward aggression (reinforcement) or where severe punishments are administered for expressing aggression (modeling).[32]

Withdrawal of affection is just as painful and anxiety-provoking to a child as physical punishment and, moreover, is probably a component to some degree of all forms of punishment. Love withdrawal is a form of discipline directly oriented toward internalization of standards, since affection is not reinstated until the child has corrected and controlled his behavior. Internalization occurs when the pleasurable feelings associated with a particular outcome are attached to the actions and thoughts leading up to it. Pleasurable feelings arise from the reduction of anxiety that is associated with types of behavior that do not lead to punishment. Studies have shown that this process is more likely to be effective when the socializing agent is nurturant than when the agent is neutral or negative, since in the latter case loss of affection is not sufficiently anxiety-provoking to motivate the child to alternate behavior.[33] An aversion to the expression of hostility arises from a training situation in which the expression of hostility subjects the individual when very young to the anxiety of loss of affection and later to the additional anxiety of shame. For males, at least, high guilt (shame) about expressing anger is associated with psychological discipline by the mother; this has been verified at the .01 level.[34]

In order to test hypothesis 3, three questions were asked; 9, 16, and 18 (see Appendix C). The major focus of this section is to test what are considered to be the legitimate bases for expression of hostility. Is expression of hostility permissible at any time when internalized ideal standards of morality are violated, or is it permissible only outside the context of specific relationships, where particularistic standards do not apply?

In the analysis of hypothesis 3 responses two out of three questions

[31] Zigler and Child, op. cit., p. 527.

[32] Robert R. Sears, Eleanor E. Maccoby, and Harry Levin, Patterns of Child Rearing, Row, Peterson and Company, Evanston, Ill. and White Plains, N.Y., 1957, p. 266.

[33] Aronfreed, Conduct and Conscience, pp. 54–56, 311–313, 320–321.

[34] Wesley Allinsmith and Thomas C. Greening, "Guilt over Anger as Predicted from Parental Discipline: A Study of Superego Development," American Psychologist, vol. 10, no. 8, August 1955, p. 320.

for both the autocentric and heterocentric cases showed significant differences among groups (16 and 18). There was also a significant difference among grade levels on two of the three questions for the heterocentric case (9 and 16) and on one question for the autocentric case (18). These aspects of hypothesis 3 will be discussed below. There were no significant differences for either case between the sexes and only one significant interaction effect—between group and grade level—in the heterocentric case for question 16. These factors will not be discussed.

On two of the three questions for the autocentric case there were significant interactions among groups. A graphical representation of how each group responded to the questions is given in Graph 16. Over

GRAPH 16   *Hypothesis 3. Comparison among Groups of Autocentric Responses, Percent*

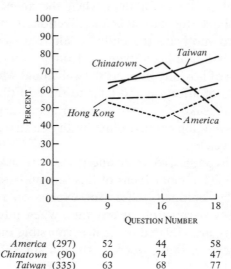

	9	16	18
America (297)	52	44	58
Chinatown (90)	60	74	47
Taiwan (335)	63	68	77
Hong Kong (362)	54	56	62

Note: Numbers in parentheses are the total number of respondents in that category.

Question 9: F = n.s.
Question 16: F = 25.61
Question 18: F = 7.56
n.s.—not significant

half the children in all groups expressed autocentric attitudes with regard to the expression of hostility, but overall this was a more pronounced characteristic for the Taiwan, Hong Kong, and Chinatown children than for the America group.

Among the four groups the average mean percentage value for all questions was 69% for Taiwan, 60% for Chinatown followed closely by 58% for Hong Kong, and 51% for America. In terms of average rank order this pattern was again manifested, with Taiwan at 1.3, Chinatown at 2.3, Hong Kong at 3.0, and America last at 3.3.

By grade level only one response was significant for the autocentric case, question 16. On this question fifth graders were highest at 65%, ahead of third graders at 64% and seventh graders at 52%; for all groups but the America group there was a decline in autocentrism by seventh grade on question 16. This pattern, although not significant, was repeated on question 18 but not on question 9, where there was a general increase in autocentrism with age. In terms of the expression of hostility, therefore, our data does not support an assumption of invariably increasing autocentrism with age except for the America group. The onset of adolescence seems rather to be a time when particularistic criteria increasingly govern the expression of hostility for all the Chinese groups, although there are marked differences among groups in this regard.

With the heterocentric case there were again two out of three questions that showed significant differences among groups; these were again questions 16 and 18. The percentages of heterocentric responses for each question for each group are shown in Graph 17. Overall the America and Hong Kong groups were the most heterocentric. The averages of the mean percentage values for all questions revealed America highest in heterocentrism with an average mean percentage value of 41%, followed by Hong Kong at 37%, Chinatown with 31%, and Taiwan with 24%. In terms of average rank order America was again first with 1.7, followed by Hong Kong with 2.0, Chinatown with 2.7, and Taiwan with 3.7.

For the heterocentric case there was a significant difference among grade levels for two of the three questions. The results for each question, plotted for each grade level, are given in Graph 18. It can be noted that while heterocentrism appears to decline by fifth grade, as would be expected, this trend is reversed by seventh grade. The averages of the

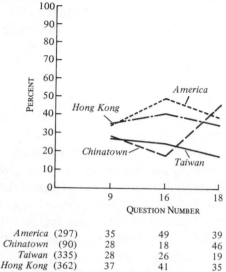

GRAPH 17   *Hypothesis 3. Comparison among Groups of Heterocentric Responses, Percent*

	9	16	18
America (297)	35	49	39
Chinatown (90)	28	18	46
Taiwan (335)	28	26	19
Hong Kong (362)	37	41	35

Note: Numbers in parentheses are the total number of respondents in that category.

Question 9: F = n.s.
Question 16: F = 48.54
Question 18: F = 9.39
n.s. — not significant

mean percentage values for each grade level were 37% for third grade, 30% for fifth grade, and 33% for seventh grade, with average rank orderings of 1.7, 2.7 and 1.7 respectively. We believe the high overall seventh-grade heterocentric value is partially related to the onset of adolescence—to a heightened uncertainty with regard to one's position and also to an increasing anxiety concerning group sanctions. At least as regards the expression of hostility, there appears for some children to be a retrogression to what may be felt to be "safer" criteria for the governance and legitimization of hostility. According to the interaction plots this shift appears most markedly for the Taiwan and Hong Kong groups, is approximately neutral for the Chinatown group, and does not hold

GRAPH 18   *Hypothesis 3. Comparison among*
Grade Levels of Heterocentric Responses,
Percent

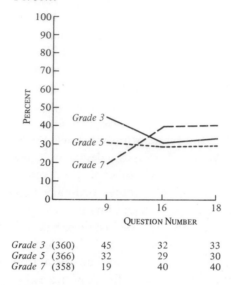

Grade 3 (360)	45	32	33
Grade 5 (366)	32	29	30
Grade 7 (358)	19	40	40

Note: Numbers in parentheses are the total number of respondents
   in that category.

Question 9: F = 12.01
Question 16: F = 10.60
Question 18: F = n.s.
n.s.—not significant

for the America group, which actually shows a decline in hetero-centrism—although the final seventh-grade position is still relatively high.

Our data on hypothesis 3 indicates that the highest degree of auto-centrism with regard to the expression of hostility is manifested by children from Taiwan, followed in order by children from Chinatown, Hong Kong, and America. This order is precisely reversed for the expression of heterocentrism, where overall the America group leads, followed by Hong Kong, Chinatown, and Taiwan. By grade levels there is not an increase in autocentrism with age; rather, there is an increase in autocentrism through fifth grade and then an apparent retrogression, which, again, we believe is at least partly related to the uncertainties and pressures of early adolescence.

The questions asked concerning hypothesis 3 relate both to modes of expression of hostility and to the legitimate bases for its expression. It is clear that children from Taiwan and, to a lesser extent, from China-town and Hong Kong will not, generally speaking, express hostility unless this expression is legitimized by the violation of some univer-salistic standard. America children, on the other hand, at least until the seventh grade, seem somewhat dependent on the designation by authority of a legitimate target for hostility and are more restrained by the personal factors involved in a relationship.

The hypothesis 3 questions are less explicit as regards mode of expression of hostility, and some attention must therefore be directed toward this problem. While emotional valence in a given situation may be one of hostility, the actual style of expression may vary from overt aggression to restrained and apparently ordinary behavior. There is, clearly, a variation in this regard depending upon society, class, sex, etc. Internalized control of aggression, for instance, has been found to exist to a greater degree among higher- rather than lower-class children.[35] Among societies control of aggression and hostile action has been found to be a particular source of difficulty for Americans.[36]

The factors that inhibit or reinforce the expression of various modes of hostility are not fully understood, but some findings are suggestive. It would appear incontrovertible that overt, aggressive punishment for aggression actually leads to aggression through the influence of modeling. Nonreacting and completely permissive adults may also increase aggression in small children by tacitly reinforcing an aggressive behavior pattern.[37] Restrictiveness may inhibit the overt expression of hostility, especially if the parents are "warm," whereas the largest amount of aggressive behavior will occur where parents are both permissive and hostile (mother lax, father punitive) and both modeling and reinforcement are able to become operative.[38] A virtually inescap-

[35] Aronfreed, *Conduct and Conscience*, p. 327.

[36] Robert F. Peck with Robert J. Havighurst, *The Psychology of Character Development*, John Wiley and Sons, (Science Editions), New York, 1960, p. 14.

[37] Sears, Maccoby, and Levin, *op. cit.*, p. 484. Also Diana Baumrind, "Effects of Authoritative Parental Control on Child Behavior," *Child Development*, vol. 37, no. 4, Dec. 1966, p. 900.

[38] Zigler and Child, *op. cit.*, p. 528.

able conclusion is that the greatest degree of internalized control over overt hostility is obtained when the authority figures are warm but not permissive, and punishments are not severe in nature. A mild threat of punishment, whereby fear, anger, and defensiveness are not aroused as dominant reactions, allows time for an understanding to develop that certain behavior is wrong. Moderate anxiety may generate a permanent change in values and produce greater internalized control over overt hostility. Rewards and punishments should not present cues which are overpowering in terms of the ends desired but should operate rather to steer the development of internalized control.[39]

Observers of Chinese society have frequently remarked upon the anxiety exhibited by traditional Chinese for actions against parents. Expressing hostility was condemned and unconditional obedience was striven for as a goal.[40] It has also been noted, however, how in some contexts, both at primary and secondary levels, the Chinese will speak with a bluntness and frankness concerning the shortcomings of another that appear almost rude to the foreigner. These two patterns of behavior are not incompatible as long as overt expression of hostility is minimized. Despite the efforts of the Communist government of China to encourage and provide opportunities for the overt expression of hostility in some contexts (mass struggle meetings, for one), it is improbable to expect that such a pattern will become a daily mode unless some very systematic changes are made in early childhood rearing. There is no evidence to suggest, however, that early patterns of punishment, permissiveness, or "warmth" have been altered in any significant way.

In Hong Kong and on Taiwan, our observations indicate that the expression of hostility by children toward authority figures is suppressed (usually verbally with such statements as "don't be rude"), but that aggression among peers will not necessarily be stopped even when it occurs directly in front of an authority figure. When aggression is stopped it is often merely to distract the offender or placate the victim rather than to actively punish. Parents and teachers stress that for a child to know he is loved is very important, more important than hitting a

---

[39] Aronfreed, *Conduct and Conscience*, pp. 288, 293, 300.

[40] Richard H. Solomon, "Mao's Effort to Reintegrate the Chinese Polity: Problems of Authority and Conflict in Chinese Social Processes," in A. Doak Barnett, ed., *Chinese Communist Politics in Action*, University of Washington Press, Seattle, 1969, pp. 284–338. See also Otto Klineberg, "Emotional Expression in Chinese Literature," *Journal of Abnormal and Social Psychology*, vol. 33, no. 4, Oct. 1938, p. 519.

child for some infraction. Unconsciously, these authority figures attempt, through warmth, through modeling, and by generally mild restrictiveness against overt hostility directed against themselves, to instill internalized controls against the overt expression of hostility, controls which subsequently break down only under special circumstances. Concomitantly there also appears to develop a certain fear of being rude or offending others and a fear under normal circumstances to verbalize freely any opposition to authority figures.

The pattern that emerges from the autocentrism/heterocentrism questionnaire and from field observation is one of a delicate balance between autocentrism and heterocentrism for Chinese children. While Chinese children occasionally express hostility, increasingly with age this expression involves a minimum display of overtness coupled with a concern for the interpersonal relationship. Remarks will be frank and to the point. Giving offense gratuitously, however, is not condoned, and an effort will be made in discussing shortcomings to invoke universalistic values as a legitimization for one's frankness.

During interviews the children were asked whether they would get angry with punishing agents or authority figures. The results for each group were as shown in Table 3.

TABLE 3   *Expression of Anger toward Punishing Agents or Authority Figures, Percent*

	CAUCASIAN AMERICAN (18)	CHINATOWN (6)	TAIWAN (18)	HONG KONG (18)
Would get angry	17	17	17	17
Would not get angry	50	17	83	83
No indication	33	66	0	0

Note: Numbers in parentheses are the total number of respondents in that category.

While this is a small sample from which to generalize, the data indicates clearly that although few children believe they would express hostility toward a punishing agent or authority figure, those from Taiwan and Hong Kong are especially convinced that they must not.

HYPOTHESIS 4:

With heterocentric attitude dispositions we expect to find the expression of opposition to authority inversely related to the strength of the interpersonal tie. With autocentric attitude dispositions we expect to find opposition to authority directly related to the extent of deviance by authority figures from positively sanctioned universalistic criteria.

Expression of hostility, as we discussed under hypothesis 3, may be exhibited in a number of ways and directed against a variety of potential targets. In this section we are specifically concerned with expressions of opposition toward authority figures. Opposition to authority does not, of course, imply hostility, but in many instances hostility may be an affective component which generates, motivates, or sustains opposition.

Opposition to authority is related to various factors in the learning process. In the most general sense the degree of opposition will depend upon the amount of respect involved in the relationship, the degree of visibility of the authority figure, and the extent of contact. Respect is a critical component and will influence greatly the style of opposition. It has been found for example, to be the basis for a "sense of duty," the feeling that a command is legitimate. If a leader presents cues similar to those of other "prestigious" leaders who have used reward for compliance, the capacity for opposition or failure to respond will be minimized. Prestige of authority is an important component of respect. It has been noted that regardless of a child's judgment concerning the intentions or consequences surrounding an act of transgression, if this judgment is contradicted by an adult the child will show a shift of judgment in the direction of the adult.[41]

If respect for authority is low and socialization has been severe the result may be an effort at counterhumiliation and counterdistress. If the authority figure is too strong for such measures to be safely undertaken, there may be suppression of aggression toward authority but projection, displacement, and release of hostility against other possible targets. In short, for opposition to occur depends upon the fulfillment of certain minimal requirements. These will determine whether opposition to authority actually takes place or not and whether, if it does take place, it is couched in terms that are constructive or hostile.

Stories for Chinese children frequently stress the love that parents, especially the mother, have for children. It is expected that love toward these authority figures will be reciprocated and will be the basis for

[41] Aronfreed, *Conduct and Conscience*, p. 264.

acceptance of the parents' leadership role. However, inculcation of respect for authority can go beyond parents. Children in Hong Kong, for instance, are enjoined as follows:

> We must love our teachers.
>
> We should obey our teachers, because what they instruct usually concerns right principles for men. If they scold us, it is with the intention to correct our mistakes. Therefore, we should accept their instruction gladly and humbly and do as directed. To obey teachers is to obey truth. It is by no means blind obedience.[42]

Or again:

> You should credit, imitate, obey and be submissive to your superior. He has the ability to lead you; the ability which you ought not to neglect. One must know that the cause for the turbulence of Chinese society is that the people have had no belief in their superiors and think that they are better than these mediocrities. In fact, you should have belief no matter whether they are good or bad, which is another question.[43]

Superiors are enjoined to respect subordinates and to be impartial toward them. Yet superiors or authority figures also enjoy a certain latitude, which in non-Communist China is often unchecked by countervailing social pressure. Observation on a beach in Taiwan showed lifeguards striking with fists and belts at swimmers unlucky enough to stray beyond the safety zone. Moreover, the swimmers so treated, although angry, said nothing, nor did the lifeguards attempt to explain or justify their actions. In Hong Kong on a busy street a large boy beat a younger one, striking him on the face, and evoking from the passing crowd only stares from two elderly women despite the small boy's tears. Not only was the exercise of authority in these two situations unchallenged, but there was no attempt on the part of others to intervene.

While a hostile challenge to authority is uncommon this should not imply meek and mute subservience. Solomon has noted how both Chinese and Americans tend to feel that criticism of superiors is neces-

---

[42] Tu Chia-chung, ed., *Economic and Public Affairs* (*Ching-chi Chih Kung-kung Shih-wu*), Book 1, Grade 7, Wen Fung Book Co., Hong Kong, 1969, p. 13.

[43] Lin Chi-sha, *Cultivation and Service of Youth* (*Ch'ing nien Hsiu-yang yu Fu-wu*), Tai Fong Publishing Society, Hong Kong, 1967, pp. 37–39.

sary for improving work.[44] Two university students in Taiwan noted emphatically that they would not fear to tell a policeman he was wrong, for, in their opinion, the police are polite and can be spoken with. Authority is also often lenient. Hong Kong school teachers rarely report school failures as due to belligerence or rebelliousness, but speak instead of withdrawal. This may be because there is, indeed, no overt challenge, but it is also partly because teachers are unwilling to stigmatize their pupils harshly to outsiders.[45] Arthur Smith noted in the nineteenth century how extreme discipline in the school was in marked contrast to the slackness of family control. Speaking of a child who did not wish to attend school, Smith wrote, "the lad absolutely declined to go, and like most Chinese parents in similar circumstances, the father was perfectly unable to force him to do what he did not wish to do."[46]

In a swashbuckling Hong Kong movie entitled, in English, *The Heroic Ones* (Shih-san T'ai-pao or Thirteen Rogues), several themes concerning leadership and followership were brought forth that are sufficiently typical to be worthy of mention. The main theme was that fighting among subordinates leads to disaster while cooperation leads to victory. Subthemes stressed that authority has the right to call for unstinted sacrifice on the part of subordinates, that supreme authority is always to be respected and the appellation of "rebel" to be strenuously avoided, that fathers have the unlimited right of punishment, and that just punishment by a superior is righteous. These are, of course, ideal patterns, which are frequently severely modified in actual practice. Children, for instance, will often crowd around teachers or guests with no sense of awe or embarrassment. Subordinates learn how to manipulate middle-level authority, as when older brothers yield to youngers because in any altercation the older one will be blamed for not having set a proper example and for failing to control the situation.[47] In Japan, where similar ideals concerning authority were held in traditional times,

[44] Solomon, *op. cit.*, p. 335.

[45] Elizabeth Rowe and Y. P. Lau, G. H. Lee, A. K. Li, W. G. Rodd in collaboration with S. C. Hu, *Failure in School: Aspects of the Problem in Hong Kong*, Hong Kong Council for Educational Research, Publication No. 3, Hong Kong University Press, Hong Kong, 1966, p. 127.

[46] Arthur H. Smith, *Village Life in China*, Fleming H. Revell Co., New York, 1899, p. 79.

[47] Margery Wolf, "Child Training and the Chinese Family," in Maurice Freedman, ed., *Family and Kinship in Chinese Society*, Stanford University Press, Stanford, California, 1970, p. 53.

it has been found that children there see rules as prohibitive (i.e., as guidelines that prohibit behavior) 43% of the time, versus 34% for white Americans and 38% for black Americans, but also see rules as beneficial (having rational social or personal reasons for existence) 45% of the time, versus only 18% for white Americans and 6% for black Americans.[48] It is clear that in the Japanese version of Oriental society the dictates of authority can be viewed as both strict and reasonable.

In interviews and written questionnaire responses the children from our four sample groups had characteristic ways of dealing with the problem of opposition to authority. The America children, for instance, often spoke of opposing authority (while also admitting that in actual practice they might well not). A third-grade boy wrote, "if a teacher hit me I could sue her." A fifth-grade boy said he would speak up to the mayor, the governor, or a Senator. "I would say something even if it would embarrass them. If I don't like what they said and I disagreed with them it would be about the best thing I could do to embarrass them." A third-grade girl, however, said, "A person can't go against the leader. A leader is a leader and you ought to do what he says. But not if it's wrong. Not even if it's just a little bit wrong."

The children from the Chinatown, Taiwan, and Hong Kong groups often stress the "feelings" of the leader and the need to maintain group harmony. Even when opposition to authority is approved it is generally sanctioned on the basis of the ultimate good of the group. A seventh-grade Chinatown boy wrote, "If you disagree with a lot of people maybe . . . it might start a fight." Here group solidarity is uppermost. A fifth-grade girl noted that it was better to speak up and "give your opinion and work things out as a group."

On Taiwan a seventh-grade girl noted that in disagreeing with an authority figure one should "speak peacefully to give him face and he can change." Another seventh-grade girl wrote, "If in speaking there is a mistake and everyone puts forth his ideas for discussion then there will not be any mistaken opinions." In an interview a seventh-grade boy reported that toward someone who was punishing him "I would get angry but I would not show it." A fifth-grade girl spoke this way when asked if she would openly disagree with the school principal or her

[48] June L. Tapp, "A Child's Garden of Law and Order," *Psychology Today*, vol. 4, no. 7, December 1970, p. 30 and chart, p. 62.

grandfather: "I can't openly disagree with them but I would express my viewpoint when nobody else is present."

In Hong Kong two seventh-grade girls had the following to say about why they would prefer not to disagree openly, with an authority figure: "Because [if spoken to alone] he will not lose face" and "if we should openly criticize it will injure his self-respect." In return children see authority figures as behaving in a considerate manner toward them. A seventh-grade girl in an interview described teachers in the following way. "Teachers should respect students and talk to them calmly and, most important of all, not make them lose face. Teachers are supposed to be their children's and pupils' model. If children fail, she should talk to them alone and express her own feelings. It is not polite to point out their mistakes, especially if they are serious."

The data from interviews with children from the four groups was summarized with respect to three questions: (1) Is it permissible to make an authority figure lose face?; (2) Can you disagree with an authority figure?; and (3) Can you openly argue with an authority figure? The

TABLE 4   *Expressions Regarding the Permissibility of Making an Authority Figure Lose Face, Percent*

	CAUCASIAN AMERICAN (18)	CHINATOWN (6)	TAIWAN (18)	HONG KONG (18)
Should not lose face	33	67	100	50
Can lose face	67	0	0	17
No indication	0	33	0	33

Note: Numbers in parentheses are the total number of respondents in that category.

TABLE 5   *Expressions Regarding Whether One Can Disagree with an Authority Figure, Percent*

	CAUCASIAN AMERICAN (18)	CHINATOWN (6)	TAIWAN (18)	HONG KONG (18)
Can disagree	61	100	72	61
Cannot disagree	0	0	28	33
No indication	39	0	0	6

Note. Numbers in parentheses are the total number of respondents in that category.

TABLE 6   *Expressions Regarding Whether One Can Openly Argue with an Authority Figure, Percent*

	CAUCASIAN AMERICAN (18)	CHINATOWN (6)	TAIWAN (18)	HONG KONG (18)
Can openly argue	83	33	17	22
Cannot openly argue	17	67	83	78
No indication	0	0	0	0

Note. Numbers in parentheses are the total number of respondents in that category.

results, given in Tables 4–6, indicate that Chinese children generally express respect and deference toward authority figures but do not believe that authority is totally unapproachable.

Although the data from Tables 4, 5, and 6 suggests that children from the Chinatown, Taiwan, and Hong Kong groups are much less

EXHIBIT C

EXHIBIT D

willing than American children to openly oppose authority figures, other results do not support this pattern. Exhibits C and D were presented to the children from the four groups. These two pictures show in one case (Exhibit C) a speaker addressing an audience with some members of the audience raising their hands, and in the second case (Exhibit D) a speaker talking with two people at the front of an auditorium. The children were asked to select one picture or the other in response to the following question: "Here is a speaker. In one picture it looks as if some people in the audience don't agree with him and are raising their hands to question him. In the other picture it appears that the audience has left but that two people who disagreed with the speaker have gone to the front of the auditorium to discuss their questions with him. If you were in the audience, which method do you think you would use if you disagreed with a speaker and if you had made up your mind that you would tell him. Mark down which method of disagreement you think is best and write down your reason for this." (The characters on the poster behind the speaker are purposely ambiguous in order not to define the situation and because these pictures were used with both Chinese and American groups.)

The pattern among groups is shown in Graph 19. There were no significant differences in responses among groups, between sexes, or among grade levels, nor were there any significant interaction effects. By grade levels the pattern was ambiguous, with an increase with age of children selecting Exhibit C (speaking out in front of the audience) from approximately 45% in third grade to about 57% in fifth grade but then a decline to about 44% in seventh grade. As we noted in the case of expression of hostility (hypothesis 3) there appears to be an increase in shyness and protection of relationships with the onset of adolescence and a heightened anxiety regarding deviation from group standards.

GRAPH 19 *Disagreement with an Authority Figure during or after a Meeting. Responses by Group, Percent.*

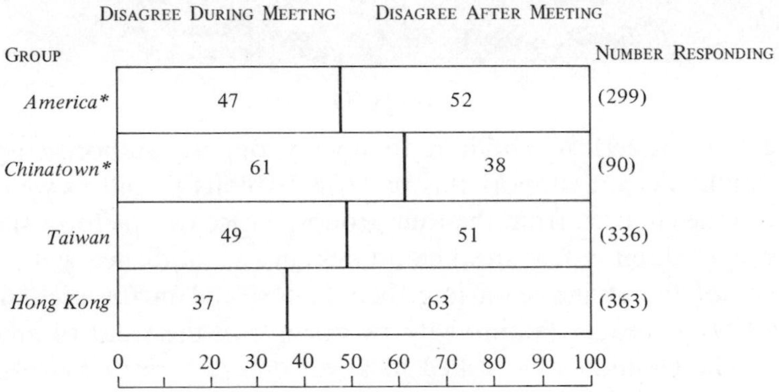

	DISAGREE DURING MEETING	DISAGREE AFTER MEETING	
GROUP			NUMBER RESPONDING
America*	47	52	(299)
Chinatown*	61	38	(90)
Taiwan	49	51	(336)
Hong Kong	37	63	(363)

0   20   30   40   50   60   70   80   90   100

*The America and Chinatown percentages do not equal 100.00 because there was one "don't know" for a female fifth grader in each group.

Disagree during Meeting: F = n.s.
Disagree after Meeting: F = n.s.
n.s.—not significant

On the autocentric/heterocentric questionnaire three questions were asked concerning hypothesis 4, questions 17, 23, and 24 (see Appendix

C). These questions were designed to test both attitudes regarding opposition to authority and levels of expression. Heterocentric responses imply muting opposition in favor of maintaining the form of a particularistic relationship, while the autocentric responses legitimize opposition to authority in terms of criteria unrelated to specific others.

For the autocentric responses two of the three questions showed a significant difference among groups (17 and 23); all three questions showed significant differences for the heterocentric case. There was one significant difference among grade levels reported for the autocentric case (17) and three for the heterocentric case. In addition, group interacted significantly with grade level on one question (17) and with sex on all three questions when tested for autocentrism.

A graph will not be given for the one significant sex–grade level interaction in the autocentric case (question 17). There will also be no representation in the text of the one instance in the heterocentric case where males and females showed a significant difference and the one significant interaction between group and sex (both on question 24).

The pattern of autocentric responses by group is shown in Graph 20. Among groups the average mean percentage value for autocentrism was 44% for Hong Kong, 43% for America, 42% for Taiwan, and 39% for Chinatown. The average rank order was 2.3 for both Hong Kong and America and 2.7 for both Taiwan and Chinatown. These differences are virtually negligible. Of more significance was the fact that on all of the interactions between group and grade level (only one of which, however, was significant) the America group showed marked increases in autocentrism with age for all cases and the Taiwan group increases for two cases, while the other two groups generally declined. By grade 7 the America group was clearly predominant on two of these questions, a factor which was not clear when looking at the gross group results.

Among grade levels there was a significant difference in autocentrism only on question 17, where the mean percentage value for grade 3 was 50%, for grade 5 60%, and for grade 7 60%. On question 23 grade 3 was again lowest, below grades 7 and 5 in that order, but on question 24 grade 3 was highest, ahead of grades 7 and 5 in that order. There is only weak confirmation overall of an increase in autocentrism with age. This increase, however, is notable for the America group. The interaction between group and grade level can be noted from Graph 21.

GRAPH 20   *Hypothesis 4.   Comparison among Groups of Autocentric Responses, Percent*

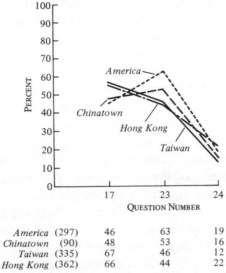

	America (297)	46	63	19
	Chinatown (90)	48	53	16
	Taiwan (335)	67	46	12
	Hong Kong (362)	66	44	22

Note: Numbers in parentheses are the total number of respondents in that category.

Question 17: $F = 102.77$
Question 23: $F = 11.89$
Question 24: $F = $ n.s.
n.s.—not significant

On all three questions there was a significant interaction between group and sex. A plot of the mean percentage values is given in Graph 22. The major pattern that emerges from the group and sex interactions for autocentric responses is the marked differences for Chinatown between males and females, a difference which is generally absent for the other groups. Chinatown females appear more autocentric than males, though this direction is reversed on the one question dealing with the family (question 24). There may well be an as yet unexamined correlation between a muting of opposition to authority within the home and its release and rather pronounced expression at the secondary level in certain social systems—such as American society—in which opposition to authority at the secondary level is relatively condoned.

GRAPH 21 *Hypothesis 4. Interaction of Group and Grade Level for Autocentric Responses, Percent*

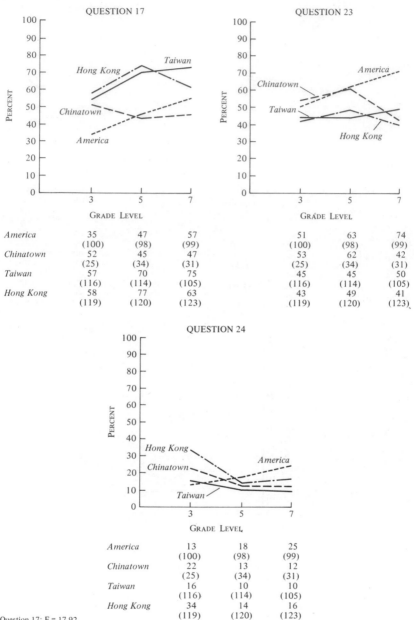

	QUESTION 17				QUESTION 23		
America	35	47	57		51	63	74
	(100)	(98)	(99)		(100)	(98)	(99)
Chinatown	52	45	47		53	62	42
	(25)	(34)	(31)		(25)	(34)	(31)
Taiwan	57	70	75		45	45	50
	(116)	(114)	(105)		(116)	(114)	(105)
Hong Kong	58	77	63		43	49	41
	(119)	(120)	(123)		(119)	(120)	(123)

QUESTION 24

America	13	18	25
	(100)	(98)	(99)
Chinatown	22	13	12
	(25)	(34)	(31)
Taiwan	16	10	10
	(116)	(114)	(105)
Hong Kong	34	14	16
	(119)	(120)	(123)

Question 17: F = 17.92
Question 23: F = n.s.
Question 24: F = n.s.
n.s.—not significant

Note: Numbers in parentheses are the total number of respondents in that category.

GRAPH 22 *Hypothesis 4. Interaction of Group and Sex for Autocentric Responses, Percent*

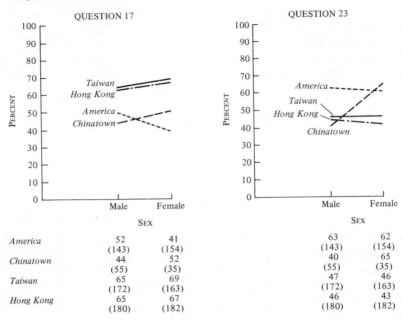

QUESTION 17

	Male	Female
America	52 (143)	41 (154)
Chinatown	44 (55)	52 (35)
Taiwan	65 (172)	69 (163)
Hong Kong	65 (180)	67 (182)

QUESTION 23

	Male	Female
	63 (143)	62 (154)
	40 (55)	65 (35)
	47 (172)	46 (163)
	46 (180)	43 (182)

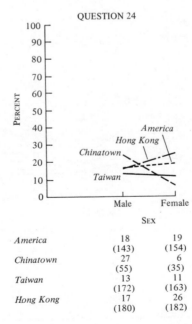

QUESTION 24

	Male	Female
America	18 (143)	19 (154)
Chinatown	27 (55)	6 (35)
Taiwan	13 (172)	11 (163)
Hong Kong	17 (180)	26 (182)

Question 17: F = 14.10
Question 23: F = 7.73
Question 24: F = 6.83

Note: Numbers in parentheses are the total number of respondents in that category

For the heterocentric case there were significant differences among groups on all three questions. Graph 23 gives the mean percentage values of heterocentrism for each group. Averaging of the mean percentage values for all questions gives Taiwan the highest value in heterocentrism with 55%, followed by Hong Kong with 52%, Chinatown with 52%, and America with 51%. The average rank order was 2.3 for Taiwan, Hong Kong, and Chinatown and 3.0 for America. On the whole the America group would appear to be very slightly lower in heterocentrism than the other groups.

GRAPH 23   *Hypothesis 4. Comparison among Groups of Heterocentric Responses, Percent*

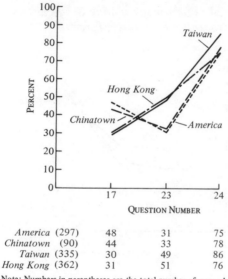

America (297)	48	31	75
Chinatown (90)	44	33	78
Taiwan (335)	30	49	86
Hong Kong (362)	31	51	76

Note: Numbers in parentheses are the total number of respondents in that category.

Question 17: F = 21.89
Question 23: F = 21.41
Question 24: F = 6.47

Among grade levels there were significant differences in heterocentrism on all three questions. The results by grade levels are given in

Graph 24. The overall mean percentage value for third grade is 56%, for fifth grade 52%, and for seventh grade 50%. The average rank order is 1.7 for third grade, 2.0 for fifth grade, and 2.3 for seventh grade, indicating an overall decrease in heterocentrism with age. It is worth noting that although there were no significant interactions between group and grade level the data in this area shows a consistent decrease in heterocentrism with age for the America group and a slight decrease for the Taiwan group, a pattern which is not noted for the Chinatown and Hong Kong groups. American children especially give evidence of a developing capacity to oppose authority when it is seen as violating universal standards.

For both the autocentric and heterocentric cases no large differences

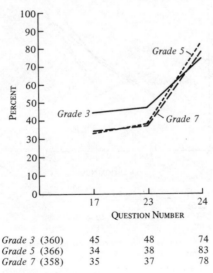

GRAPH 24   *Comparison among Grade Levels of Heterocentric Responses, Percent*

	17	23	24
Grade 3 (360)	45	48	74
Grade 5 (366)	34	38	83
Grade 7 (358)	35	37	78

Note: Numbers in parentheses are the total number of respondents in that category.

Question 17: F = 12.87
Question 23: F = 9.43
Question 24: F = 5.96

exist among any of our control categories. Overall the America group appears to be slightly more autocentric and slightly less heterocentric than the other groups; third graders appear slightly more heterocentric than higher grades. One interesting but not statistically significant pattern was the general increase in autocentrism with age (and decrease in heterocentrism) of the America group. The children in all groups were predominantly heterocentric on the one question related to the family (24), in contrast to the other questions, where heterocentrism overall is lower than autocentrism. At the primary level, opposition to authority appears to be restrained for all children by the particularistic ties involved.

DISCUSSION AND SUMMARY

In the expression of hostility (hypothesis 3) most children express autocentric attitudes, with children from Taiwan the highest, followed by Chinatown, Hong Kong, and America. By grade level autocentrism increases to fifth grade but declines by seventh with the onset of adolescence. There were no significant patterns of differences between the sexes.

Although there are marked differences among groups, most children tend to feel that the expression of hostility should be legitimized by a violation of universalistic standards. The America children overall invoke universalistic standards least—barely over half compared to nearly 70% for Taiwan—and at the third- and fifth-grade levels are nearly as likely to justify hostility on the basis of particularistic factors in a relationship.

In the case of opposition to authority (hypothesis 4), a higher percentage of children from all groups express heterocentric rather than autocentric attitudes. There is, however, a variation among role levels, with a marked degree of heterocentrism expressed in the family context. Overall America and Hong Kong were the highest in autocentrism. Taiwan, Hong Kong, and Chinatown were virtually equal in being slightly more heterocentric than the American children. The differences in either case, however, were not large. More interesting was the fact that the America group (and to a lesser extent the Taiwan group) tended to show a consistent pattern of increasing autocentrism (and decreasing heterocentrism) with age.

It is noteworthy that hypothesis 4 is the first in which the America group is not near or at the bottom in terms of autocentrism and at or near the top of in terms of heterocentrism. It is also the first case in which the Taiwan group is not at the top in autocentrism and at the bottom in heterocentrism. Clearly opposition to authority is something that children generally see as unfavorable, although Chinese societies appear to have slightly more negative sanctions concerning opposition than is the case for American society. It does not seem an unreasonable assumption that the emphasis in Chinese learning on shaming sanctions relates to training in not manifesting overt hostility to authority, and to inculcating that the demands of particularistic ties can be overridden only by explicit reference to universalistic criteria. In other words, universalistic values provide legitimization and psychic protection in situations where particularistic and ideally warm relations are violated either by the authority figure in punishment or by the subordinate in opposition. The capacity to express opposition, however, is severely modified, and increasingly so with age, by conflicting values of loyalty, respect, and obedience with regard to specific authority figures.

SECTION FOUR.   HYPOTHESES 5 AND 6

HYPOTHESIS 5:

With either heterocentric or autocentric attitude dispositions conformist behavior will be observed. With heterocentric attitude dispositions conformity to group patterns is legitimized by institutionalized group leaders (parents, teachers, etc.). Conformity to leader behavior by followers is positively sanctioned. Nonconformity to specific legitimized leaders receives heavy negative sanction. With autocentric attitude dispositions conformity to group patterns may also be legitimized by institutionalized group leaders. However, nonconformist behavior in terms of transcending universalistic values may be permissible.

Richard Solomon appears to have grasped one of the basic strands in the Chinese socialization process with his emphasis on the fear of "luan" or confusion and disharmony that is so pervasive in the injunctions and training methods used with Chinese children.[49] This fear, of

[49] Solomon, *op. cit.* See also Solomon, "One Party and 'One Hundred Schools': Leadership, Lethargy, or Luan?" *Current Scene*, vol. 7, nos. 19–20, Oct. 1, 1969.

course, actually reflects the much deeper psychic fear of abandonment for behavior that alienates socializing agents and other group members. Fear of "luan" is, in fact, an aspect of shame anxiety, the tension generated whenever ideal aspirations and actual behavior are non-congruent; it is not fear of "luan" as such which motivates social conformist behavior but deep anxiety about being in a "shameful" situation. To "know shame," as the Chinese express it, means, in a deeper sense, to know how to be in harmony with one's ideals and with others, not confused and disruptive. So pervasive is this sentiment that conformity or harmony become in themselves positive ideals concerning identity, while chaos and conflict are negative ideals and identities.

It is well known that the effect of isolation on a human being can be devastating. It is less easy to prove rigorously a direct link between the anxiety of fear of abandonment and tendencies to affiliation and finally to conformity. Our ideas here are therefore tentative, although we feel the evidence that does exist strongly suggests only a limited set of possible outcomes for the social resolution of fear of abandonment.

Stanley Schachter has suggested a drive for "self-evaluation," positively related to anxiety and hunger, that becomes broadened during growth to a drive for cognitive clarity, which in turn impels affiliative behavior involving social contact and discussion to reduce ambiguities of behavior and thought.[50] If we assume a desire for self-evaluation arising from a variable punishment-and-reward learning process, this desire can be fulfilled only through social comparison prompted by pressure from socializing agents and other group members to reduce discrepancy from expected norms in the direction of conformity to the culturally acceptable state. When self-evaluation reveals a discrepancy and anxiety is aroused, one will either have to change one's own opinions and/or behavior, change others', or cease evaluation.[51]

Conformity has been defined as "the convergence of individual judgments toward a central value."[52] While we are not certain why people strive to make socially desirable responses—why they will give up or renounce behavior and goals toward which they are motivated in order to be like others—we assume that it is because of the reward

[50] Stanley Schachter, *The Psychology of Affiliation*, Stanford University Press, Stanford, California, 1959, pp. 5, 103.

[51] *Ibid.*, pp. 104, 113–114.

[52] Roger Brown, *Social Psychology*. The Free Press, New York, 1965, p. 678.

that accrues when the anxiety associated with deviance is reduced and the threat of punishment eliminated. It is impossible, of course, to speak of complete conformers or complete deviants; in practice everyone is a conformer and a deviant to some degree, and the tendency in either direction is a function of complex influences, of which the most important are social and geographic location, cognitive ability, personality characteristics, conflicting norms, and social-psychological factors such as adaptability, interpretive capacity, etc.[53]

A child may be taught to avoid the pain of inconsistency by training in developing and utilizing certain coping mechanisms. For some children this may mean merely an overt situational change, while for others it may mean a complete change of privately held beliefs. The likelihood of the latter condition prevailing is dependent partly on the extent and duration of the pressure to conform and also, very critically, on the earliness in the life cycle when the pressure is begun. Individuals excessively concerned about threats to self-esteem will show a heightened desire for social support, self-protection, and avoidance of failure, in which the need for love and affection is singularly important.[54] Such persons may develop a set of attitudes "in which an idealized version of the self [ego-ideal] . . . is maintained and defended."[55] There may also be low striving for independence, low assertiveness, and difficulty in acknowledging personal feelings as well as difficulty in recognizing and contending with hostility. Where the fear of failure is high the resolution for the attendant anxiety may be through submission to the group.[56] We assume that socialization practices in some societies may emphasize acquiring particular sets of coping mechanisms—such as inhibiting expression of hostility to authority and conforming to group standards.

In any society where coordinated cooperative effort is valued there will be pressure during childhood training for compliance. Compliance to demands for conformity may arise from overt social pressure alone as well as from a desire to defend the ego-deal against anxiety.[57] These

[53] Giuseppe Di Palma and Herbert McClosky, "Personality and Conformity: The Learning of Political Attitudes," *American Political Science Review*, vol. 64, no. 4, December 1970, p. 1060.

[54] Douglas P. Crowne and David Marlowe, *The Approval Motive: Studies in Evaluative Dependence*, John Wiley and Sons, New York, 1964, p. 202.

[55] *Ibid.*, p. 190.

[56] *Ibid.*, pp. 202, 203.

[57] Norman S. Endler and Elizabeth Hoy, "Conformity as Related to Reinforcement

two factors may ultimately become linked, since social pressure need not always entail the physical presence of others. Individuals have internal reference structures composed of memories, symbols, and values that the individual may recognize as attributes of the self or of others.[58]

Conformity may lead to reduction of anxiety and thus be rewarding, but it may also have certain negative results that are less readily apparent. Tomkins states that overconformity is negatively related to a genuine interest in others.[59] Bronfenbrenner has noted that while use of love-oriented techniques in training may foster internalization of adult standards and develop socialized behavior, it may also put stress on conformity and thus accentuate anxiety and reduce self-sufficiency.[60]

Even within a well-defined social milieu conformity is in no sense a uniform phenomenon. Younger children are more conforming than older children and girls are consistently and significantly more conforming than boys.[61] And for American children, for example, peer-group norms may favor deviance from adult standards, so that there is considerable adult-peer cross-pressure. It has been hypothesized that this "standard experience" for American children may ultimately help develop more secure and self-regulating behavior than is developed by children who are more thoroughly oriented to either adult or peer standards, who are better behaved but less self-regulatory.[62]

As an example of cultural differences in adult-peer cross-pressures, Clausen, citing work by Bronfenbrenner, has noted how American and Soviet children respond differently to a hypothetical situation concern-

and Social Pressure," *Journal of Personality and Social Psychology*, vol. 7, no. 2, Oct. 1967, p. 200; and Kay H. Smith and Barrie Richards, "Effects of Rational Appeal and of Anxiety on Conformity Behavior," *Journal of Personality and Social Psychology*, vol. 5, no. 1, Jan. 1967, p. 122.

[58] Richard Lake, "The Varieties of Communicative Experience," *Comparative Group Studies*, vol. 1, no. 3, August 1970, p. 308.

[59] Silvan S. Tomkins, *Affect Imagery Consciousness*, vol. 2: *The Negative Affects*, Springer Publishing Co., New York, 1963, p. 211.

[60] Urie Bronfenbrenner, "The Changing American Child—A Speculative Analysis," in Neil J. Smelser and William T. Smelser, eds., *Personality and Social Systems*, John Wiley and Sons, New York, 1963, p. 352. (Originally published in *Journal of Social Issues*, vol. 17, no. 1, 1961, pp. 1–18.)

[61] Edward C. Devereux, "The Role of Peer-Group Experience in Moral Development," in John P. Hill, ed., *Minnesota Symposia on Child Psychology*, vol. 4, University of Minnesota Press, Minneapolis, 1970, pp. 116–118, 129. Also Halla Belloff, "Two Forms of Social Conformity: Acquiescence and Conventionality," *Journal of Abnormal and Social Psychology*, vol. 56, no. 1, January 1958, pp. 99–104.

[62] Devereux, *op. cit.*, pp. 126–127.

ing socially disapproved behavior. Soviet children are less willing to say they will engage in such behavior and are even more unwilling if told that classmates will see their responses. For American children, on the other hand, the knowledge that classmates will see their answers results in a greater likelihood of their saying they will engage in disapproved be-behavior.[63] In Chinese as well as other societies there may be relatively great pressure to conform in some situations, such as in a classroom, whereas in other situations, such as sleeping in a park, some self-indulgence in terms of posture and place is permitted.

On the autocentric/heterocentric questionnaire three questions (7, 10, and 25) related to conformity (see Appendix C). Strictly speaking, these particular questions for hypothesis 5 are not designed to test conformity as such but rather whether the value basis of conformist behavior derives from adherence to universalistic or particularistic criteria. The questions are posed in both a negative and positive way in order to elicit the most truthful value orientation.

There was a significant difference among groups for only one question (25) for both the autocentric and heterocentric cases. There were no significant differences between the sexes or among grade levels. Despite the general lack of significance the *pattern* of responses for both groups and grade levels is revealing, and graphs will be presented for this material. On question 10 there was a significant interaction between group and sex and between sex and grade level for the heterocentric case; graphs for this material will not be presented in the text since the patterns are not duplicated in the other material.

The interaction between group and grade level was not significant for any of the questions for either the autocentric or heterocentric cases. Nevertheless one pattern of note did emerge. For the autocentric case the Taiwan children increased in autocentrism with age on two of the three questions, while the Hong Kong children decreased. This pattern was reversed for the heterocentric case. The America children declined in heterocentrism with age on all three questions, a pattern not repeated by the other groups. By seventh grade the Taiwan children were notably highest on autocentrism and lowest on heterocentrism on all three questions, while the Hong Kong children were highest in heterocentrism on all three questions and lowest in autocentrism on two of the three

[63] John A. Clausen, "Perspectives on Childhood Socialization," in John A. Clausen, ed., *Socialization and Society*, Little, Brown and Co., Boston, 1968, p. 171.

questions. It would appear that conformity among these two groups is clearly based upon very different attitudinal criteria, with the children from Taiwan increasingly invoking universalistic criteria as their reason for conforming—or their reason for deviating—while Hong Kong children conform and are prevented from deviating because of particularistic factors.

For the combined autocentric responses there was a significant difference among groups only for question 25. A plot of the responses for the three questions by groups is given in Graph 25. The general pattern among the four groups is similar, but the predominance of autocentrism for the Taiwan group is readily apparent. The average of the

GRAPH 25 *Hypothesis 5. Comparison among Groups of Autocentric Responses, Percent*

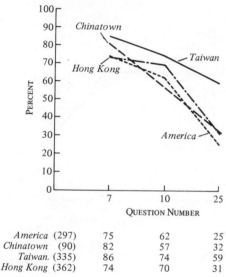

	7	10	25
America (297)	75	62	25
Chinatown (90)	82	57	32
Taiwan. (335)	86	74	59
Hong Kong (362)	74	70	31

Note: Numbers in parentheses are the total number of respondents in that category.

Question 7: F = n.s.
Question 10: F = n.s.
Question 25: F = 16.32
n.s.—not significant

mean percentage values for each group showed Taiwan clearly in the lead with 73%, ahead of Hong Kong with 58%, Chinatown with 57%, and America with 54%. The average rank order for each group was Taiwan 1.0, followed by Chinatown at 2.7, Hong Kong at 3.0, and America at 3.3. On an overall basis the Taiwan group was clearly the most autocentric and the America group least, although it must be kept in mind that by seventh grade the Hong Kong children are uniformly, for all questions, the least autocentric.

Among grade levels there were no significant differences for any of the questions under hypothesis 5. For this reason we shall restrict ourselves to an examination of the general pattern among grade levels.

GRAPH 26   *Hypothesis 5. Comparison among Grade Levels of Autocentric Responses, Percent*

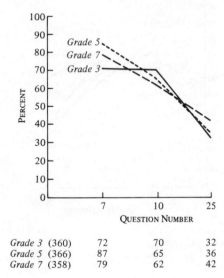

	7	10	25
Grade 3 (360)	72	70	32
Grade 5 (366)	87	65	36
Grade 7 (358)	79	62	42

Note: Numbers in parentheses are the total number of respondents in that category.

Question 7: F = n.s.
Question 10: F = n.s.
Question 25: F = n.s.
n.s.–not significant

This pattern can be seen in Graph 26, where the responses to each question by grade level are presented. On two of three questions grade 3 is in the expected position of lowest in autocentrism, while on one question it is highest. Averaging of the mean percentage values places grade 3, with 58%, below seventh grade with 61% and fifth grade with 63%. The average rank order also gives third grade the least autocentrism with 2.3, below grade 7 with 2.0 and grade 5 with 1.7. While these results must be viewed as providing only weak confirmation, they do indicate the expected lower autocentrism for younger children.

For the heterocentric responses there was only one question of three (25) which showed a significant difference among groups. The

GRAPH 27   *Hypothesis 5. Comparison among Groups of Heterocentric Responses, Percent*

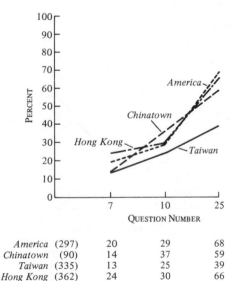

America (297)	20	29	68
Chinatown (90)	14	37	59
Taiwan (335)	13	25	39
Hong Kong (362)	24	30	66

Note: Numbers in parentheses are the total number of respondents in that category.

Question 7: F = n.s.
Question 10: F = n.s.
Question 25: F = 7.43
n.s.–not significant

responses for each question by group are shown in Graph 27. The general pattern among all four groups is similar, but the magnitude of responses clearly shows the Taiwan children to be lowest in heterocentrism. The average of the mean percentage values places Hong Kong as the most heterocentric with an average value of 40%, ahead of America with 39%, Chinatown with 36%, and Taiwan, markedly the lowest, with 26%. The average rank order also places Hong Kong first with 1.7, followed by America with 2.0, Chinatown with 2.3, and Taiwan with 4.0.

For the combined heterocentric responses there were no significant differences by grade level. Overall, however, the younger children tended

GRAPH 28   *Hypothesis 5. Comparison among Grade Levels of Heterocentric Responses, Percent*

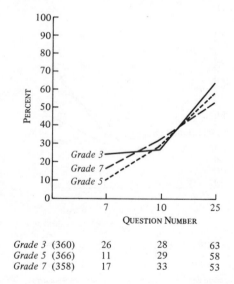

Grade 3 (360)	26	28	63
Grade 5 (366)	11	29	58
Grade 7 (358)	17	33	53

Note: Numbers in parentheses are the total number of respondents in that category.

Question 7: F = n.s.
Question 10: F = n.s.
Question 25: F = n.s.
n.s.—not significant

to be more heterocentric than children in higher grades, as is shown in Graph 28. The differences among grades are not large, although, as expected, grade 3 is the most heterocentric, with an average mean percentage value of 39 %, ahead of grade seven with 34 % and grade 5 with 33 %. The average rank orders are third grade at 1.7, seventh grade at 2.0, and fifth grade at 2.3. While the differences are not significant, younger children do seem to have a higher degree of heterocentrism in regard to conformity than do older children.

Overall children from all four groups tended to have generally autocentric attitudes concerning conformity. That is, there is a tendency to justify conformity—or failure to conform—on the basis of universalistic criteria. Children from Taiwan are clearly the most autocentric (and least heterocentric), while the other three groups are similar, with Hong Kong the most heterocentric. By seventh grade the degree of heterocentrism is pronounced and increasing for the Hong Kong children, but generally decreasing for the America and Chinatown children.

Although autocentric responses predominated overall for all groups, there was a sharp departure from this rule for the one question (25) dealing with peer interaction. There heterocentrism was pronounced for all groups but Taiwan. In Hong Kong, America, and Chinatown peer interaction would appear to be an area where particularistic criteria predominate in establishing patterns of conformity.

There were no significant differences between the sexes in the expression of autocentrism or heterocentrism. There were also no significant differences among grade levels, although a pattern did emerge indicating slightly greater heterocentrism (and less autocentrism) for younger children. Although the difference is very slight it is in the expected direction.

Attitudes toward conformism do not give a direct indication of the extent of or tendency toward conformist behavior. In order to obtain some data in this area two pictures were presented that measure the tendency to conform as reflected by the desire to be like, or not like, other members of a group. The two pictures (Exhibits E and F) show one group in similar clothes and an alternate group in varied dress. The children were asked to select one or the other of the pictures in response to a question phrased as follows: "Here are two groups. Both of these groups have asked you to join them. You have decided that you would like to join a group but you can only join one. Which one of these

EXHIBIT E

groups would you join? Mark down which group you would like to join and write down your reason for this."

Clearly conformism can exist within either of the groups depicted in Exhibits E and F. Group norms may call for conformism in terms of variety or in terms of uniformity. We assume, however, that the desire to join a group where uniformity is manifest rather than one where variety is apparent implies a need to make one's conformist behavior easily recognized. The pictures do, therefore, provide a first indication of overt conformism to group pressure but must be supported by additional data.

Overall, an average of 74% of all the children from all four groups chose the similarly dressed group and an average of 24% of all children selected the variedly dressed group. There was a significant difference among groups, however, in the response rate. A majority of American children chose the variedly dressed group, whereas only an insignificant number of children from the Taiwan and Hong Kong groups made this choice. There was no significant difference between the sexes or among grade levels. Females selected the uniformly dressed group only slightly

EXHIBIT F

less than males (71% versus 77%). This pattern between the sexes was true for every grade level and for every group except Taiwan (where the difference was slight). By grade level the selection of the uniformly dressed group decreased sharply with age for the America group, decreased slightly with age for the Taiwan group, was virtually stationary with age for the Hong Kong group, and increased slightly with age for the Chinatown group. The distribution of responses among groups was as shown in Graph 29.

The children were requested, after indicating their desire to join either a similarly dressed or a variedly dressed group, to write down the reasons for their particular choice. Below are some of these responses, selected both because they are typical and because they reflect how children buttress their choices by imputing to the group they select qualities that they feel are highly desirable.

A third-grade girl from Taiwan said simply in explaining her choice of the similarly dressed group, "Because their clothes are the clothes of the group," and a third-grade boy wrote, "Because the clothes they are

GRAPH 29   *Conformism. The Desire To Be a Member of a Similarly
Dressed or Variedly Dressed Group. Responses by Group, Percent.*

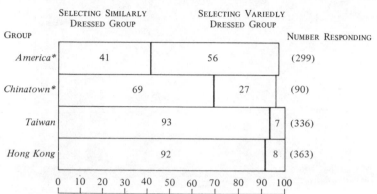

*America Group: 3 percent Don't Know
Chinatown Group: 4 percent Don't Know
Selecting Similarly Dressed Group: F = 23.27
Selecting Variedly Dressed Group: F = 18.83

wearing are comparatively orderly." Two fifth-grade girls from Taiwan
replied as follows: "Because their clothes are orderly they will not be at
sixes and sevens," and "If clothes are orderly then people will have an
orderly feeling." A seventh-grade boy noted, "Because this group's
clothes are orderly; if you join and go to other places then people can
see which group it is." A seventh-grade girl wrote, "I feel that in order
for a group to have regulation there must be respect and protection and
where clothes are confused it reveals that there is no order."

In Hong Kong a fifth-grade boy justified his choice of the similarly
dressed group as follows, "Because if everyone has on the same clothes
then we can know that they are our people." A seventh-grade boy said,
"Because their clothes are orderly and clean; moreover, everyone is alike
and their spirits are satisfied." Two seventh-grade girls gave the following reasons: "Because those who wear the same kind of clothes express
unity," and "Because their clothes are the same it proves that they are
well behaved."

In Chinatown a fifth-grade boy had the following to say concerning
why he selected the uniformly dressed group: "So everybody could be

the same and I think that is the right way and it looks better." A fifth-grade girl wrote, "The people in this picture dress neater than the others and I think they are better." A seventh-grade boy had the following comments: "Because they are dressed more neatly so I assume they behave better than the other group." In selecting the variedly dressed group a seventh-grade girl wrote, "Because they are neatly dressed and can be trusted," while a fifth-grade boy noted, "I like to join a group where the people all agree on everything the law said." Clearly, membership in either group is seen as association with "better" people.

In the America group less than half of the children selected the uniformly dressed group. Those children who selected this option, like their Chinese counterparts, frequently cited organization or unity as the reason for their choice. A fifth-grade girl wrote, "Because it would be organized and everybody would have to behave or else they would be kicked out of the club." A fifth-grade boy noted laconically, "It would be more orderly," while a seventh-grade boy wrote, "Because other people would think that your group was organized if you all have the same type clothes. People usually like an organized group."

The majority of America children selected the variedly dressed group. For these children the emphasis in their reasons was on variety, individuality, and freedom; in short, on nonconformity. A fifth-grade girl wrote, "Because there are different people that think differently and like different things." A fifth-grade boy said, "I would have more freedom," and a fifth-grade girl noted, "You don't have to be the same to join a group. You should do what you feel like doing and not be the same." A seventh-grade girl commented, "Because they show individuality and freedom," and a boy wrote, "Because it seems that this group has a variety of opinions while in the other one everyone thinks the same. But I would have to meet the people first." Finally, a seventh-grade girl said, "Because it looks like a more liberal group and they wouldn't make everybody act and look alike."

In both Hong Kong and Taiwan children wear uniforms to school, and this fact undoubtedly influences their high selection rate for the uniformly dressed group. This factor does not, however, explain the high percentage of choices for this picture by the group from Chinatown, where uniforms are not worn. Nor does this factor easily explain the stress on group unity, organization, and good behavior so frequently given by Chinese children in their explanations for the selection of the uniformly dressed group as the one that would be desirable to join. Whether attitudes toward conformity are autocentric, as with Taiwan children, or more heterocentric, as with children in Hong Kong, there appear to be powerful factors in Chinese society making conformity to the group a very highly valued virtue. Some of the ways by which conformism as a virtue is inculcated have been extensively covered in previous research.[64] Other studies point out how English language subjects have been tested and found to be more open-minded and less dogmatic than Chinese language subjects.[65] There seems to be little question that many American children have very different ideas concerning their role within a group structure than do Chinese children; they are far less willing to perceive of conformism and group unity and organization as desirable in and of themselves. For many American children the group is secondary to the individual, whereas for many Chinese children unity and organization appear to be overriding concerns whether this cohesion is legitimized by universalistic or particularistic criteria.

One of the factors favoring conformity to group norms in the Chinese context is the belief that opposition to the group and to its leaders is to be avoided whenever possible. During interviews the children were asked whether one can go against the group. When the data from all four groups is summarized we obtain the results given in Table 7, which show clearly the heavy negative sanctions against opposition to the group in Chinese society.

TABLE 7   *Expressions Regarding Whether One Can Go against the Group, Percent*

	CAUCASIAN AMERICAN (18)	CHINATOWN (6)	TAIWAN (18)	HONG KONG (18)
Can go against the group	72	50	17	33
Should not go against the group	28	50	83	67
No indication	0	0	0	0

Note: Numbers in parentheses are the total number of respondents in that category.

[64] Richard W. Wilson, *Learning to be Chinese: The Political Socialization of Children in Taiwan*, Massachusetts Institute of Technology Press, Cambridge, Mass., 1970.

[65] Margaret J. Earle, "Bilingual Semantic Merging and an Aspect of Acculturation," *Journal of Personality and Social Psychology*, vol. 6, no. 3, July 1967, p. 311.

It is interesting to note that those children in Hong Kong who mentioned that one could go against the group stressed as their reason the lack of morality of the leader or group—not their own individual aspirations. Similarly, the opposers in the Taiwan group all clearly reflected autocentric attitudes in their emphasis that opposition could be justified only on legal grounds.

HYPOTHESIS 6:

Reciprocity between authority and nonauthority figures differs with attitude disposition. With heterocentric attitude disposition mutual obligation receives the heaviest positive sanctions regardless of any contradictory universalistic values. With an autocentric attitude disposition we would not expect to find reciprocity defined solely in terms related to the interpersonal relationship itself. Rather, we would expect to find reciprocity also defined in terms of universalistic criteria.

There are two stories told in a third-grade reader in Hong Kong that set forth with great clarity ideal Chinese concepts with regard to reciprocity. In the first of these stories there is described the "traditional" lack of reciprocity between those who have no prior relationship and the relative lack of concern of bystanders. In the second story the relationship between the two individuals is tenuous (although they are schoolmates), but the weaker is able to invoke a standard which, by creating shame anxiety in the stronger, brings about reciprocity. So much has been said about dependency in Chinese relationships that it is worth pointing out explicitly that the situation that develops in the second story is not one of dependency as such, but arises rather from the capacity of the weaker to invoke universally held standards of behavior that are adhered to by the stronger because nonadherence is anxiety-provoking for him.

The first story, entitled "Hunchback and Big Beard," is a play that takes place on a lane in a country marketplace with several onlookers. The hunchback is carrying two baskets of mollusks and is walking slowly along the lane.

HUNCHBACK: Today I got up early and am carrying my baskets for sale in the marketplace. Do not tease me about my hunchback. I manage to sell my goods very fast.

(*Big Beard is riding a donkey and comes from the opposite end of the lane*).

BIG BEARD: You, Hunchback, blocking my way! Hurry aside and let me pass or else my donkey will knock you down.

HUNCHBACK: You mind your riding and I'll mind my baskets. What are you yelling at?

(*Both of them refuse to yield. Big Beard, riding his donkey, goes straight toward Hunchback, who is unable to avoid him and is knocked down. The baskets are overturned and the mollusks are scattered on the ground. The people look at them curiously.*)

BIG BEARD: If only you had given way I would not have knocked you down and overturned the baskets. What should we do now?

HUNCHBACK: I carried my baskets while you quickly rode your donkey. My mollusks did not touch your donkey but your donkey knocked the baskets over. I earn money to raise my family with these goods. Now you have done me serious harm. I think it would be right if you compensate me with your donkey.

BIG BEARD: Are your goods worth a donkey? I can't agree with that. I can only give you my hat so it will settle our dispute.

HUNCHBACK: Who wants your hat? If you refuse to give me your donkey I'll pull your beard off.

(*Hunchback drags Big Beard from the donkey and the dispute carries on.*)

BIG BEARD: You are acting like a rascal. I am not afraid of you, I am going to show you something. Watch out for your back because I am going to beat you on your hunchback.

(*They fight. The mollusks are trampled to pieces and the donkey, frightened, runs away.*)

ONLOOKERS: One of you frightens the donkey away and the other ruins the goods. Since neither of you yielded see what the result is. We suggest that you, Hunchback, pick up your broken mollusks and that you, Big Beard, chase back the donkey. Don't spend your time quarreling.[66]

The story conveys the moral of the desirability of cooperation and the sense that some mutual obligation should have existed. It is very different in tone from the following:

[66] Editorial Board of Ling Kee Publishing Col., ed., "Hunchback and Big Beard," in *A New Chinese Reader* (*Hsin-pien Kuo-yu*), First Term, Grade 3, Ling Kee Publishing Co., Hong Kong, 1968, pp. 34–36.

One evening, when everybody was sitting in the parlor watching television, Chung-sheng went to his bedroom after finishing his work. His brother was puzzled by this and followed him. Chung-sheng was writing his diary. His brother said, "What are you doing?" Chung-sheng handed the diary over to him. In it was written: "9 November, Wednesday. Fine. This afternoon, when I was playing on the playground, a senior student dashed by and knocked me down. At that moment I was very angry and I shouted at him, 'Why do you bully me?' He quickly came to help me up and apologized, 'I am sorry, I didn't mean to do that. Please excuse me.' While he was talking he showed a touch of shame on his face. At once my anger subsided and I replied, 'It's all right, it's really my fault.' After this incident, we became good friends and walked home together after school."[67]

In a technical sense, reciprocity merely implies a reaction similar in intent or kind to any given initiating action. It can have negative connotations, as to reciprocate another's bad will, or, as is usually the case in social science literature, it can refer to individuals responding favorably to each other. In this latter usage, reciprocity is an aspect of such concepts as cooperation or harmony. Our usage of reciprocity is in consonance with this second pattern, although in a broader sense we are examining simply the form of attitudes that defines any type of reciprocity in a relationship.

No group is completely harmonious. Positive relations among group members arise both from the reward involved in performing positively sanctioned behavior and from the anxiety associated with performance of negatively sanctioned behavior. Training to behave in an approved way begins early and to a greater or lesser extent is maintained throughout life. There may be many situational factors involved in the activation of reciprocity behavior and it is not our purpose here to detail all of these. We assume that visibility and contact between individuals are required, although the necessary magnitude of these factors may vary by society. We assume also that the negative or positive state of the affectional bond of those involved in the potential reciprocal relationship will be important. Beyond these basic criteria, however, reciprocity may be activated—and legitimized—by internalized universalistic value criteria, the violation of which would be anxiety-provoking.

[67] Editorial Board of Ling Kee Publishing Co., ed., "Diary Writing," in *A New Chinese Reader, op. cit.*, p. 40.

These criteria may legitimize reciprocity both in an affectionally positive or affectionally neutral situation and, more rarely, in an affectionally negative situation. To some extent such universalistic criteria operate in any large social system, for it is impossible to have positive affectional bonds with all members of any relatively complex group. Yet it is also true that where universalistic criteria concerning reciprocity are of limited salience, reciprocity outside of positive recognized affectional bonds will be sharply reduced.

In traditional Chinese society emphasis in interpersonal relations was not on being liked (although loss of love might be an important factor in anxiety-arousal, motivating one to behave in certain ways), but rather on strict definition of role behavior in hierarchical terms, with a resultant sanctioning of dependency, passivity, and conformism for those of lower status. Ideally, reciprocity was based on a belief in "harmony" and on the performance of mutual obligations whose root was affectional in nature. In practice, while affectional factors were perhaps more important than is generally realized, there came to be an emphasis on correct performance of one's role and on mutual—but not equal—dependence of those in reciprocal role relationships. Authority might or might not be affectional, but correct role performance and mutual dependence were required regardless of the magnitude and valence of affectional content, with rather severe punishments for noncompliance.[68] A consequence of this pattern in traditional China was that where role relationships were not defined and mutual dependence was not a factor—at least for one of those in the relationship— there were only weakly competing values against the avoidance or absence of reciprocity.

The force of traditional patterns governing reciprocity is noticeable in modern Chinese society in the lack of trust that many older Chinese report they feel in unfamiliar interpersonal contexts. Situations can be witnessed in which a driver will block a street or entrance and will not move his vehicle for another despite abundant room and his knowledge of the other person's desires. Similar situations have been frequently observed in both Taiwan and, especially, Hong Kong. Street behavior and waiting in lines are areas where we have noted public manifestation of lack of reciprocity. On the other hand, an equal number of childhood

---

[68] Lucian W. Pye, op. cit., p. 18. Also Francis L. K. Hsu, Clan, Caste, and Club, D. Van Nostrand Co., Princeton, N.J., 1963, p. 51.

game situations have been observed where older and younger children not related to each other show high degrees of reciprocity without any outward manifestation of "dependent" behavior.

In interviews and written materials, the responses of the children from our sample groups show a strikingly consistent pattern, with the Taiwan, Hong Kong, and Chinatown groups responding in one way and the America sample in another. Although Chinese children mention affection as a motive for reciprocity, the primary reasons given are mutual help, cooperation, and minimization of conflict. These reasons are related to traditional values of mutual dependence and obligation, but with the very significant difference that they are no longer stressed primarily with regard to reciprocal primary-level roles but rather operate within a much broader group context (as, e.g., all Chinese, although on other occasions even this broad reference is missing).

In speaking of people in group relationships a third-grade boy in Hong Kong said "They should love each other and help each other. The most important thing is to have a good relationship. They should cooperate and help each other; this is the most important." A third-grade girl spoke as follows: "People should help each other, work in harmony, and correct each other's mistakes." A fifth-grade boy said that a good group is made up of people "who are obedient, are willing to correct their mistakes, follow regulations, and don't fight with each other." A fifth-grade girl noted that group members "must fit in with each other, help others to correct, and improve themselves and never quarrel. They must work together and be good friends in order to live like a big family They must be cooperative." Finally, a seventh-grade girl said, "members should help each other and work together like close friends. They must have a good and close relationship between each other so that they will not quarrel or disagree with each other."

In contrast to this emphasis on helpfulness, cooperativeness, and passivity, American children stress likability (people are nice) and friendliness. As one seventh-grade girl said, "If you like them and they like you it's a good group. They should like each other. It's the most important thing." Likeableness and friendliness (as desirable characteristics) were also stressed in the reasons, given by seventh-grade children of the America group for selecting the variedly dressed group in the pictorial questionnaire (Exhibits E or F). (Girl) "Because they look neater and friendlier"; (Boy) "Because they seem like they are a really friendly group"; (Girl) "Because they look very clean and friendly"; (Boy) "Because they look friendly"; (Girl) "Because it looks like you would be able to wear colorful clothing and the kids look nicer." The Taiwan, Hong Kong, and Chinatown groups, in contrast, emphasized order, cooperation, unity, and good behavior in their reasons for selecting the uniformly dressed group.

Although the bases for reciprocity appear to be different within the Chinese and American social contexts, the feeling that reciprocity is necessary is uniformly high. Most of the children from the four groups who were interviewed—78% of the American sample (18), 83% from Chinatown (6), and 100% of both the Taiwan and Hong Kong samples (18 in each)—expressed a need for reciprocity as they defined it. The children from Taiwan and Hong Kong placed an especially high emphasis on this value, which for them is largely subsumed under mutual help, cooperation, and good behavior (not being troublesome or aggressive).

Differences in attitudes concerning reciprocity were revealed on questions 19, 21, and 28 of the autocentric/heterocentric questionnaire.[69] There were significant differences among groups on two of the questions (19 and 21) for both the autocentric and heterocentric cases. There were no significant differences between the sexes. Among grade levels there was a significant difference only on question 19 for the autocentric case, where autocentrism *declines* sharply with age. There were no significant interaction effects for either the autocentric or heterocentric cases. Only graphs for the differences among groups will be presented. Generally the remainder of the data did not exhibit significant differences between sexes or among grade levels, nor where there any consistent patterns that might indicate a nonsignificant but suggestive trend in the response patterns.

The mean percentage values of autocentric responses for each question for each group are given in Graph 30. The response patterns among groups are similar with some variation, but the Taiwan and Hong Kong groups are dominant in terms of autocentrism. For all three questions the average mean percentage values are 68% for Taiwan, 57% for Hong Kong, 47% for Chinatown, and 43% for America. These differences are reflected in the average rank orders, with Taiwan at 1.0, Hong Kong at 2.0, Chinatown at 3.3, and America at 3.7.

[69] See Appendix C.

GRAPH 30   *Hypothesis 6.   Comparison among Groups of Autocentric Responses, Percent*

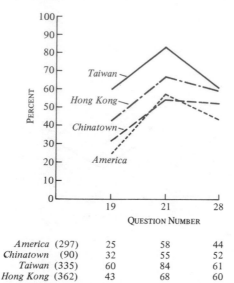

	19	21	28
America (297)	25	58	44
Chinatown (90)	32	55	52
Taiwan (335)	60	84	61
Hong Kong (362)	43	68	60

Note: Numbers in parentheses are the total number of respondents in that category.

Question 19: F = 50.83
Question 21: F = 23.47
Question 28: F = n.s.
n.s.—not significant

Graph 31 gives the mean percentage values of heterocentric responses for each question plotted by groups. As with the autocentric case the general pattern among groups is similar, but there is a large difference in magnitude, with the America group largest in heterocentrism and the Taiwan sample least. The average of the mean percentage values puts America first in heterocentrism with 46%, ahead of Chinatown with 42%, Hong Kong with 40%, and Taiwan with 28%. The average rank orders are America 1.0, Chinatown 2.3, Hong Kong 2.7, and Taiwan 4.0.

All four groups, then, express a need for reciprocity in their relations with others, with children from Taiwan and Hong Kong slightly more expressive of this desire than the Chinatown and America groups.

GRAPH 31   *Hypothesis 6.   Comparison among
Groups of Heterocentric Responses, Percent*

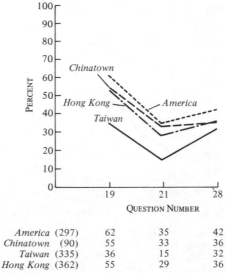

America (297)	62	35	42
Chinatown (90)	55	33	36
Taiwan (335)	36	15	32
Hong Kong (362)	55	29	36

Note: Numbers in parentheses are the total number of respondents
in that category.

Question 19: F = 13.46
Question 21: F = 5.63
Question 28: F = n.s.
n.s.—not significant

In interviews the children from Taiwan and Hong Kong and, to a lesser
extent, from Chinatown tended to define reciprocity in universalistic
terms relating to mutual help, cooperation, and the restraint of hostility.
In contrast, the America group puts stress in reciprocity on the friendliness and likability of others. These patterns were confirmed by the data
on autocentrism and heterocentrism, which showed the Taiwan and
Hong Kong children having much higher percentages of autocentric
responses in regard to reciprocity than the America and, to a lesser
extent, Chinatown groups. While none of the groups scored over 50%
in heterocentric attitude responses, the America group was highest,
followed closely by Chinatown and Hong Kong and with the Taiwan
group markedly the lowest. Only the America group had a heterocentric

response rate higher on the average than the autocentric rate, although the difference in autocentrism and heterocentrism for the Chinatown children was only a few percentage points. In contrast, the children from Taiwan and Hong Kong were markedly higher in autocentrism than in heterocentrism.

DISCUSSION AND SUMMARY

Hypotheses 5 and 6 investigated attitudes toward conformism and reciprocity. In the case of conformism most children from all four groups tended to emphasize autocentric attitudes. Conformism was positively sanctioned—and deviance condemned—primarily in terms of universalistic standards. The Taiwan children tended to be the most autocentric among groups, while the Hong Kong children tended to be least. Overall the Hong Kong children exhibited the greatest heterocentrism regarding conformity, followed by the America, Chinatown, and Taiwan groups.

In terms of intensity of conformism the data indicated a greater reluctance on the part of children from Taiwan and Hong Kong to believe that opposition to a group is permissible. In comments on why one might wish to join a group, there is a stress by these children on the virtues of unity, organization, and good behavior, whereas many America children speak of individuality and freedom.

All children in our groups stressed the value of reciprocity, but there were marked differences concerning what the bases of reciprocity are. Children from Hong Kong and especially Taiwan (the Chinatown group was closer to the America sample) were markedly autocentric, viewing reciprocity largely in terms of the fulfillment of universalistic criteria. The goals of reciprocity were frequently noted as mutual help, cooperation, and the suppression of hostility. America children, on the other hand, were the least autocentric of the four groups and were the only group where heterocentric attitude responses were greater than autocentric ones. The stress in reciprocity for the America sample was on likability, friendliness, and the niceness of others, all factors associated with the specific aspects of relationships.

For both conformism and reciprocity there were no significant differences or patterns between the sexes, and for reciprocity there was no significant difference among grade levels. In the case of conformism there is a pattern of change by age, with younger children very slightly less autocentric and more heterocentric than older children.

Both Chinese and American societies are in the throes of change. The tight hold of primary groups, and the overriding need for mutual dependency among primary-group members, has been severely modified in the United States and is under great pressure in all Chinese societies. This common social phenomenon may provide the basis for conjectures concerning anomalies in the data on conformism and reciprocity. Why, for instance, in the case of conformity, do children from Hong Kong tend to view unity, organization, and good behavior in ways more related to specific relationships than do children from Taiwan, who, relatively speaking, see these attributes as universals not tied to specific individuals? Yet both of those groups stress cooperation and mutual help among individuals as universalistic attributes of reciprocity. American children, on the other hand, are relatively more nonconformist than Chinese children and see reciprocity in terms of likability of and friendliness toward specific others.

What we are witnessing in the Chinese case is a differential breakdown of the authority and inclusiveness of the primary group, in which the attack on the primary group is legitimized in terms of criteria that have been freed from a particularistic mooring and elevated to the status of universalistic criteria. This has been largely achieved through a schooling process in which monopolistic loyalty to the primary group is challenged and there is inculcated and ultimately established a broader sense of group membership and loyalty. The exceptionally massive efforts in this direction on Taiwan (and in the People's Republic of China) may well explain both the similarities and the differences in the response patterns between Taiwan and Hong Kong.

In the United States the challenge to and breakdown of monopolistic loyalty to primary groups are largely completed (there are, of course some very significant differences in the general pattern of primary-group organization in "traditional" America and China). In modern America what we are observing, many feel, is the reintegration of specific ties in a broader and more amorphous peer culture, where the habit of nonconformity is institutionalized but the need for close affectional relations has reasserted itself.

CONCLUSION

Children from Taiwan, Hong Kong, Chinatown (New York City), and New Jersey were tested and observed in order to ascertain whether their attitudes with regard to selected aspects of role behavior were referred primarily to learned, internalized standards or to the opinions and behavior of authority figures as guidelines for appropriate responses. These two general types of attitude disposition, were referred to as *autocentrism* and *heterocentrism*, respectively. The major purpose of this analysis was to discover if there were significant differences or patterns among the four groups, different age levels, and males and females. An attempt was also made through interviews, observation, and the use of a pictorial questionnaire to obtain a measure of the intensity of the feelings held regarding certain types of behavior and of some of the salient symbols or attributes associated with these types of behavior.

The measurement of attitudes in a nonlaboratory setting is difficult at best, and is especially so when the research objective is to examine differences in areas of behavior which are relatively commonplace in the lives of the subjects. Attitude measurement increases in complexity the farther we depart from well-defined areas of high interest to the subject or of high salience within the social unit in question. We are only too aware of the inadequacies of the testing instruments we have used (despite elaborate pretesting), of the limitations imposed by the time available for testing, and of the consequent necessity to limit the number of questions and the full range of cross checks that would be available and desirable in other research contexts. At times one cannot escape the feeling of having tried to weigh a hair with an ordinary bathroom scale.

Despite the research limitations which existed, there emerged from the data a definite pattern of responses among the four groups and among age levels. The pattern in these two areas was sufficiently pronounced for us to have confidence that the tests we utilized have tapped real and significant differences in these areas. Our findings, however, emerge as variations in degree and not in kind; that is, we have not found that children in our four samples are characterized by polarities of attitude but rather, that their attitudes vary in magnitude while tending in a common direction. It is, of course, this very pattern that makes the analysis of crosscultural attitudes difficult and helps to underline the fact that although social systems may be very similar in many respects, differences in degree, even though slight, may be crucial in terms of our understanding of them.

Surprisingly, our data overall revealed no significant differences or patterns of responses between the sexes. There were, of course, differences between males and females among our groups and by grade level, but these were neither consistent nor, generally, very large. Other research has shown clear differences between the sexes with regard to certain attitudinal areas, but we were forced to conclude that sex differences were simply not as important for the attitudes tested here as differences in cultural setting or in age level. Perhaps a test geared to highly defined and specific behavior might be more revealing, but the more generalized attitude dispositions that we were concerned with do not reveal sex variations of any significance.

It is worth noting briefly why further analysis in terms of intelligence quotient or sibling position was not attempted. No doubt our data, analyzed in terms of such categories, would provide further insights. Yet it is our belief that at the level of analysis dealt with here examination of our material in terms of such criteria would be both premature and overly refined. The need is to uncover basic patterns and to gain a more precise understanding of underlying social psychological dynamics.

Most of the children in all our samples generally express autocentric attitudes. When we examine the grand means for each of the twenty attitude questions, sixteen questions, or 80%, show an overall autocentric response pattern above 50%, while the grand means for the heterocentric responses show that on seventeen questions, or 85%, there was a general heterocentric response rate below 50%. Children from all groups, therefore, tended *not* to cite particular others as the authority for their attitudes toward behavior. Fifty-five percent of the autocentric cases showed significant differences among groups and 35% showed significant differences among grade levels. For the heterocentric case 65% of the twenty questions showed significant differences among groups and 40% showed significant differences among grade levels.

It is helpful to look first at the overall patterns for the four groups and for grade levels for both autocentrism and heterocentrism. Averages of mean percentage values and of average rank orders will be noted first for the significant responses and then for all responses. It will be observed that in almost all cases the differences between the averages for the significant questions and the averages for all questions are

TABLE 8   *Autocentric Responses by Group for Significant and All Responses*

SIGNIFICANT RESPONSES
(ELEVEN QUESTIONS)

GROUP	AVERAGE MEAN PERCENTAGE VALUE	AVERAGE RANK ORDER	NUMBER RESPONDING
Taiwan	73	1.5	335
Hong Kong	61	2.6	362
Chinatown	57	2.6	90
America	53	3.3	297

ALL RESPONSES
(TWENTY QUESTIONS)

Taiwan	69	1.4	335
Hong Kong	61	2.7	362
Chinatown	59	2.7	90
America	55	3.2	297

extremely small, indicating the general validity of the overall pattern that emerges.

For the autocentric case the differences among groups were as shown in Table 8. Among grade levels the autocentric response pattern indicated the distribution given in Table 9.

For the autocentric case the *overall* pattern indicates the dominance

TABLE 9   *Autocentric Responses by Grade Level for Significant and All Responses*

SIGNIFICANT RESPONSES
(SEVEN QUESTIONS)

GRADE LEVEL	AVERAGE MEAN PERCENTAGE VALUE	AVERAGE RANK ORDER	NUMBER RESPONDING
5	66	1.7	366
7	63	1.9	358
3	58	2.4	360

ALL RESPONSES
(TWENTY QUESTIONS)

5	64	1.5	366
7	61	2.1	358
3	58	2.4	360

of the Taiwan sample, the similarity of the Hong Kong and Chinatown groups, and the relatively lower autocentrism of the America group. By grade level fifth grade is *overall* dominant in autocentrism, ahead of both seventh grade and third grade. The data does tend to indicate that autocentrism increases with cognitive development and is largely completed by ages 10 to 12.

For the heterocentric case the overall differences among groups were as given in Table 10.

TABLE 10   *Heterocentric Responses by Group for Significant and All Responses*

SIGNIFICANT RESPONSES
(THIRTEEN QUESTIONS)

GROUP	AVERAGE MEAN PERCENTAGE VALUE	AVERAGE RANK ORDER	NUMBER RESPONDING
America	41	1.9	297
Hong Kong	37	2.1	362
Chinatown	35	2.6	90
Taiwan	27	3.7	335

ALL RESPONSES
(TWENTY QUESTIONS)

America	37	2.1	297
Hong Kong	36	1.9	362
Chinatown	32	2.6	90
Taiwan	27	3.7	335

Two patterns emerge rather clearly. First, Taiwan was markedly the least heterocentric. Secondly, the America group overall tended to be the most heterocentric, although the position of the Hong Kong and America groups was very close.

The overall response pattern by grade level is shown in Table 11.

By grade level third grade is clearly the most heterocentric, with fifth grade and seventh grade virtually at the same level. The differences in age levels are in the expected direction, with younger children more heterocentric (and less autocentric) than older children. The major difference here is between third and fifth grade. By the latter age (10–12), children appear to have acquired a knowledge of universalistic criteria and an effective if still somewhat rigid internalization of these precepts. While the overall differences in mean percentage values by grade level

TABLE 11   *Heterocentric Responses by Grade Level for Significant and All Responses*

SIGNIFICANT RESPONSES
(EIGHT QUESTIONS)

GRADE LEVEL	AVERAGE MEAN PERCENTAGE VALUE	AVERAGE RANK ORDER	NUMBER RESPONDING
3	43	1.5	360
5	33	2.2	366
7	31	2.3	358

ALL RESPONSES
(TWENTY QUESTIONS)

3	38	1.4	360
5	31	2.1	358
7	31	2.5	366

are not great, we believe the persistent dominance of third graders in heterocentrism and their lower autocentric scores to be highly important. This pattern implies for older children an increased cognitive ability and capacity to apply an integrated set of abstract principles to the management and selection of modes of behavior. It is through this development with age that human beings develop a behavioral orientation increasingly independent of external sanctions, in which anxiety concerning behavior is aroused not by detection by others but by a capacity to measure behavior and thought against a learned standard.

By seventh grade, all groups had predominantly autocentric attitudes with regard to behavior. This observation lends credence to the assumption that a motivation to correct behavior, arising from a need to reduce shame anxiety when actual behavior is perceived as discrepant with internalized standards, is present by late childhood and early adolescence in all our groups, although with varying levels of intensity. The variations, however, are highly important and reflect the influence of different learning situations and the probability that different types of behavior in any given situation may tend to characterize given populations.

Gross differences or similarities among groups or grade levels mask to some extent the complexity of attitude dispositions. Table 12 summarizes the empirical data for groups and grade levels arranged by behavior area.

TABLE 12   *Summary of Universalistic/Autocentric and Particularistic/Heterocentric Responses for Groups and Grade Levels*

SIX QUESTIONS	GROUP OR GRADE LEVEL	AVERAGE MEAN PERCENT VALUE	AVERAGE RANK ORDER	GROUP OR GRADE LEVEL	AVERAGE MEAN PERCENT VALUE	AVERAGE RANK ORDER
VALUES	UNIVERSALISM			PARTICULARISM		
	Taiwan	76	1.7	Chinatown	31	2.2
	America	72	2.0	Hong Kong	29	2.2
	Hong Kong	69	2.8	Taiwan	20	3.0
	Chinatown	61	3.5	America	19	2.6
	7	73	1.5	3	32	1.2
	5	71	1.8	5	23	2.0
	3	65	2.7	7	20	2.8
	AUTOCENTRISM			HETEROCENTRISM		
HYPOTHESIS 1:						
	Taiwan	79	1.2	America	28	2.4
CONGRUENCE	Hong Kong	74	3.2	Hong Kong	24	1.4
WITH VALUES	Chinatown	72	2.0	Chinatown	21	3.0
(FIVE	America	66	3.6	Taiwan	18	3.2
QUESTIONS)	5	76	1.4	3	31	1.0
	7	75	1.8	5	19	2.6
	3	67	2.8	7	19	2.4
HYPOTHESIS 2:						
	Taiwan	77	1.7	Hong Kong	30	1.6
PUNISHMENT	Chinatown	67	3.0	America	32	2.7
(THREE	America	67	2.6	Chinatown	21	2.7
QUESTIONS)	Hong Kong	66	2.7	Taiwan	19	3.0
	5	74	1.0	3	28	1.0
	7	67	2.7	7	21	2.0
	3	67	2.3	5	20	3.0
HYPOTHESIS 3:						
	Taiwan	69	1.3	America	41	1.7
HOSTILITY	Chinatown	60	2.4	Hong Kong	37	2.0
(THREE	Hong Kong	58	3.0	Chinatown	31	2.6
QUESTIONS)	America	51	3.3	Taiwan	24	3.7
	5	62	1.4	3	37	1.7
	3	59	2.3	7	33	1.7
	7	58	2.3	5	30	2.6

TABLE 12   *Continued*

Six Questions	Group or Grade Level	Average Mean Percent Value	Average Rank Order	Group or Grade Level	Average Mean Percent Value	Average Rank Order
VALUES	AUTOCENTRISM			HETEROCENTRISM		
HYPOTHESIS 4:						
	Hong Kong	44	2.3	Taiwan	55	2.3
Opposition	America	43	2.3	Hong Kong	52	2.3
to	Taiwan	42	2.7	Chinatown	52	2.4
Authority	Chinatown	39	2.7	America	51	3.0
(Three	5	43	2.0	3	56	1.7
Questions)	7	43	1.7	5	52	2.0
	3	40	2.3	7	50	2.3
HYPOTHESIS 5:						
	Taiwan	73	1.0	Hong Kong	40	1.7
Conformism	Hong Kong	58	3.0	America	39	2.0
(Three	Chinatown	57	2.7	Chinatown	36	2.3
Questions)	America	54	3.3	Taiwan	26	4.0
	5	63	1.7	3	39	1.7
	7	61	2.0	7	34	2.0
	3	58	2.3	5	33	2.3
HYPOTHESIS 6:						
	Taiwan	68	1.0	America	46	1.0
Reciprocity	Hong Kong	57	2.0	Chinatown	42	2.3
(Three	Chinatown	47	3.3	Hong Kong	40	2.7
Questions)	America	43	3.7	Taiwan	28	4.0
	3	55	2.0	7	40	2.0
	5	52	1.7	3	40	1.7
	7	51	2.3	5	37	2.3

Number of respondents: America, 297; Chinatown, 90; Taiwan, 335; Hong Kong, 362. Grade 3, 360; grade 5, 366; grade 7, 358.

Intensity of autocentrism declines from hypothesis 1 (Congruence with values) to hypoethesis 2 (Punishment) to hypothesis 5 (Conformity) to hypothesis 3 (Hostility) to hypothesis 6 (Reciprocity), with hypothesis 4 (Opposition to authority) lowest (this order roughly reverses for heterocentrism, although hypotheses 3 and 5 and hypotheses 2 and 1 are closely paired). Within each hypothesis the difference among groups is most marked for hypothesis 6 (reciprocity) and is least for hypothesis 4 (opposition to authority). In the areas of hostility, conformism, and reciprocity behavior American children do not seem to invoke universalistic criteria to the same degree as the Chinese groups. On the other hand, large numbers of children from all groups tend to cite others as the authority for behavior (heterocentrism) when the situation involves opposing authority. Among grade levels the major difference occurs for hypothesis 1 (with third grade markedly lowest in autocentrism); the difference is least for hypothesis 4 (opposition to authority).

Some of the overall patterns noted above for groups and for grade levels take on added significance when the response data for all questions within each hypothesis is aggregated and the groups compared on the basis of the age-related changes within each group for each hypothesis. This data is given in Graph 32.

For the four groups as a whole it appeared that fifth- and seventh-grade responses were quite close, with seventh grade slightly retrogressive in terms of autocentrism. When age changes within each group are compared, however, it can be noted that the shift away from high autocentrism in fifth grade is almost exclusively a characteristic of the Chinese groups and is particularly noteworthy in the areas of punishment, hostility, and opposition to authority, although not confined to these areas. What we infer from this data is the presence of conflicting forces in the learning process. Although there are large differences among the Chinese groups, the advent of adolescence is apparently accompanied for many Chinese children by a shift away from earlier, heavily stressed autocentric attitudes. This shift appears to be especially true for the children from Hong Kong, which we feel are in many ways the most traditional of our Chinese groups.

The data for hypothesis 1 is straightforward and follows the analysis presented earlier. The Chinatown and especially the America group showed incongruities in relative group position when tested for values and attitudes. The America children expressed highly universalistic values (and low particularism), but in terms of attitudes with regard to behavior were relatively lower in autocentrism and higher in heterocentrism. The Chinatown sample was relatively lower in heterocentrism than its particularistic value position indicated. We feel that both these incongruities relate to changes in the group life of those involved. For Americans generally behavior patterns may well have changed toward referencing specific others faster than ideal values concerning behavior would indicate. For the Chinatown children

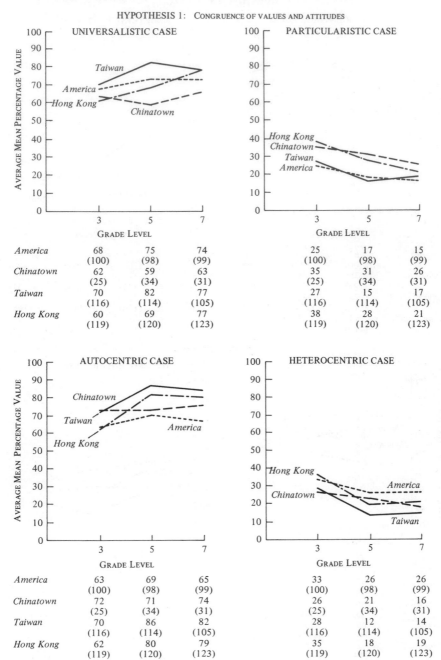

GRAPH 32 *Average Mean Percentage Values for Groups by Grade Levels for All Hypotheses for the Autocentric and Heterocentric Cases*

HYPOTHESIS 1: CONGRUENCE OF VALUES AND ATTITUDES

UNIVERSALISTIC CASE

America	68	75	74
	(100)	(98)	(99)
Chinatown	62	59	63
	(25)	(34)	(31)
Taiwan	70	82	77
	(116)	(114)	(105)
Hong Kong	60	69	77
	(119)	(120)	(123)

PARTICULARISTIC CASE

America	25	17	15
	(100)	(98)	(99)
Chinatown	35	31	26
	(25)	(34)	(31)
Taiwan	27	15	17
	(116)	(114)	(105)
Hong Kong	38	28	21
	(119)	(120)	(123)

AUTOCENTRIC CASE

America	63	69	65
	(100)	(98)	(99)
Chinatown	72	71	74
	(25)	(34)	(31)
Taiwan	70	86	82
	(116)	(114)	(105)
Hong Kong	62	80	79
	(119)	(120)	(123)

HETEROCENTRIC CASE

America	33	26	26
	(100)	(98)	(99)
Chinatown	26	21	16
	(25)	(34)	(31)
Taiwan	28	12	14
	(116)	(114)	(105)
Hong Kong	35	18	19
	(119)	(120)	(123)

Note: Numbers in parentheses are the total number of respondents in that category.

GRAPH 32—*Continued*

HYPOTHESIS 2: PUNISHMENT

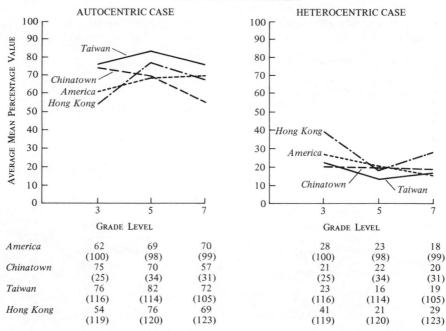

America	62	69	70		28	23	18
	(100)	(98)	(99)		(100)	(98)	(99)
Chinatown	75	70	57		21	22	20
	(25)	(34)	(31)		(25)	(34)	(31)
Taiwan	76	82	72		23	16	19
	(116)	(114)	(105)		(116)	(114)	(105)
Hong Kong	54	76	69		41	21	29
	(119)	(120)	(123)		(119)	(120)	(123)

HYPOTHESIS 3 HOSTILITY

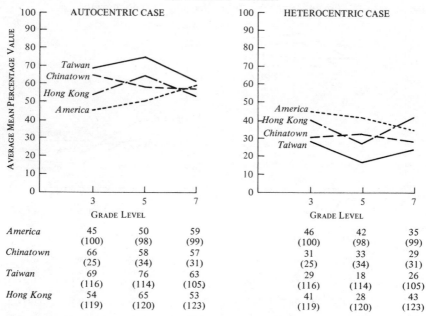

America	45	50	59		46	42	35
	(100)	(98)	(99)		(100)	(98)	(99)
Chinatown	66	58	57		31	33	29
	(25)	(34)	(31)		(25)	(34)	(31)
Taiwan	69	76	63		29	18	26
	(116)	(114)	(105)		(116)	(114)	(105)
Hong Kong	54	65	53		41	28	43
	(119)	(120)	(123)		(119)	(120)	(123)

Note: Numbers in parentheses are the total number of respondents in that category.

GRAPH 32—*Continued*

HYPOTHESIS 4: OPPOSITION TO AUTHORITY

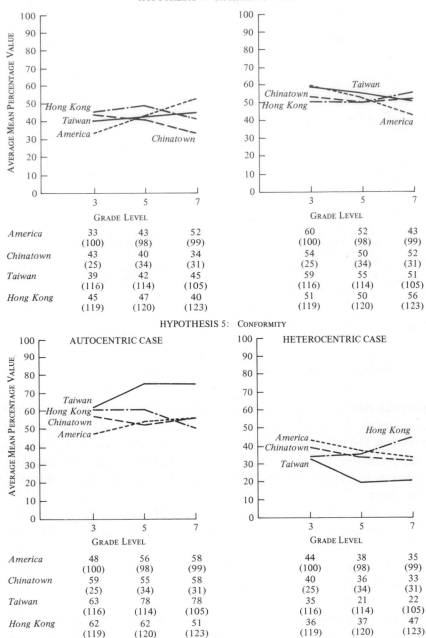

America	33	43	52	60	52	43
	(100)	(98)	(99)	(100)	(98)	(99)
Chinatown	43	40	34	54	50	52
	(25)	(34)	(31)	(25)	(34)	(31)
Taiwan	39	42	45	59	55	51
	(116)	(114)	(105)	(116)	(114)	(105)
Hong Kong	45	47	40	51	50	56
	(119)	(120)	(123)	(119)	(120)	(123)

HYPOTHESIS 5: CONFORMITY

AUTOCENTRIC CASE   HETEROCENTRIC CASE

America	48	56	58	44	38	35
	(100)	(98)	(99)	(100)	(98)	(99)
Chinatown	59	55	58	40	36	33
	(25)	(34)	(31)	(25)	(34)	(31)
Taiwan	63	78	78	35	21	22
	(116)	(114)	(105)	(116)	(114)	(105)
Hong Kong	62	62	51	36	37	47
	(119)	(120)	(123)	(119)	(120)	(123)

Note: Numbers in parentheses are the total number of respondents in that category.

GRAPH 32 *Continued*

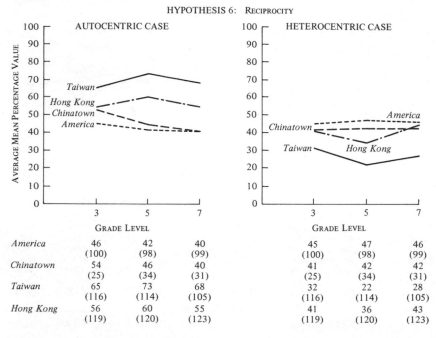

HYPOTHESIS 6: RECIPROCITY

Note: Numbers in parentheses are the total number of respondents in that category.

	Grade Level				Grade Level		
	3	5	7		3	5	7
America	46	42	40		45	47	46
	(100)	(98)	(99)		(100)	(98)	(99)
Chinatown	54	46	40		41	42	42
	(25)	(34)	(31)		(25)	(34)	(31)
Taiwan	65	73	68		32	22	28
	(116)	(114)	(105)		(116)	(114)	(105)
Hong Kong	56	60	55		41	36	43
	(119)	(120)	(123)		(119)	(120)	(123)

particularistic criteria may appear more attractive as an ideal within an immigrant and enclave community without this ideal being verified in practice. The relatively higher heterocentrism of the America group may also be related to the decline in specific morals training (where autocentrism is emphasized) that has characterized changes in American education.

In the area of punishment (hypothesis 2), we note that the children from Taiwan, Hong Kong, and Chinatown, but not those from America, show a declining pattern of autocentrism by seventh grade. For the Hong Kong and especially the Taiwan children this occurred after pronounced increases in autocentrism to fifth grade. It would appear that with age Chinese children experience group punishment sanctions in which the particularistic aspects of relationships are increasingly important. The influence of such sanctions appears especially important for the Hong

Kong children, who show a marked increase in heterocentr

For hypotheses 3 and 4 (hostility and opposition to auth. America children show a clear trend of increasing autocentrism relative to the other groups. In the case of opposition to authority, the America children are the most autocentric and least heterocentric by seventh grade. In the area of hostility Taiwan and Hong Kong children show a marked shift away from an earlier increasing autocentrism by seventh grade. For both Taiwan and Hong Kong, but most notably for the Hong Kong children, there is a corresponding increase in heterocentrism with age. The Chinatown children show relatively steady decreases in auto-centrism for both hostility and opposition to authority.

For hypotheses 5 and 6 (conformism and reciprocity) Taiwan children are lowest in heterocentrism for both hypotheses and also are highest in autocentrism. Hong Kong children are high in autocentrism for reciprocity, but decline to the lowest position in the area of confor-mity, concomitantly showing a marked increase in heterocentrism with age. For these children conformity to particularistic demands is still highly important, but this is not true of the children from Taiwan, who overwhelmingly base conformism as well as reciprocity on the fulfillment of universalistic criteria. For America and Chinatown children, on the other hand, there appears to be a high degree of tolerance for relativity of intent in the areas of conformity and reciprocity, with the result that autocentric attitudes, especially with regard to reciprocity, are not highly predominant. In the areas of conformism and reciprocity these two groups are identical by seventh grade.

A word must be said concerning areas where particular levels of intensity of feeling were indicated. The data supports the conclusion that for children from Taiwan and Hong Kong and, to a lesser extent, Chinatown, punishment by group sanctions is early, intensely, and increasingly feared, the consequences of open opposition to either the group or its authorities are likewise increasingly feared (this is markedly the case for the Hong Kong children), and conformity in group behavior is viewed very positively as having direct relevance to desired goals of unity and organization. For the America and Chinatown children, on the other hand, the threat of group sanctions—although increasingly feared—is less massive, authority and groups are seen as openly challengeable, and diversity in group life, especially for the America group, is perceived as relatively desirable. Unlike the case for Chinese children there is a strong stress in interpersonal relations on friendliness and likability. These patterns are set forth for each group by grade level in terms of the pictorial questionnaire responses presented earlier in Graph 33.

The age trends of the four groups are revealing and tend to bolster our earlier conclusions made on the basis of the overall findings. Readers, of course, are aware that our conclusions are tentative and open to more than one interpretation. We defend our assumptions on the basis that the patterns we set forth appear to us to be the most probable outcomes in terms of the learning environments outlined in chapter 3.

For America children reciprocity appears especially to be an area where consideration of specific others is highly important. We have noted before the emphasis in American group relationships on likableness and friendliness. There is, however, an increasing capacity on the part of these children to express hostility generally and opposition to authority specifically when others in the relationship are deemed to have violated universalistic standards. We feel that opposition on the basis of universal criteria is stressed because likableness in relationships is emphasized and the breaking of bonds involving affiliation is difficult without invoking such criteria as proof that authority is genuinely "unlikable." On the basis of these findings we would expect Americans to seek friendliness in others, including authority figures (the policeman and President, to name two frequently cited figures in political socialization research), but to feel that the expression of hostility or opposition toward others is justified if the individual or group has overstepped moral limits. On the other hand this opposition will normally be tempered by a continuing search for friendliness and likability in reciprocal relationships. The greatest hostility and mistrust, in fact, is likely to be reserved for those individuals or groups who reject, or, are perceived as rejecting, any ultimate outcome of friendliness or compromise.

Children from Chinatown share the general patterns concerning conformism and reciprocity held by other American children. This appears to be the result of a largely common educational experience. Certain attitudinal patterns, however, are in sharp contrast with those manifested by Caucasian and Negro American children. This difference

GRAPH 33 *Mean Percentage Values for Groups by Grade Level for Pictorial Questionaire Responses*

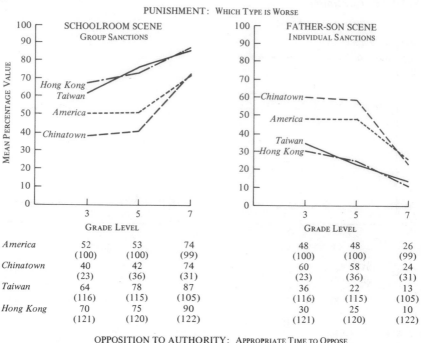

PUNISHMENT: WHICH TYPE IS WORSE

SCHOOLROOM SCENE — GROUP SANCTIONS

FATHER-SON SCENE — INDIVIDUAL SANCTIONS

	3	5	7		3	5	7
America	52	53	74		48	48	26
	(100)	(100)	(99)		(100)	(100)	(99)
Chinatown	40	42	74		60	58	24
	(23)	(36)	(31)		(23)	(36)	(31)
Taiwan	64	78	87		36	22	13
	(116)	(115)	(105)		(116)	(115)	(105)
Hong Kong	70	75	90		30	25	10
	(121)	(120)	(122)		(121)	(120)	(122)

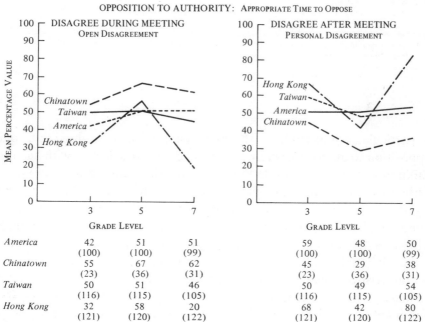

OPPOSITION TO AUTHORITY: APPROPRIATE TIME TO OPPOSE

DISAGREE DURING MEETING — OPEN DISAGREEMENT

DISAGREE AFTER MEETING — PERSONAL DISAGREEMENT

	3	5	7		3	5	7
America	42	51	51		59	48	50
	(100)	(100)	(99)		(100)	(100)	(99)
Chinatown	55	67	62		45	29	38
	(23)	(36)	(31)		(23)	(36)	(31)
Taiwan	50	51	46		50	49	54
	(116)	(115)	(105)		(116)	(115)	(105)
Hong Kong	32	58	20		68	42	80
	(121)	(120)	(122)		(121)	(120)	(122)

Note: Numbers in parentheses are the total number of respondents in that category.

GRAPH 33   *Continued*

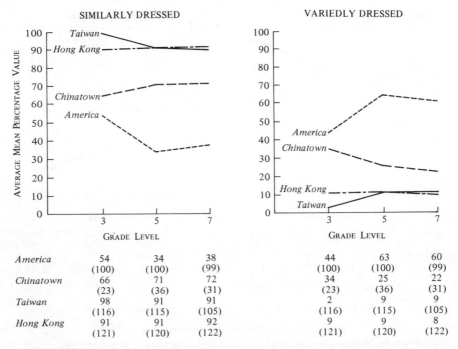

America	54	34	38	44	63	60
	(100)	(100)	(99)	(100)	(100)	(99)
Chinatown	66	71	72	34	25	22
	(23)	(36)	(31)	(23)	(36)	(31)
Taiwan	98	91	91	2	9	9
	(116)	(115)	(105)	(116)	(115)	(105)
Hong Kong	91	91	92	9	9	8
	(121)	(120)	(122)	(121)	(120)	(122)

Note: Numbers in parentheses are the total number of respondents in that category. There were significant differences among groups for the Punishment and Conformism questions and among grade levels for the Punishment question. There were no significant interaction effects.

is particularly noticeable in the areas of punishments, hostility, and opposition to authority, where autocentric attitudes decline with age for children in Chinatown while they rise for other American children. In Chinatown the search for an identity is made more difficult by the rejection of traditional Chinese values, by the relative stress on particular bonds, and by the feeling that authority can be challenged combined with a relative inclination to oppose authority on the basis of particular rather than universal standards. In all probability these patterns may be characteristic of many immigrant groups. The resultant step for many Chinese Americans may well be a more complete absorption of the dominant culture's behavioral and value patterns together with a shift in the locus of identity from particular others to one's own ethnic group as a source of pride in itself and as a component of a larger grouping deserving of loyalty.

The children from Taiwan and Hong Kong represent, to some extent, two aspects of transition in Chinese society. Taiwan is an example of an independent, modernizing Chinese society, while Hong Kong, as a colony, has seen great economic change but less systematic effort to mold behavior and value patterns. In both social systems we have noted an emphasis on morals training, and the manner in which particularistic values, in the course of such training, are raised to the level of universal truths. The effect of such training, more intensely and systematically carried out in Taiwan, appears to be reflected for both groups in rapid increases in autocentrism to fifth grade. At this point there is generally a shift away from this pattern toward decreasing autocentrism and, most especially marked for the children in Hong Kong, an increase in hetero-centrism. Overall the children from Taiwan remain high in autocentrism, especially in the areas of conformism and reciprocity, but this cannot be said for the children from Hong Kong. For both groups this leveling off or reversal phenomenon appears, in our opinion, to be related to the increasing demands for adherence to well-defined behavior patterns and the threat of group ostracism and shaming sanctions against deviants. We believe it is the increasing strength of such anxiety that helps explain declining autocentrism for both groups in the areas of punishment and expression of hostility and, for the Hong Kong children, in the area of opposition to authority.

The major difference between the Taiwan and Hong Kong samples is in the area of conformism. Taiwan children legitimize this type of behavior by largely autocentric attitude dispositions, whereas Hong Kong children increasingly base conformist behavior on the expectations of specific others, to a degree even greater than for American children. The pattern is less clear for reciprocity, where both groups are relatively high in autocentrism, although even here the Hong Kong children show a marked increase in heterocentrism.

In Taiwan conformism is based on adherence to universalistic codes of behavior. Expression of hostility is increasingly muted by awareness of group sanctions, but opposition to authority is increasingly with age felt to be legitimate if universalistic standards are violated. We expect that past a certain point, if opposition is vented, it will be little

ed by particularistic bonds, especially because the targets will usually be deemed to have violated standards for conformism and will thus achieve outgroup status. This pattern has been evidenced we feel, though with some differences, of course, in many movements in the People's Republic of China, a society which also greatly emphasizes the learning of universal moral standards.

In Hong Kong conformism and opposition to authority are increasingly based on particularistic rather than universalistic criteria. Where hostility is expressed or opposition to authority occurs, we would expect universal values to be invoked less frequently than in Taiwan as a legitimization for these types of behavior—and, given the patterns of heterocentrism for conformity and reciprocity, that much effort would be exerted, when hostility or opposition occurs, to maintain the form of relationships.

Despite a rough correspondence of *feelings* for children from Taiwan and Hong Kong regarding types of punishment, opposition to authority, and conformism (based on the pictorial questionnaire), their different levels of autocentrism and heterocentrism reveal differences in the ways in which social stability, the legitimacy of authority, and individual goals are related. Where autocentrism is high, as in Taiwan, we believe that anxiety concerning group sanctions, overt opposition, and conformism would tend to produce a somewhat rigid invocation of universalistic criteria in behavior regardless of the relationships involved. Standards, we expect, would be seen as socially inclusive and encompassing all role levels, and value consistency and purity demanded of both leaders and led. Political authority would be seen as relatively unchallengeable as long as its moral quality is not in question. Where heterocentrism is relatively high, as in Hong Kong, we expect that the same anxieties would be reflected in special emphasis on fulfillment of primary-level obligations, special consideration of particular relationships, and a belief that standards regarding behavior are defined in terms of specific roles. Political authority would be held accountable as a general model, we expect, but social control left essentially in the hands of primary groups. Where heterocentrism is relatively high and there is an emphasis on likability and individualism and relatively lower anxiety concerning group sanctions, overt opposition, and conformism, as in America, we believe that behavior is likely to be expressive of individual desires and particularistic criteria will infuse role relations at all levels. Authority will be expected to be both likable and moral; challengeability of authority at any level will appear as possible. Group differences in magnitude of autocentrism or heterocentrism, then, may be small, but their social and political implications are large.

A question must be raised, finally, concerning the overall general validity of these findings. Is it not possible that these are ideal patterns unrelated to actual behavior? Furthermore, can one accept the validity of the Taiwan findings if one posits that these particular responses are merely "approved" ones reflecting the pressure of life in an authoritarian social system? These objections, which are serious and cannot be totally invalidated, deserve some consideration. Attitudes, clearly, are not behavior, and we have made no suggestion here that we are in fact measuring anything but attitudes. As we pointed out at the beginning of this chapter, we do feel there is a linkage between the attitudes we have revealed and behavior patterns, but the data we have presented has not addressed itself directly to this point. Nevertheless we feel that the attitude dispositions we have uncovered make "sense" as reflections of the learning environments set forth by us earlier. Moreover, our observations carried out in previous research and for this project strongly suggest the validity of our findings. Space and our research focus have not permitted as full a presentation of this material as some readers might wish, but within these limitations, we have tried to present both ideal and actual aspects of behavior that bear upon the focus we have selected.

We certainly feel that the social environment on Taiwan has influenced responses of children from there, but we believe this to be due more to the nature of the school learning environment than to any simplistic relationship to an authoritarian political system, even recognizing the tight political control of the educational system. As we hope to show in the following chapter, the responses of the children on Taiwan, far from being invalid as a reflection of political fear, in fact reflect the intense school training that these children receive.

5 Role Learning and

Attitude Orientation

The degree to which attitude dispositions will be generally autocentric or heterocentric is related, we assume, to the extent, type, and intensity of primary- and secondary-role learning. Primary-group relationships have a high degree of personal orientation and generally also a considerable amount of affective content. In situtations such as family interaction, we would therefore expect attitude dispositions to be somewhat heterocentric in nature. Secondary-level role learning, on the other hand, requires greater cognitive structuring than does primary-group role learning (learning the role behavior of an official versus that of a son, for instance) and is also less invested with affect. The greater cognitive structuring required in secondary-group role learning arises because direct cues from others are frequently much less available and the role behavior itself requires actions directly and positively associated with abstract concepts. In other words, the learned dispositions that are required in secondary-level learning imply the development of sets of less personalized value orientations that ultimately come to define and legitimize behavior. To some degree, of course, the freeing of values from attachment to specific others is also true of primary-group role learning, but we believe it is much less in evidence at that level, both because the number of personal cues is greater and because the affective content of role relationships is higher. Secondary-role learning may involve learning role attributes as complete abstractions unrelated to others—the

226

good citizen is patriotic, loyal, involved—or as aspects of particularistic relationships raised to the level of general principles—the good citizen is loyal as he would be to his father or to God. In the latter case attitude dispositions are apt to have the form of codes or taboos.

In all but the most primitive societies, individuals, to some extent, learn both primary- and secondary-group roles. Role learning for the two levels is significantly different in the degree of value abstraction required, but it is not totally different in kind; the attributes of either level of learning can be found to a degree in the other. Anxiety concerning behavior will be less to the extent that there is congruity and reinforcement among values at both role levels. However, individual training and experience with secondary-level role behavior will vary greatly depending upon age, sex, social status, educational level, societal type, etc. To the extent that a person has been trained or given experience in secondary-level roles we would expect that depersonalized dispositions would govern much behavior at both the secondary and primary levels. For not only must secondary-role learning be salient for the strong development of autocentric attitude dispositions, but these dispositions, once learned, come to constitute the ideals for appropriate role behavior at all levels. In other types of social situations —such as for a peasant in traditional society—secondary-role learning will be much more random and the opportunity for actual involvement in secondary roles infrequent. In such cases we would expect to a greater degree generalized attitudinal dispositions related to primary-level role behavior.

In the three sections which follow the patterns of autocentrism and heterocentrism for each role-learning level shall be presented. A general discussion can be found in the Summary and Discussion section at the end of this chapter.

THE FAMILY—ATTITUDE ORIENTATIONS

If the concepts of autocentrism and heterocentrism introduced in chapter 4 are used to analyze primary-level role learning an interesting pattern emerges for groups and grade levels that lends further support to our assumptions. The questions from our questionnaire that dealt with primary-level behavior were 10, 11, 14, 18, 21, and 24 (see Appendix C).

For these questions there was a generally autocentric disposition for all groups, as indicated by the fact that on four of the six questions (10, 14, 18, 21) the grand mean for autocentrism was over 50%. On only one question, number 24, was the grand mean for heterocentrism over 50%. Nevertheless, there was generally higher heterocentrism with regard to family-level role behavior than in any other learning area. Significantly, the one exception to this was the area of school learning for the America children, where heterocentrism was higher than in the family area.) One question, number 21, involved primary- and secondary-level role conflict but was included among the primary-level questions because of its emphasis on primary relationships.

For the autocentric case there were significant differences among groups on three of the six questions (14, 18, and 21), but no significant differences between the sexes or among grade levels. For the hetero-centric responses there were four significant differences among groups (questions 14, 18, 21, and 24) and one significant difference between sexes and one among grade levels both number (24). In the tables that follow only group and grade-level responses are analyzed.

The mean percentage values and the average rank orders for primary-level responses for groups and grade levels are as given in Table 13.

The differences among the Hong Kong, Chinatown, and America children are very slight for both the autocentric and heterocentric cases. The same relative lack of difference is true across grade levels and reflects the fact that attitudes with regard to primary-role behavior are relatively stable by third grade. Generally the Taiwan group was highest in auto-centrism and lowest in heterocentrism. However, if the mean percentage values and the average rank orders for the various groups are plotted by grade level different patterns emerge. These patterns are indicated in Graphs 34 and 35.

It is clear that overall Taiwan is both highest in autocentrism and lowest in heterocentrism. For the America group there is an increase in autocentrism with age and for the Chinatown group a decrease. For the heterocentric case the Hong Kong children show an increase with age while the other groups are more stable. It would appear that the saliency of universal codes governing primary-level behavior increases to fifth grade for the America, Taiwan, and Hong Kong children but decreases subsequently with age for the latter two groups. For both of these there

TABLE 13   *Autocentric and Heterocentric Cases: Mean Percentage Values and Average Rank Orders for Primary-Level Responses for Groups and Grade Levels*

GROUP OR GRADE LEVEL	MEAN PERCENTAGE VALUE	AVERAGE RANK ORDER	NUMBER RESPONDING
AUTOCENTRIC CASE			
Taiwan	62	1.8	335
	(77)		
Hong Kong	54	2.5	362
	(63)		
America	53	2.5	297
	(63)		
Chinatown	51	3.0	90
	(60)		
5	56	1.5	366
3	56	2.0	360
7	52	2.5	358
HETEROCENTRIC CASE			
Hong Kong	44	2.2	362
	(44)		
Chinatown	41	2.3	90
	(42)		
America	41	2.7	297
	(42)		
Taiwan	36	2.8	335
	(36)		
7	41	1.7	358
3	40	1.8	360
5	39	2.5	366

Note: The percentages in parentheses under "Mean Percentage Value" refer to significant responses only.

is a sharp rise in heterocentrism from fifth to seventh grade, indicating the resurgence of particularistic criteria governing behavior in primary-level relations. In absolute terms this is most marked for the Hong Kong sample. Children from the America group, on the other hand, show no such pattern, indicating an apparently more decisive break from family ties. For the Chinatown children there is an apparent ambiguousness, with a decrease by seventh grade in both autocentrism and heterocentrism.

GRAPH 34   *Average Mean Percentage Values for Groups by Grade Level for Primary-Level Role-Behavior Responses for the Autocentric and Heterocentric Cases*

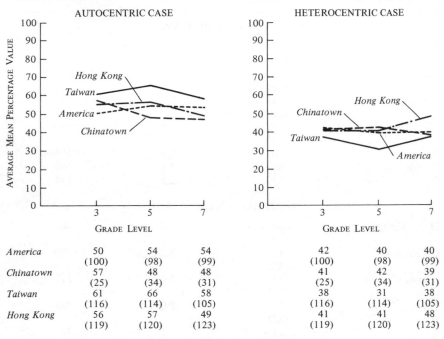

	3	5	7		3	5	7
America	50	54	54		42	40	40
	(100)	(98)	(99)		(100)	(98)	(99)
Chinatown	57	48	48		41	42	39
	(25)	(34)	(31)		(25)	(34)	(31)
Taiwan	61	66	58		38	31	38
	(116)	(114)	(105)		(116)	(114)	(105)
Hong Kong	56	57	49		41	41	48
	(119)	(120)	(123)		(119)	(120)	(123)

Note: Numbers in parentheses are the total number of respondents in that category.

THE SCHOOLS—ATTITUDE ORIENTATIONS

There were seven questions that were related to aspects of secondary-level role learning in the schools. These were 8, 9, 15, 17, 19, 25, and 27 (see Appendix C). Of these, five had significant differences among groups for the autocentric case (8, 17, 19, 25, and 27), and six had significant differences among groups for the heterocentric case (8, 9, 17, 19, 25, and 27). Overall the area of secondary-level role learning was the one in which the four groups showed the greatest disparity. Across grade levels there were four questions for the autocentric case (8, 17, 19, and 27) and three for the heterocentric case (8, 17, and 27) where a significant

GRAPH 35   *Average Rank Orders for Groups by Grade Level for Primary-Level Role-Behavior Responses for the Autocentric and Heterocentric Cases*

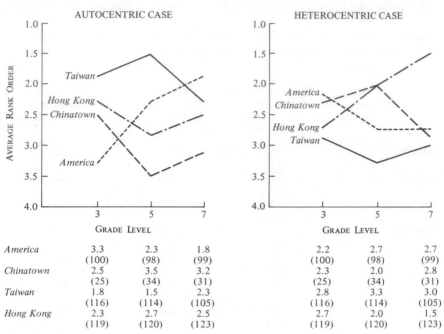

	3	5	7		3	5	7
America	3.3	2.3	1.8		2.2	2.7	2.7
	(100)	(98)	(99)		(100)	(98)	(99)
Chinatown	2.5	3.5	3.2		2.3	2.0	2.8
	(25)	(34)	(31)		(25)	(34)	(31)
Taiwan	1.8	1.5	2.3		2.8	3.3	3.0
	(116)	(114)	(105)		(116)	(114)	(105)
Hong Kong	2.3	2.7	2.5		2.7	2.0	1.5
	(119)	(120)	(123)		(119)	(120)	(123)

Note: Numbers in parentheses are the total number of respondents in that category.

difference was indicated. There were no significant differences between the sexes for autocentrism, but three questions indicated significant male-female differences for the heterocentric case (8, 9, and 27). Males appear to be slightly more heterocentric than females, being higher in heterocentrism on two of the three significant-difference responses and on five of the seven total responses. In the tables that follow only group and grade-level responses will be analyzed.

The data shows that the children from all four groups tended toward autocentrism, although this was less the case for the America group. For only two of the seven questions did the grand mean for autocentrism fall below 50% and the grand mean for heterocentrism exceed 50%. Most children from our samples have clearly developed by ages eight or nine internalized attitude dispositions with regard to role behavior that generally allow them to operate without needing to cite external authority as the legitimization for behavior. The mean percentage values and the average rank orders for all questions for attitudes

TABLE 14   *Autocentric and Heterocentric Cases: Mean Percentage Values and Average Rank Orders for Secondary-Level Role Learning for Groups and Grade Levels*

GROUP OR GRADE LEVEL	MEAN PERCENTAGE VALUE	AVERAGE RANK ORDER	NUMBER RESPONDING
	AUTOCENTRIC CASE		
Taiwan	74 (73)	1.0	335
Hong Kong	63 (60)	2.6	362
Chinatown	56 (48)	2.7	90
America	50 (41)	3.7	297
7	64 (63)	1.6	358
5	62 (62)	1.9	366
3	56 (55)	2.6	360
	HETEROCENTRIC CASE		
America	43 (44)	1.3	297
Chinatown	35 (36)	2.4	90
Hong Kong	33 (33)	2.3	362
Taiwan	22 (21)	4.0	335
3	39 (40)	1.3	360
5	32 (26)	2.3	366
7	29 (23)	2.4	358

Note: The percentages in parentheses under "Mean Percentage Value" refer to significant responses only.

relating to secondary-level role learning for groups and grade levels are given in Table 14.

The differences among the four groups are marked, with Taiwan clearly the most autocentric and least heterocentric and America the least autocentric and most heterocentric. Overall the children from Chinatown and Hong Kong are in the middle position, with Hong Kong between Chinatown and Taiwan and Chinatown between Hong Kong and America. There appears to be a continuum by grade level from third to fifth to seventh, with third grade highest in heterocentrism and lowest in autocentrism and seventh grade highest in autocentrism and lowest in heterocentrism. Generally the values for fifth and seventh grade were relatively close in comparison to the values for third grade, indicating that in the area of secondary-level role learning autocentric development has largely been completed by grade 5 (ages 10–11, approximately). There are, however, differences in patterns of development. If the average mean percentage values and the average rank orders of the various groups are plotted by grade level, the patterns shown in Graphs 36 and 37 emerge.

The plots of average mean percentage values and average rank orders show that Taiwan remains the most autocentric and least heterocentric of the groups with age. America is the most heterocentric with age. The Chinatown children decrease in autocentrism with age, indicating, we feel, the influence of the American school system and its lack of congruence with primary-level role learning for these children. While autocentrism remains the dominant response for children from Chinatown and Hong Kong, both groups are much lower than Taiwan, indicating the less heavy emphasis on autocentrism in the schools for these children.

THE POLITY—ATTITUDE ORIENTATIONS

Seven questions, 7, 12, 16, 22, 23, 26, and 28, dealt with attitudes related to secondary-level behavior in the polity. Of these, three questions (16, 23, and 26) showed a significant difference among groups for both the autocentric and heterocentric cases. Questions 12, 16, and 22 showed a significant difference among grade levels for the autocentric case, and

GRAPH 36   *Average Mean Percentage Values for Groups by Grade Levels for Secondary-Level Role-Learning Responses for the Autocentric and Heterocentric Cases*

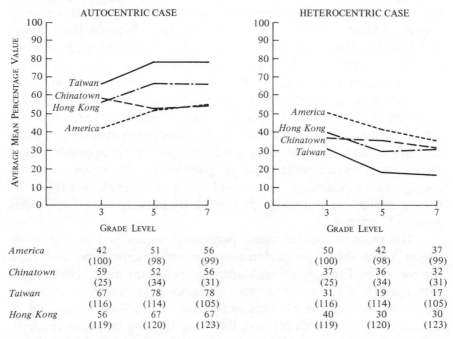

	America					
America	42	51	56	50	42	37
	(100)	(98)	(99)	(100)	(98)	(99)
Chinatown	59	52	56	37	36	32
	(25)	(34)	(31)	(25)	(34)	(31)
Taiwan	67	78	78	31	19	17
	(116)	(114)	(105)	(116)	(114)	(105)
Hong Kong	56	67	67	40	30	30
	(119)	(120)	(123)	(119)	(120)	(123)

Note: Numbers in parentheses are the total number of responses in that category.

questions 16, 22, and 23 showed a significant difference among grade levels for the heterocentric case. For both the autocentric and heterocentric cases there was a significant difference between the sexes only on question 26. Although the mean percentage differences between the sexes were generally extremely small, it is of interest that of the seven questions females were higher than males on six questions for the autocentric case and lower on six questions for the heterocentric case. While the differences are slight, the overall pattern suggests that females are somewhat more autocentric with regard to attitudes concerning secondary-level behavior.

The general prevalence of autocentrism in secondary-level role

GRAPH 37   *Average Rank Orders for Groups by Grade Level for Secondary-Level Role-Learning Responses for the Autocentric and Heterocentric Cases*

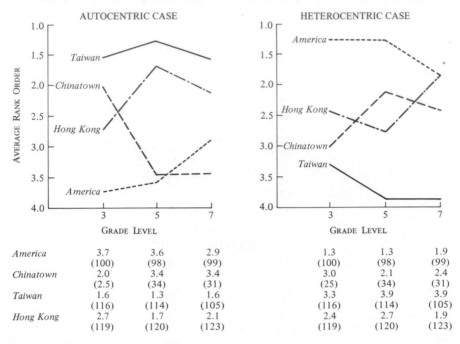

		3	5	7		3	5	7
America		3.7	3.6	2.9		1.3	1.3	1.9
		(100)	(98)	(99)		(100)	(98)	(99)
Chinatown		2.0	3.4	3.4		3.0	2.1	2.4
		(2.5)	(34)	(31)		(25)	(34)	(31)
Taiwan		1.6	1.3	1.6		3.3	3.9	3.9
		(116)	(114)	(105)		(116)	(114)	(105)
Hong Kong		2.7	1.7	2.1		2.4	2.7	1.9
		(119)	(120)	(123)		(119)	(120)	(123)

Note: Numbers in parentheses are the total number of responses in that category.

behavior is indicated by the fact that for no question was the grand mean for autocentrism under 50% or the grand mean for heterocentrism over 50%. The mean percentage values and the average rank orders for all questions for attitudes relating to secondary-level role behavior for groups and grade levels are given in Table 15.

Generally the results confirm our expectations concerning the relative degrees of autocentrism and heterocentrism among groups. Taiwan had the highest amount of autocentrism; Hong Kong and America were relatively lower than Taiwan in autocentrism and somewhat higher in heterocentrism. The Chinatown children were overall lowest in heterocentrism and on a level with Taiwan in terms of auto-

TABLE 15   *Autocentric and Heterocentric Cases: Mean Percentage Values and Average Rank Orders for Secondary-Level Role-Behavior Responses for Groups and Grade Levels*

GROUP OR GRADE LEVEL	MEAN PERCENTAGE VALUE	AVERAGE RANK ORDER	NUMBER RESPONDING
AUTOCENTRIC CASE			
Taiwan	71 (68)	1.4	335
Chinatown	68 (69)	2.3	90
Hong Kong	64 (60)	3.0	362
America	62 (61)	3.3	297
5	72 (71)	1.1	366
7	64 (63)	2.3	358
3	63 (63)	2.6	360
HETEROCENTRIC CASE			
Hong Kong	32 (37)	1.3	362
America	29 (32)	2.6	297
Taiwan	25 (27)	3.1	335
Chinatown	23 (21)	3.0	90
3	33 (38)	1.1	360
7	26 (27)	2.1	358
5	23 (26)	2.7	366

Note: The percentages in parentheses under "Mean Percentage Value" refer to significant responses only.

centrism, primarily due to relatively high scores in autocentrism for younger children.

By grade level there was a surprising decrease in autocentrism after grade 5. Apparently the degree of autocentrism in secondary-level role behavior reaches a peak in childhood around the age of 10 or 11 and decreases with the onset of adolescence. At this stage we can only be tentative concerning the reasons for this. It may be that insecurities associated with puberty occasion a slight turning away from auto-centrism in role relationships. On the other hand, it may also be that by seventh grade the intensity of loyalty to various group memberships has become relatively fixed. Where the secondary level is an ambiguous source of identity and focus of loyalty there may be a partial rejection of attitudes and behavior patterns appropriate to that level and a return to a reduced level of autocentrism as the general pattern for behavior. It will be noted in any case that the shift between fifth and seventh grade is a relatively small one, indicating that basic secondary-level attitudes and behavior patterns are set by approximately ages ten to eleven. One further and perhaps significant explanation derives from the work of Piaget and Kohlberg. It may well be that age shifts in autocentrism reflect a change away from conventional and rather rigid morality in fifth grade to a more mature and relative conception of relationships by grade seven. This shift, however, is not uniform for all groups or in all contexts. In the realm of the polity the shift from a highly autocentric fifth-grade stance appears most strongly in those groups for which explicit morals training has been a significant aspect of training.

The average mean percentage values and the average rank orders of the four groups plotted by grade level are shown in Graphs 38 and 39.

The data suggests that there is a variation among the four groups relative to each other in the acquisition of attitudes relating to secondary-level role behavior. In Taiwan and Hong Kong morals training relating to secondary-level behavior is a significant aspect of school training, more pronounced and explicit in Taiwan than in Hong Kong. Relative to the other groups both Taiwan and Hong Kong increase in autocentrism and decrease in heterocentrism by fifth grade. With increasing age, however, the children in Hong Kong show a de-crease in autocentrism and an increase in heterocentrism, a pattern which we believe is related to the failure of the school system in Hong Kong to impart an unambiguous sense of membership at the secondary level which would give meaning and significance to the learning of secondary-level attitudes and behavior patterns. In Taiwan, on the other hand, where a sense of secondary-level membership is firmly acquired, the relative ranking of first place for the autocentric case is more pro-

GRAPH 38 *Average Mean Percentage Values for Groups by Grade Level for Secondary-Level Role-Behavior Responses for the Autocentric and Heterocentric Cases*

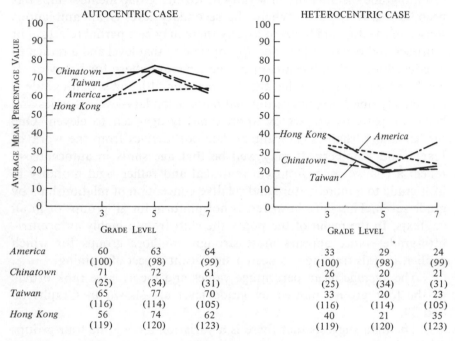

| | America | | | Chinatown | | | Taiwan | | | Hong Kong | | |

America	60	63	64		33	29	24
	(100)	(98)	(99)		(100)	(98)	(99)
Chinatown	71	72	61		26	20	21
	(25)	(34)	(31)		(25)	(34)	(31)
Taiwan	65	77	70		33	20	23
	(116)	(114)	(105)		(116)	(114)	(105)
Hong Kong	56	74	62		40	21	35
	(119)	(120)	(123)		(119)	(120)	(123)

Note: Numbers in parentheses are the total number of respondents in that category.

nounced with age, although there is an absolute decline in autocentrism from fifth to seventh grade.

Children from New Jersey and Chinatown both experience training in the American public school system, where there is little explicit formal effort to develop a uniform set of attitudes and behavior patterns appropriate for membership at the secondary level. Although autocentrism for both of these groups increases slightly to fifth grade, there is a relative decrease in autocentrism and increase in heterocentrism at that grade level in comparison with the Taiwan and Hong Kong groups, where the children are acquiring autocentric attitude dispositions in a more systematic fashion. Although the amount of heterocentrism for all

GRAPH 39   *Average Rank Orders for Groups by Grade Level for Secondary-Level Role-Behavior Responses for the Autocentric and Heterocentric Cases*

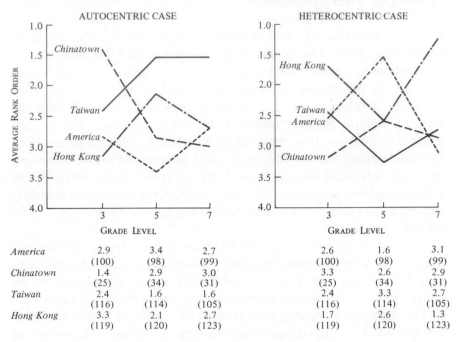

	Grade Level 3	Grade Level 5	Grade Level 7		Grade Level 3	Grade Level 5	Grade Level 7
America	2.9	3.4	2.7		2.6	1.6	3.1
	(100)	(98)	(99)		(100)	(98)	(99)
Chinatown	1.4	2.9	3.0		3.3	2.6	2.9
	(25)	(34)	(31)		(25)	(34)	(31)
Taiwan	2.4	1.6	1.6		2.4	3.3	2.7
	(116)	(114)	(105)		(116)	(114)	(105)
Hong Kong	3.3	2.1	2.7		1.7	2.6	1.3
	(119)	(120)	(123)		(119)	(120)	(123)

Note: Numbers in parentheses are the total number of respondents in that category.

groups is not high, Chinatown, America, and Taiwan are all absolutely and relatively much lower than Hong Kong by grade seven. The America sample shows a slight increase in autocentrism with age as the more randomly acquired secondary-level autocentric attitudes and behavior patterns become better established and there is a greater understanding of their relevance in terms of secondary-level occupational roles and in terms of a still rather diffuse but growing sense of common membership at the secondary level. For Chinatown children heterocentric attitudes are low by grade seven but autocentric attitudinal responses also show a decrease with age. This decline, we believe, mirrors the difficulty that many Chinese-American children have in developing an identity at the secondary level that can anchor secondary-level attitude and behavior patterns.

SUMMARY AND DISCUSSION

Readers will not have to be told that wide gaps exist in our understanding of the ways in which people internalize values and that many of our assumptions concerning the learning process are speculative. Nevertheless, among the groups and grade levels studied here there are some persistent differences that appear to be logically connected with the learning patterns we have observed. We make no claim, and in fact, specifically disavow, that our work to date has set bare the causal links between learning and attitudes concerning behavior. What we do believe have been advanced here are lines of argument for further investigation and assumptions concerning the ways in which the learning of attitudes and behavior patterns associated with group membership levels may be related.

In this book some facets of learning in New Jersey, Chinatown (New York City), Taiwan, and Hong Kong have been set forth with regard to the learning of roles in the family, in the school, and in the polity. Some of the aspects discussed were punishments, including the role of shaming; modeling; peer groups; the extent of morals training; and the effects of differential commitments to various levels of group memberships. When these and other factors associated with learning were assessed in terms of group and grade level, it was found that the Taiwan children were generally predominant in autocentrism and lowest in heterocentrism regardless of the learning area. Overall the America group was least in autocentrism, although not always greatest in heterocentrism. There were, however, important variations by behavioral area, and in the age patterns within each group. Differences between the sexes were not a pronounced feature. The number of significant differences between males and females were few and random. The overall pattern indicated that females were slightly more autocentric than males, but the differences were in almost all cases small.

In Table 16 are set forth the average mean percentage values for each group and grade level for the responses related to the family, for those related to the school, and for those related to the polity. In calculating these average values all responses relating to a particular learning area were used. It will be noted that overall the children are predominantly autocentric by both group and grade level.

TABLE 16 *Average Mean Percentage Values for Groups and Grade Levels for Role-Learning Responses Related to the Family, School, and Polity*

GROUP OR GRADE LEVEL	ROLE-LEARNING CATEGORY		
	Family	*School*	*Polity*
AUTOCENTRIC CASE			
America	53	50	62
Chinatown	51	56	68
Taiwan	62	74	71
Hong Kong	54	63	64
3	56	56	63
5	56	62	72
7	52	64	64
HETEROCENTRIC CASE			
America	41	43	29
Chinatown	41	35	23
Taiwan	36	22	25
Hong Kong	44	33	32
3	40	39	33
5	39	32	23
7	41	29	26

Number of Respondents: America, 297; Chinatown, 90; Taiwan, 335; Hong Kong, 362. Grade 3, 360; grade 5, 366; grade 7, 358.

At all grade levels the greatest autocentrism and the least heterocentrism occur in the area of role learning in the polity. Only in the area of school learning, however, is there a progressive increase in autocentrism from third to fifth to seventh grade. In both family and polity autocentrism increases to fifth grade but decreases by seventh grade. This is a complex phenomenon and varies according to group. Generally we have hypothesized that this decline in autocentrism by seventh grade is related to anxieties associated with the onset of adolescence, to lack of full commitment to secondary-level membership, and to cognitive changes in moral growth away from strict conventional morality and toward a greater understanding of reciprocity and interdependency in relationships. These assumptions must remain tentative, however, since, evidence from the school learning environment indicates no such decline in autocentrism from fifth to seventh grade.

Among groups Taiwan is the highest in autocentrism in all categories. The Hong Kong group is the highest in heterocentrism in the family and the polity while the America group is highest in heterocentrism in the school. The America sample is the only one in which overall the responses for autocentrism in the school are lower than for the family. The Taiwan group is the only one in which autocentrism in the school is higher than for the family or polity. The highest degree of difference among groups is found for school learning, with Taiwan clearly the highest in autocentrism followed by Hong Kong, Chinatown, and America. We believe that these prominent differences in the various learning areas are related to the explicit use of shaming in school education in Taiwan and Hong Kong, to morals training in Chinese schools, to the relative importance of autonomous peer groups in American society and especially in American schools, and to the inability of children in Chinese societies (particularly Hong Kong and Chinatown) to maintain a firm sense of identity and commitment to secondary-level membership. The patterns themselves can be more clearly perceived if the variations between family, school, and polity are set forth for each group by grade level (Graph 40).

Third-grade children in American society are apparently lower in autocentrism in all areas than are Chinese Americans or children from Taiwan and Hong Kong. We believe the reason for this is that family and school education in the United States is less specific about behavioral codes and less prone to the use of open and consistent shaming when ideals of behavior are violated. In the areas of school and polity American children show a slight increase in autocentrism with age. In Chinatown and in Taiwan and Hong Kong there is a higher level of autocentrism in third grade than in American society and a higher degree of fluctuation in autocentrism with age. For Chinatown children, there is a general decrease in autocentrism in all areas until by seventh grade the levels of autocentrism (and heterocentrism) are very close to those that exist in the rest of American society. For the children in Taiwan and Hong Kong there is a "bow" effect, with autocentrism most marked in fifth grade and then declining in the areas of the family and polity by seventh grade. This decline may reflect, as we have said, the development of greater perceptivity concerning the desirability or not of

AMERICA
(297 RESPONDENTS)

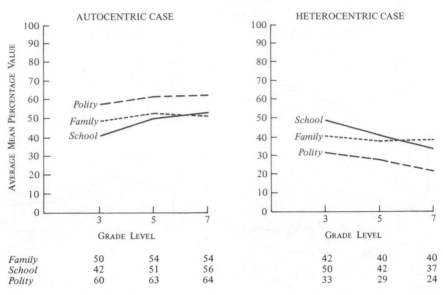

	AUTOCENTRIC CASE				HETEROCENTRIC CASE		
Family	50	54	54		42	40	40
School	42	51	56		50	42	37
Polity	60	63	64		33	29	24

CHINATOWN
(90 RESPONDENTS)

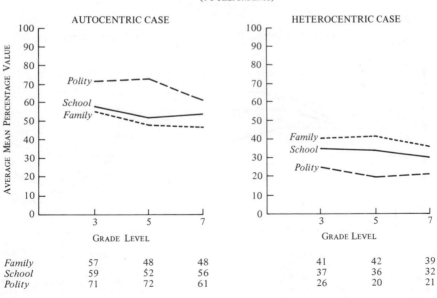

	AUTOCENTRIC CASE				HETEROCENTRIC CASE		
Family	57	48	48		41	42	39
School	59	52	56		37	36	32
Polity	71	72	61		26	20	21

GRAPH 40 *Continued*

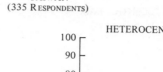

TAIWAN
(335 RESPONDENTS)

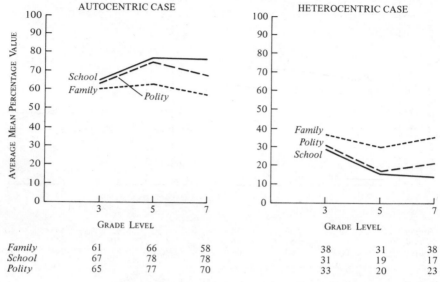

	AUTOCENTRIC CASE			HETEROCENTRIC CASE		
Family	61	66	58	38	31	38
School	67	78	78	31	19	17
Polity	65	77	70	33	20	23

HONG KONG
(362 RESPONDENTS)

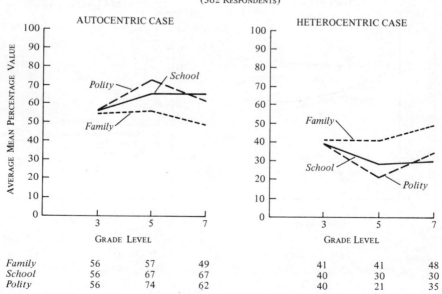

	AUTOCENTRIC CASE			HETEROCENTRIC CASE		
Family	56	57	49	41	41	48
School	56	67	67	40	30	30
Polity	56	74	62	40	21	35

applying rigid moral codes and, especially for the children in Hong Kong, a partial failure to develop a secondary-level group identity that would make the learning of autocentric behavioral codes salient. Taiwan is generally higher in autocentrism, is the only group for which autocentrism is highest in the schools. It is also in Taiwan that morals training in the schools is most explicit.

Within the family autocentrism for the American group increases slightly with age, but for the children in the other three groups family-related autocentrism shows a decline by seventh grade. For the Taiwan and Hong Kong children there is an increase in family-related hetero-centrism with age. This is especially marked for the children from Hong Kong. There is an apparent decline in the importance of the home for American children and a shift to the peer group of many of the affective patterns that in Chinese groups remain largely in the family. Within the home, in Taiwan, Hong Kong, and Chinatown mothers are particularly able to manipulate affect in such a way that shaming becomes an increasingly powerful molder of behavior. The salience of the family—especially in Hong Kong—and the use of shaming in both its negative and positive modes combine to make an awareness of interpersonal interactions increasingly important.

Clearly one of the more interesting aspects of our findings is that nowhere do they point to the Chinese father-child relationship as central in the learning process. Strong pressures for conformism, either to specific primary-group role demands or to universal standards of conduct, appear to have their origin in the affective nexus between the child and its mother and in the subsequent capability of educators, one of whom in a broad sense is the father, to utilize the anxieties from this relationship to obtain conformity and adherence to desired standards of behavior. Obtaining and holding the approval of others by correct performance is very early related to the threat of loss of nurturance in such a way that deviance is anxiety-provoking. Authority figures—including fathers—are generally expected to be sufficiently good models that correct behavior is clearly differentiated from deviant behavior. It is the affect within the mother–child relationship, however, that sets the stage for strong motivation to adhere to "appropriate" behavioral patterns.

In the school context only the America group shows a clear progression in the development of autocentrism with age. For the China-town children there is a slight decrease with age and for the children from

Taiwan and Hong Kong an increase in autocentrism to a high level by fifth grade followed by relative stability. The Hong Kong and especially the Taiwan children show marked degrees of autocentrism within the school learning context. We believe this prominence of school-related autocentrism is related to the greater stress on morals training in schools in Taiwan and Hong Kong. There also appears to be a relationship between high autocentrism in the school and the explicit use of shaming for the violation of codes that are expected to be learned and acted upon without prompting. This shaming, however, may lead to a heightened concern about punishment by particular others and about the expression of hostility.

Studies of spatial perceptivity with regard to leadership position and closeness or looseness of group membership (chapter 3) indicate that children in Taiwan and, to a lesser degree, in Hong Kong perceive leadership as being within the group. This is less the case for the America and Chinatown groups, who are more apt to perceive leadership as outside the group context. Children in Hong Kong, Taiwan, and Chinatown are also more prone than the America children to perceive ideal group relationships as close. These patterns emphasize the importance of group relations for Chinese children and make clearer why group sanctions involving shaming are powerful motivators of behavior in their social contexts.

For the Hong Kong and Taiwan children it is the group as an inclusive unit, with leadership within, with which one identifies and toward which one conforms. The concept of "leadership within" implies a leader-follower relationship in which the leader is able to influence members along internal lines of control. This is quite different from situations of "leadership without," in which the group as a whole—which may of course have its own informal leaders—deals as an entity with (outside) leadership. In such a case the group, through the force of its own internal codes and sanctions, buffers the sanctions and codes of the leadership. This type of corporate relationship to authority is to some extent a characteristic of American peer groups in their relations with adult authority. Such groupings provide affective and normative alternatives to both the family and the school in a way unknown in either Hong Kong or Taiwan. For American children, where the process is most pronounced, the peer groups that form among schoolmates are subsocial units within the larger school context. We believe that the influence of peer groups offers a very plausible explanation for why children from New Jersey, unlike those from Chinatown, Hong Kong, or Taiwan, are in third and fifth grade more heterocentric in the schools than in any other area. In fact, while Americans may seem community-minded, patriotic, and strong adherents of social harmony and together-ness in comparison to other Western societies, these attributes must be seen as only relative in comparison to children from other cultural contexts.[1]

Children generally exhibit high degrees of autocentrism with regard to behavior at the level of the polity. This is especially the case, relative to the family or the school, for the Chinatown and America groups. For the Taiwan group at all grade levels and for the Hong Kong children by grade 7 autocentrism as related to citizen behavior is lower than for school behavior. Unlike the America group, where autocentrism with regard to the polity shows a slight but steady increase with age, the pattern for the other three groups shows an increase to fifth grade—this is especially marked for Taiwan and Hong Kong—followed by a pronounced decrease in seventh grade. By grade 7 only Taiwan is larger in autocentrism with regard to the polity than is America, although the differences among all the groups are not large. The relatively lower auto-centrism of Americans in earlier years may well be related to the effec-tiveness of peer groups or of other subnational identifications in inhibiting the development of an unambiguous sense of secondary-level membership and a sense of the importance of that membership. Instead role relationships tend to be personalized at both the primary and secon-dary levels. In Chinatown, Hong Kong, and Taiwan there is explicit stress on secondary-level behavioral codes. However, in all three of these groups the family, to some extent, remains an effective challenger to unambiguous identity and sense of membership in a larger grouping. We believe that this challenge is least effective in modern Taiwan, due to the intensity of the educational system, and most effective in Hong Kong and Chinatown, where identity and sense of membership and its im-portance at the secondary level are blocked, despite the educational system, by conflicts relating to either minority status in Chinatown or colonial status in Hong Kong.

It is especially worthy of mention that America is the only group in

[1] Joseph Adelson, "The Political Imagination of the Young Adolescent," *Daedalus*, vol. 100, no. 4, Fall 1971, pp. 1046–1049.

which the levels of autocentrism increase overall with age for family, school, and polity. This is a general pattern that would be of considerable significance if continued through adolescence. On the other hand, Chinatown is the only group that shows a decrease in autocentrism with age in all three learning areas. The children in Taiwan and Hong Kong decrease overall in family-related autocentrism but increase with age (from third to seventh grade, but with fifth grade the highest) in school- and polity-related autocentrism. Despite their dissimilar patterns the Chinatown and America samples are relatively close in all categories, by seventh grade, the Taiwan group is the highest in autocentrism by seventh grade in all categories, and the Hong Kong group by seventh grade is similar to America and Chinatown in the areas of the family and polity but intermediate between these two groups and Taiwan in the area of school-related autocentrism. It is interesting to note that despite the absolute differences in mean percentage values the Chinatown, Hong Kong, and Taiwan children—but not the America children—show overall a decrease in autocentrism and increase in heterocentrism with age with regard to the family. With differences, depending on social location and on the political and educational system, it is clear that primary groups continue to exert an influence in Chinese society in very special and interesting ways.

The notion of the development of internalized moral codes that act, as one metaphor puts it, like a gyroscope setting the individual on course regardless of the situation, clearly needs qualification in terms of the groups analyzed in this study. It is true that children in all four samples taken together are generally autocentric in attitude disposition and that this autocentrism clearly increases overall with age to approximately age ten or eleven. However, there are important variations in areas of learning and among groups concerning these changes, with at least one group, Chinatown, failing generally to follow this pattern. In looking at groups separately, one of the patterns that emerges at the seventh-grade level is the higher degree of "don't know" responses indicated for the America and Chinatown groups than for the Taiwan and Hong Kong children (the "don't know" for a given group in the area of family, school, or polity at a given grade level can be obtained by adding the mean percentage values for autocentrism and heterocentrism and subtracting the result from 100). We believe that these "don't know" responses for the two American samples reflect an ambiguity concerning the values involved in a given situation and may be indicative of the *type* of moral reasoning being employed by some of the children. Kohlberg and Gilligan have noted how at age 13 (about seventh grade) an awareness of the relativism of personal values and opinions characterizes about ten percent of a given sample in the United States but less than five percent of a Taiwanese sample. At the same time, on Taiwan there is a strikingly large percentage of children at age thirteen who are concerned with conformity to stereotypical images of what is conceived to be majority or right behavior. In America, these scholars assert, there is a continuing development after age thirteen of notions of moral relativism, while on Taiwan conformity to stereotypical images remains relatively constant and is augmented by the development of notions of dutiful performance and respect for authority.[2]

These different conceptions of morality suggest that autocentrism may be qualitatively different in American and Chinese societies. That is, while in both cases behavior may be without reference to particular authorities American children may well show a continuing increase in autocentrism based on conceptions of relativity of morality, whereas Chinese samples may indicate a relative leveling off of autocentrism by age 12 with a greater emphasis on the importance of adhering to certain defined rules, although with some slight shifts with age. These differences appear, in our opinion, to be related to the intensity of conventional morals training in Taiwanese schools and to the influence in American society of peer groups, in which competing moral standards may be tested and evaluated in an atmosphere somewhat free of adult authority.

In Hong Kong and Taiwan adult behavioral standards receive no real competition from an effective independent peer culture, although there are signs that such a culture is developing. In America, on the other hand, an independent peer culture is a major aspect of childhood socialization, accepted as normal by most families and schools (most parents and teachers having experienced the phenomenon themselves). In the case of Chinatown this peer culture, if not totally accepted, effectively competes with socialization by adults within the family. In contrast, explicitly in Taiwan and more implicitly in Hong Kong there is an effort to make family and school patterns of behavior congruent and relatively exclusive. Patterns such as "respect for authority" that

2 Lawrence Kohlberg and Carol Gilligan, "The Adolescent as a Philosopher: The Discovery of the Self in a Postconventional World," *ibid.*, pp. 1066–1071.

have a particularistic reference within the family are stressed as the ideal pattern for all social relations. On Taiwan, where there is little room for individual exploratory development, great effort has been expended in the school system to make secondary-level attitude and behavioral patterns the model for all relationships. In order for this to be accomplished, however, there must be a sense of membership at the secondary level and a feeling that the patterns applicable to that level should be and are worth being adhered to. If this is not done, then particularistic criteria derived from the more dominant sense of primary-group membership will tend to intrude.

On Taiwan there is evidence that a firm focus of loyalty at the secondary level based on a sense of Chinese nationhood has been achieved, even if this focus is challenged. In Hong Kong this focus has not been obtained. There may be similarities among systems in training styles and techniques, though, regardless of the relative degree to which they have succeeded in changing focuses of loyalty. This point is a crucial one, for in both Taiwan and Hong Kong one notes techniques of training that are particularly likely to bring group pressure to bear upon the individual and make formal and stereotypical conformity to demands operative; conformity, however, can be directed toward the fulfillment of different demands. Where loyalty to secondary-level membership has been achieved, as in Taiwan, there may be a relatively rigid application of universalistic criteria in all relationships; where this shift in focus has not been made (as in Hong Kong) there may exist a relatively greater pressure for conformity to particularistic demands.

Many of our arguments are admittedly hypothetical. If the reasoning we have employed is persuasive, however, then a virtually inescapable conclusion is that the modern school is of critical importance in the socialization process. It not only teaches the skills necessary for fulfilling roles in a modern society but also, and equally important, reinforces types of attitude dispositions, sets patterns for relations with secondary-level authorities, and helps mold, under appropriate conditions, firm senses of commitment and identity at various levels of social existence.

PART IV CONCLUSION

CHAPTER **6** Concluding

Comments

Much of the data that might be summarized here has been presented earlier in section summaries and chapter conclusions. We will not try to duplicate this information, but will instead attempt to assess the validity of some of our assumptions, highlight areas of special significance, and speculate in broad terms concerning some of the patterns and problems presented in this work. In meeting these objectives we will confine ourselves to brief comments in two areas. These are the relationship between shame and socialization and the relationship between role learning and the acquisition of attitude orientations. Some additional comments concerning the implications of our findings for the groups studied will also be presented. These remarks will touch on the relationship between autocentrism and heterocentrism and the ways in which authority is legitimized in periods of changing social patterns and values.

In considering the relationship between shame and socialization, we posited that guilt versus shame was a false dichotomy, in that guilt anxiety concerning transgression was actually a subcategory of a broader and ubiquitous shame anxiety concerning abandonment. We pointed out that earlier studies differentiating social systems on the basis of guilt or shame foundered on a host of contradictions, the most notable being the conception of internalized sanctions as predominant in "guilt" cultures and external sanctions as predominant in "shame" cultures. Instead we noted, empirical evidence suggests that internalized and external sanctions can coexist with varying levels of intensity in all social systems, and that the essential distinction was not one between guilt and shame but rather related to the ways in which role learning and socialization practices interact in terms of a ubiquital shame anxiety to produce different attitude and behavioral outcomes. We noted that shame anxiety as a factor in socialization could be intensified by certain socialization practices, and that this intensification would heighten the tension involved in learning in such a way that certain "approved" patterns of thought and behavior would become intensely acquired and deviation would be highly anxiety-provoking. We assumed that shame anxiety would be aroused and be motivating in the learning process either by the threat of external "social" sanctions or because the individual has learned a set of ideals of behavior that serve as a standard against which actual behavior can be measured. In the latter case, failure to approximate these ideals would be anxiety-provoking regardless of the existence or nonexistence of external sanctions. We further assumed that these two sources of shame anxiety were not mutually exclusive but could exist simultaneously with differential levels of salience in different social systems and also at different stages of the socialization process. In asserting the importance of shaming in socialization, we have not made the assumption that this conception explains all of the variance in the learning process. Quite clearly we have made only a start, and more refined conceptual and methodological tools are needed.

We have posited the learning of social attitude orientations concerning behavior that would have an affective valence (positive or negative) and that would increase in complexity with cognitive development. We posited that strongly operative positive attitude orientations would exist to the degree that role training inculcated a sense that behavior in terms of these attitudes is desirable and necessary. We further assumed that there is a relationship between behavioral conformity to ideal internalized standards and the style and content of socialization. This relationship depends on the degree of congruence in role learning at various social levels, the extent of inclusiveness of the socialization process (the freedom of the individual to experiment with alternate role behaviors), the capacity of the socialization process to arouse motivating anxiety (based on patterns of reinforcement and punishment involving levels of affective display, love withdrawal, and induction training), the importance given in socialization to ideal

standards as guides for behavior, and the explicitness with [
standards are made known.

We defined heterocentric attitude orientations as those in which
particular others are cited as the authority for behavior and autocentric
attitude orientations as those in which particular others are not so cited.
These orientations were studied for third,- fifth-, and seventh-grade
children in Taiwan, Hong Kong, Chinatown (New York City), and
New Jersey in terms of their congruence with value types (universalism
and particularism) and their relationship to punishment, hostility,
opposition to authority, conformity, and reciprocity behavior. We also
studied the distribution of attitude orientations in terms of role learning
in the primary group (family), secondary group learning environment
(school), and larger secondary group (polity).

Overall most children tended to be autocentric in their attitudes
toward behavior. As expected, this autocentrism tended to increase with
cognitive development (i.e., with age), and to be more characteristic of
role behavior at secondary than at primary levels. Both of these groups
and age levels, however, showed some significant differences in rates and
levels of acquisition of learned ideals. In many cases these dissimilar
results appeared to be related to differing styles and content of
socialization, in regard to which differential arousal of shame anxiety is
an important aspect. Our findings also lent support to our contention
that shame anxiety can operate in socialization both where behavior is
oriented to external sanctions—as is often the case in primary groups
—and where behavior is regulated by adherence to learned standards, as
frequently occurs in secondary-level groups.

Of the four groups investigated in this study, the children from
Taiwan were generally the most autocentric in attitude orientation.
It is our belief that this degree of orientation is due to the operation of
several socialization influences, of which the most important are the
shame-arousing punishments used in both primary- and secondary-level
role-learning situations, intensive induction training, explicit emphasis
on moral codes, and heavy emphasis on loyalty to secondary-level
group membership. One or more of these factors was less emphasized in
the learning environment of the other groups, resulting, we believe, in
lower levels of autocentrism for them. Shame-arousing punishments,
for instance, are approximately equally emphasized in Taiwan and
Hong Kong, but training in Hong Kong puts less emphasis on explicit

morals training and secondary-level group membership. Certain patterns, such as conformism and weak opposition to authority, characterize both the Taiwan and Hong Kong groups, but the children on Taiwan are more apt to legitimize behavior by reference to universalistic criteria than are children from Hong Kong. American children, who overall are relatively lower in autocentrism, are exposed to lower levels of explicit morals training than children in Hong Kong and Taiwan, and in school experience less frequent shame-arousing punishments. Induction training for American children is frequently an informal aspect of peer-group relationships, whereas in Taiwan induction training in the school, and to a lesser extent in the home, is heavily stressed and is associated with the more formal learning of moral injunctions.

In our samples we found an increase in autocentrism and a decrease in heterocentrism from third to fifth grade and a very slight retrogression of this pattern to seventh grade. In effect, by ages ten to eleven (fifth grade) cognitive development appears to have progressed to the point where formal moral learning is virtually complete. Among the four groups in this study, however, there were considerable differences in intensity of moral development depending upon the particular behavioral area considered. Group differences in levels of autocentrism were most marked in the area of reciprocity and were least marked in the area of opposition to authority. In the areas of hostility, conformity, and reciprocity, children in Taiwan invoke universalistic values to a greater degree than do children from Hong Kong, Chinatown, or New Jersey. It is in the area of opposition to authority that all children show the greatest propensity for citing others as the authority for behavior, although this propensity decreases markedly with age for the American children. Opposition is evidently seen as sufficiently serious that it cannot or should not take place unless some alternate authority figure sanctions this behavior. Invoking universalistic criteria is not sufficient, for "loyalty" itself is considered a prime virtue, the violation of which under normal circumstances is justification for punitive action by authority figures.

There is some evidence from Solomon that the acquisition of power is seen as desirable by many Chinese, partly, no doubt, to reduce the anxiety of being in a relatively powerless position.[1] This same anxiety

---

[1] Richard H. Solomon, "Mao's Effort to Reintegrate the Chinese Polity: Problems of Authority and Conflict in Chinese Social Processes," in A. Doak Barnett, ed., *Chinese Communist Politics in Action*, University of Washington Press, Seattle, 1969, p. 360.

appears to lie at the root of the need to legitimize both reciprocity behavior and the expression of hostility by reference to formal moral precepts. It is our belief that patterns of Chinese group behavior involving hierarchic interrelations stress "moral" behavior as the best way to reduce anxiety, and that this stress gives Chinese moral learning its heavily formalistic flavor. For anxiety to be minimized behavior must be referred to values that are explicit in content and closed in terms of alternatives. For Americans, on the other hand, moral learning for many individuals becomes highly tinged with the notion of relativity, especially in the area of reciprocity. Behavior reflects attitudes that are frequently implicit in value content and open in terms of alternatives. This is perhaps related to the high need for affiliation that characterizes Americans. Likableness and friendliness are seen as desirable values in group activity (rather than unity and discipline, which are given as group goals by many Chinese children). In order to behave in accordance with ideal standards that place a premium on good intention, flexibility in accordance with situational factors is required and behavioral values emphasize relativity of intent. There is pressure to prevent social ruptures from being defined in "moral" terms and to keep cleavages at a personal or policy-oriented level for the sake of larger-group stability. Yet precisely because affiliation is stressed and overall conformity to an unambiguous and inclusive set of precepts is minimized, there may be distrust where affiliation is seen as lacking. We believe that it is differing socialization practices, stressing either formality or relativity of intent, that influence the quality (and the amount) of "moral" development, rather than a strict defined set of invariant stages with attendant levels of development.

Socialization in Taiwan and Hong Kong, with its stress on obedience and group unity, makes deviation from group norms especially anxiety-provoking. Unity, cooperative behavior, and achievement for the group are highly valued, whereas the gratuitous expression of non-sanctioned hostility is increasingly subject to shaming punishments. In previous work we have discussed some of the behavioral consequences that result from the development of an inflexible and exclusive code of secondary-level moral attributes.[2] It is not our intention to reproduce those findings here, but it is germane to note that cynicism with regard

2 Richard W. Wilson, *Learning to be Chinese: The Political Socialization of Children in Taiwan*, Massachusetts Institute of Technology Press, Cambridge, Mass., 1970, pp. 99-136.

to ingroup behavior and highly focused hostility with regard to selected outgroups (either within or outside the society) are two possible outcomes. In some cases anxiety about how well one has adhered to group norms appears to be reduced by projecting self-punitiveness against others, especially those who are deemed to be "morally" impure and to embody negative identity components. It is entirely possible that in societies like Taiwan there is too much rigidity with regard to values and behavior, although we might equally well assert that American society is characterized by too great fluidity, a lack of selflessness in terms of secondary-level group needs, and an inordinate amount of overt interpersonal hostility. In either case we must be critically aware of the level of group membership of which we are speaking and of the individual's commitment to membership at that level.

In social systems where membership in secondary-level groups is highly emphasized for large segments of children during socialization, the attitudes relating to authority relations may show a progressive shift from an emphasis on particularistic criteria to an emphasis on universalistic criteria. We have assumed that this shift is related to age changes in cognitive capacity combined with the learning of secondary roles and the fostering of a commitment to the performance of those roles. Secondary-role learning in turn may be characterized by particular styles, so that attitude orientations may be especially intense in areas such as reciprocity or the expression of hostility.

In modernizing societies, schools, where secondary-level role learning takes place, are extremely important in the learning process. Educational authorities are frequently charged with the task of ensuring that traditional family or clan-directed loyalties are minimized in favor of commitment to higher levels of social organization. Yet regardless of political ideology, universalistic values are likely to become components of behavioral attitude dispositions to the extent that they are developments from initially particularistic orientations. In other words, an orientation such as "respect," which at the level of secondary learning may be learned as applicable to others generally, is strengthened by its relationship to an initial sense of respect directed toward specific individuals such as the mother or father. Universalistic values that develop from highly articulated family codes and taboos are strengthened by their reinforcement in a variety of learning areas. These values, however, may also be invested with high degrees of affectivity, making deviance highly anxiety-provoking and a stress on moral purity highly imperative.

Scholarship on historical family patterns indicates a relatively uniform traditional pattern of female and childhood subservience to dominate adult males. This pattern of hierarchy, however, existed within a primary-group context in which the nuclear family was by no means the sole source of emotional satisfaction. These patterns have widely changed in the direction of greater equality for family members and a conception of the nuclear family as a prime source of emotional nurturance. In part, at least, these changes have paralleled a more general process of "modernization," in which decisive breaks have occurred in traditional authority patterns in the realms of religion, economics, and politics at the same time that new forces of production were coming into being. In a very real sense, modernization is the breakdown of primary-group and primary group–type loyalties in favor of the development of a new type of loyalty commitment to higher levels of social group membership.

For many people the very concept of socialization implies consensus and conservatism. Yet in the last two hundred years consensus in many societies has never been less apparent and social change never more rapid. Clearly one of the reasons for lack of consensus has been the difference in attitudinal dispositions of individuals trained in modern schools as compared with those who have not been. A factor abetting rapid social change has been the effectiveness of the school system in training individuals to new loyalties and membership patterns. In this sense socialization is at the heart of the revolutionary process, and the modern school, where new attitudes, conceptions, and beliefs are acquired, has become the critical learning area. To a great extent this process is largely completed by about age thirteen, when levels of development are sufficiently advanced for a basic understanding of role conceptions to have been acquired. One special function of the school is to provide an encompassing framework of attitudes (one aspect of which is sometimes referred to as "nationalism") that can serve to integrate and legitimize behavior at all levels of group activity. The child is taught that patterns which apply at the highest levels of group membership legitimize the performance of similar behavior at lower levels, and that indeed such behavior is required if loyalty to the group at the secondary level is to be fulfilled.

Relative *explicitness* about the values associated with secondary-level role behavior is a fundamental feature of a modernizing school system. The saliency of "morals" education in certain "transitional" social systems derives in part from the perception by leaders of differential patterns of loyalty within the society, differences that are not nearly as noticeable (nor as emphasized by educational authorities) in largely "traditional" or largely "modernized" systems, where value consensus is more assumed and where strong primary-group loyalties are not seen as threatening. The school's impact, however, lies not merely in its capacity to impart content but also in its capacity to structure the learning environment in such a way that affective and intellectual valences are progressively narrowed to prescribed ends.

Morals training was an aspect of formal learning that permeated Chinese schools in traditional times. This training frequently presented morals in a highly particularistic context, though with sufficient tinges of universalism as to give some aspects of traditional Chinese life (such as the operation of the bureaucracy) a markedly modern cast. The necessity for learning morals is a deeply ingrained aspect of the Chinese educational tradition, and while the content and emphasis have changed in modern times, educators remain firmly in a tradition in which "Man pays special attention to morality and virtue which are the criteria which differentiate human nature from barbarous nature."[3] Schram has noted how the nineteenth-century Chinese hero Tseng Kuo-fan and the modern hero Mao Tse-tung both share a similarity in that both believe that "practical activity must be penetrated from beginning to end with moral values."[4]

The application of abstract ideas to behavior is more characteristic of behavior in the school environment or the polity than in the family. Universal values are apparently acquired with special reference to secondary-level role learning and behavior. This is especially true of Taiwan, an intensely modernizing society. There the acquisition of autocentric attitudes is noticeably higher than in Hong Kong, Chinatown, or New Jersey. Significantly, autocentrism for the Taiwan children is highest among all groups for behavior in the school learning environment itself.

[3] Lin Chi-sha, ed., *Cultivation and Service of Youth* (*Ch'ing-nien Hsiu-yang yu Fu-wu*), Tai Fong Publishing Society, Hong Kong, 1967, p. 17.
[4] Stuart R. Schram. *Thought of Mao Tse-tung*, Praeger, New York, 1963, p. 84.

In one sense the distinctions among our samples in the patterns for autocentrism and heterocentrism are reminiscent of Riesman's distions between inner-directedness and other-directedness. Moralizing, as Riesman noted, is "a virtually uniform political style for the inner-directed."[5] If American children are compared against children in Taiwan, there would seem to be a correspondence between high autocentrism and inner-directedness in Taiwan and lower autocentrism and other-directedness in America. The distinction appears particularly compelling in light of the friendliness and likableness in others that American children desire in group relations as against the emphasis on competence and efficiency in the Taiwanese children's remarks.

Riesman's typology does appear to have a certain utility. In the breakdown of the traditional pattern of primary-group commitment the secondary level is exalted, but with increasing economic growth and urbanization an undifferentiated commitment to the secondary level may itself be questioned in favor of the individual himself. Such a shift requires extensive economic growth, widely shared values, and a highly institutionalized distributive economy in which individual well-being is less strongly dependent on political authority. Role models in such a case are likely to be peer models, sanctioned by peer-specific values relatively unrelated to economic or political power but closely associated with social power. This would be the case for other-directeds. On the other hand, where commitment to secondary-level membership is heavily and unambiguously emphasized, models are likely to be representative of the goals and aspirations of the group at that level and to be closely associated with economic, political, and/or military success. Idols of production or politico-military leaders will be preeminent. This would be the case for inner-directeds.

One of the major problems of using the concepts of inner- and other- directedness is their relationship to a stage sequence in modernization. It is entirely possible, in fact, that Chinese society may always have had large components of inner-directedness, and in like manner American society may well have been characterized historically by large components of other-directedness. Viewed on a single-society basis there appears to be some validity to the hypothesis of movement during modernization from inner- to other-directedness, but viewed com-

[5] David Riesman, *The Lonely Crowd*, Yale University Press, New Haven, 1950, p. 191.

paratively among societies this distinction is blurred by the very different levels of inner-or other-directedness at comparable stages of growth.

In both Hong Kong and Taiwan there is a mix of the traditional and the modern, most obvious to the observer in terms of generational differences. Despite the fact that certain institutions such as the family are undergoing a diminution of importance as a focus of loyalty for the individual, there still remains in many areas a remarkable "traditionalism" in style, albeit shifted to new dimensions. It is this factor that makes socialization practices in Taiwan and Hong Kong appear highly similar in many respects, despite the very different outcomes we have noted with regard to social behavior. A concern for authority within a well-defined hierarchy, for clear-cut ideological guides, and for group cohesion are noticeable in both places, but with different social implications.

While vastly different in many respects, the People's Republic of China and Taiwan share certain similarities in socialization that lead us to speculate that the patterns of autocentrism and heterocentrism in these two systems might well be more congruent with each other than either would be with the less intensely "morals"-oriented and less secondary-level–oriented socialization in Hong Kong. John Lewis has described some facets of social transformation in the People's Republic that in a different ideological context could easily be applicable to Taiwan. There has been, he notes, an emphasis on expansion of social horizons, in which the attempt is made to create a sense of a nationwide collectivity demanding new relationship patterns. Traditional loyalties and obligations are being transformed from personal and particularistic ones to common loyalties and obligations deriving from a new identity as one of "the people."[6] For both Taiwan and the People's Republic, however, this shift in commitment patterns continues to stress the traditional virtues of loyalty, cohesion, discipline, and unity.

It is noteworthy that the children from Taiwan, Hong Kong, Chinatown (New York City), and New Jersey tend to vary in the same direction with regard to autocentrism and heterocentrism. Within this shared tendency, however, there were significant distinctions, which, while they tend to be ones of degree rather than kind, result in very significant variations in total group behavior. We believe our findings point both to the complexity of understanding the bases of aggregate

[6] John Wilson Lewis, *Leadership in Communist China*, Cornell University Press, Ithaca, New York, 1963, p. 253.

social behavior and to the error of believing that the bases of significant social differences must be essentially bipolar in nature. This caveat is especially true with respect to the vast literature on modernization. As our work has we hope, indicated, such concepts as universalism and particularism cannot be uncritically applied as measurements of "modernization." There may be considerable variation in respect of these concepts among societies that appear similar in other respects and among social levels within a given society.

In the Introduction we raised the question of whether there is a uniform Chinese political culture. The answer, for this period of rapid social change, seems clear: rather large differences exist among several Chinese societies. At the least our findings suggest that a warning flag should be raised for any who might still see Chinese society as uniform and homogeneous and who would base analyses of China on such an assumption. In terms of our criteria, children on Taiwan are very different from those who live in Hong Kong or in Chinatown. Indeed, with respect to the latter a good argument can be made that although Chinese Americans by adolescence show differences from Caucasian or Negro Americans, these are far smaller and less significant than the differences between children in Chinatown and those on Taiwan.

Yet one cannot simply dismiss all similarity among Chinese groups, even when their educational and social experiences are radically different. There is, for instance, still a relative uniformity in primary-group interaction, especially with regard to the use of induction training combined with love withdrawal and the early attachment of moral precepts to interpersonal obligations. There is also a general tendency in socialization to stress the value of imitative learning, with particular emphasis on models. Clearly these early and relatively similar experiences are modified by class position, by sex, and by different school systems, whose goals may differ and whose training styles may vary in terms of congruence with primary-group socialization practices. Despite the effect of such variable influences, however, we may well find children in very disparate Chinese societies exhibiting similar tendencies regarding the expression of hostility or the inclusiveness of groups and the positions of leaders within these groups.

It may be true that political socialization is largely completed by age thirteen to fourteen, but at least one critical development still remains. It has been noted that in American society support for authority and social institutions, particularly the police, shows a dip in late adolescence and young adulthood.[7] This is a complex and as yet imperfectly understood phenomenon, but it appears to be related to the development of a critical capacity with regard to social institutions and their leaders. In our own data we noted a downturning of auto-centrism with age in the area of secondary-level behavior (the polity) for children in Taiwan, Hong Kong, and Chinatown. For the first two groups this downturn occurred after sharp rises to fifth grade (approximately ages ten to eleven). Without further data we can only speculate on the reasons for this, but it seems at least plausible that in the polity area, where personal control of events is largely absent, increased understanding with age reveals a gap between the rigid moral standards learned and the actual, perceived behavior of individuals in secondary-level roles. The result, we feel, may be the development of an attitude of cynicism, in which affective support is withdrawn from the secondary level and a greater emphasis is placed upon particularistic loyalties and relationships. Perhaps in any rapidly modernizing society, where loyalty to secondary-level membership has not been uniformly acquired, there will be a tendency for some forms of hostility or withdrawal to occur. There is no predetermined way in which individuals will respond to the perception of a gap between the actual behavior of others and learned values regarding behavior. The response may be the development of an awareness of relativity of intent that allows for individual flexibility, or it may be an increased drive for moral awareness and purity in the society as a whole.

[7] David Easton and Jack Dennis, *Children in the Political System: Origins of Political Legitimacy*, McGraw-Hill Book Co., New York, 1969, pp. 297–303.

Appendix

Material for this study was essentially obtained in four ways:
(1) primary and secondary written sources; (2) interviews; (3) observation; and (4) questionnaires. As the primary and secondary sources in both Chinese and English have been noted in footnotes and in the bibliography, no further reference to this data will be made. It should, however, be pointed out that considerable effort was expended in Taiwan, Hong Kong, New York City, and New Jersey in obtaining a cross section of literature relevant to this study.

For each of the four groups studied, every effort was made to obtain as random a sample as possible within the constraint that the children should come from the most modernized geographical areas within their societies. Schools selected for testing were those in which, according to information supplied by educational authorities, the children were approximately matched in terms of socioeconomic criteria and sex distribution. By and large the children were from lower-middle-class backgrounds. The exceptions to this were the children from Princeton, New Jersey who came from middle-class backgrounds but who were included as representative of the most advanced sectors of suburbia in the United States. Within the schools themselves, classroom selection was random.

The purpose of the study was to examine attitude distributions among several Chinese societies in order to ascertain which types of attitudes have greatest salience and what factors in the learning process are likely to influence attitude change. It was for this reason that Taiwan, Hong Kong, and Chinatown (New York City) were selected, as each is geographically separate from the others and has a different political structure. Obviously we would have liked to do work in the People's Republic of China, but this was impossible. The sample of Negro and Caucasian-American children from New Jersey was included in order that one non-Chinese sample could be utilized for comparative purposes. Testing was done for three different age levels in order that our theoretical notions concerning moral development could be tested for age changes. We were interested both in how attitude type generally changes with age and, more specifically, in how these changes occur within each group depending upon the learning area and upon the specific type of behavior in question.

In the analysis of questionnaire data we chose an analysis of variance technique in which tests were run for each question on the main effects of group, sex, and grade level and the interaction among these effects. For each question there were five responses in which there were two possible responses for each of two value or attitude categories (universalism/particularism or autocentrism/heterocentrism) plus a don't know response. In the statistical analysis the data for the two responses for each category was aggregated. For each question there was therefore a percentage distribution among two aggregated attitude or value categories plus a don't know/no response category. For each question both autocentrism and heterocentrism (or universalism and particularism) were tested separately in order to determine differences in attitude (or value) distribution for each of the main effects (that is, for each question what was the distribution of responses for each attitude—or value—category among groups, among grade levels, and between the sexes). The analysis of interaction effects tested whether there was an unusual variation among the effects. For instance, in testing the interaction between group and grade level for a given attitude category, if the age changes by group were relatively similar despite a significant difference among the groups themselves then no significant interaction effect would be reported.

Extensive pretesting was done and led to some important changes in both the structure and content of the questionnaires. In addition, the questionnaires, general methodology, and theoretical approach were set forth for criticism before a wide number of scholars.

Our techniques with regard to interviews, observation, and the questionnaires themselves are briefly set forth below.

A. INTERVIEWS

Sixty interviews of approximately one hour in length were conducted. These interviews were divided as follows: eighteen in Hong Kong, eighteen in Taiwan, eighteen in New Jersey, and six with Chinese–American children. The smallness of the number of Chinese–American interviewees was due to the great difficulty in obtaining respondents from this group. Generally the interview sample was divided equally among third, fifth, and seventh graders and was divided equally by sex at each grade level. Within the limits of these restrictions the further selection of interviewees was random. The interviews were conducted by myself for the two American groups and by research assistants in Hong Kong and Taiwan.

In each of the interviews the pictures from the pictorial questionnaire were used to structure the responses. The function of the pictures was to be suggestive rather than limiting. Where possible the autocentric/heterocentric questionnaire was also utilized and the interviewee asked to respond to a number of questions and then to elaborate on his response. Responses were recorded in writing.

A set number of interview questions were used, but the interviewer was allowed to probe for further information and to ask questions in associated areas if a given direction appeared promising. There was no set phraseology or order for the questions, which were as follows:

  a. Questions asked with regard to the father–scolding–son picture and the teacher–scolding–pupil question:
  1. Which is worse, suffering pain or being ashamed?
  2. Why does one feel ashamed in front of others?
  3. Can one feel ashamed alone? (Several examples would then be given.)
  4. Do you ever worry about gods or spirits punishing you? Which is worse—worrying about God punishing you or worrying about being punished in front of others?
  5. Do you worry about what your Mother, Father, or Teacher will think of you if you do something wrong?

      6. Do you get angry with the person who is punishing you?

  b. Questions asked with regard to the questioning-of-authority-during-a-meeting picture and the questioning-of-authority-after-a-meeting picture:

    1. Can you disagree with anyone if they do something wrong—Father, Mother, Teacher, the Principal, the Police, the Mayor, a Senator, etc.?

    2. Should you get angry when you disagree?

    3. Should you make a leader "lose face"?

    4. Are leaders supposed to set a good example for group members and can you openly disagree with them if they don't? For instance, your Grandfather, the Principal, etc. If you believe you can disagree, give an example.

  c. Questions asked with regard to the similarly dressed–group picture and the variedly dressed–group picture:

    1. What is a good group?

    2. In a group is the most important thing for group members to have a good relationship? If not, what is the most important?

    3. Should leaders and followers have a good relationship? Why?

    4. Is it right for group members to go against what the group wants? Against what the leader feels the group should do? When would it be right?

B.   OBSERVATION

Systematic observation was made of the children in all four research areas on streets, in playgrounds and schoolrooms, etc. No observations were made directly within homes, but family interaction was observed in a variety of non-home settings. The major patterns observed concerned the quality and quantity of interpersonal interaction in terms of punishments and in terms of positive reinforcements of behavior. Observations were conducted by myself in all areas and with the additional help of research assistants in Taiwan and Hong Kong.

C.   QUESTIONNAIRES

Two types of questionnaires were administered. Both types were pre-tested in various formats with approximately two hundred children, divided equally between Princeton, New Jersey and Chinatown, New York City. Adjustments were made in the development of the final questionnaires based on the results of the pretests.

a. *Pictorial Questionnaire*

With this questionnaire three sets of two pictures each were used. The children were asked to select one picture from each set in response to a question relating to that set. They were also asked to write down the reasons for their selection. The answers were anonymous. Below are noted the three questions asked for each picture set.

1. *Set One:* Containing one picture showing an adult male with his hand raised above a male child and another picture showing a student standing in class with the teacher pointing at him. [See *Exhibit A* on page 151 and *Exhibit B* on page 152.]

    Question Asked: Here are two situations. In one of them a father or older brother is talking to his son or younger brother. Let us suppose it is the father. In the picture the father looks like he is scolding his son and might even be going to spank him. In the other picture it looks like a child may have done something wrong in the class. The teacher has asked the child to stand and is scolding him. Now, if you were in both of these pictures which way do you think would be the *worse* way to be punished? Mark down which punishment you feel is *worse* and write down your reason for this.

2. *Set Two:* Containing one picture showing people raising their hands during a meeting and one picture with two people talking to a speaker in an empty hall. [See *Exhibit C* on page 172 and *Exhibit D* on page 173.]

    Question Asked: Here is a speaker. In one picture it looks as if some people in the audience don't agree with him and are raising their hands to question him. In the other picture it appears that the audience has left but that two people who disagreed with the speaker have gone to the front of the auditorium to discuss their questions with him. If you were in the audience, which method do you think you would use if you disagreed with a speaker and if you had made up your mind that you would tell him. Mark down which method of disagreement you think is best and write down your reason for this. (The characters on the poster behind the speaker are purposely ambiguous in order not to define the situation and because these pictures were used with both Chinese and American groups.)

3. *Set Three:* Containing one picture with a group of people similarly dressed and one picture with a group of people in varied dress. [See *Exhibit E* on page 192 and *Exhibit F* on page 193.]

Question Asked: Here are two groups. Both of these groups have asked you to join them. You have decided that you would like to join a group but you can only join one. Which one of these groups would you join? Mark down which group you would like to join and write down your reason for this.

b. *Autocentric/Heterocentric Questionnaire*

A twenty-nine–item questionnaire was administered in classrooms in Taiwan, Hong Kong, Chinatown (New York City), and New Jersey. The children were asked to pick the one response for each question which they felt was most appropriate, and their responses were anonymous. Below is the English language version of this questionnaire. (The designations (U)–Universalistic, (P)–Particularistic, (A)–Autocentric, and (H)–Heterocentric were not included on the questionnaire given to the children.)

Please answer these questions about yourself:
Your age_____ Grade in School_____
Boy_____ or Girl_____
Where were you born? State_____Country_____
Where was your father born? State_____Country_____
What does your father do?_____
If you have brothers, how old are they?_____
If you have sisters, how old are they?_____
On the next few pages there are some questions. We want to know how you really feel about them. This is *not* a test. There are *no* right or wrong answers. Please answer every question the best you can.
A. The six questions below ask what *should* happen. Choose the answer that is closest to what you think *ought to* happen.
 1. Can the President do as he wishes or do you believe rules should be alike for everyone?
_____the President cannot do as he wishes (U)
_____rules should always be the same for everyone (U)
_____the President can do as he wishes (P)
_____rules are not always the same for everyone (P)
_____don't know

2. If a policeman catches his best friend speeding *in a school zone*, he should:

_____be angry with him this time but let him go (P)

_____ask another policeman to give him a ticket (U)

_____warn him that he shouldn't do this (P)

_____give him a ticket like everyone else (U)

_____don't know

3. A person should be selected as a leader of the country because:

_____he is very courageous (U)

_____he received very high grades in school (U)

_____his family is very powerful (P)

_____friends who are leaders want him to be one (P)

_____don't know

4. In choosing teams for a game, I should pick:

_____the best player (U)

_____someone I like (P)

_____someone who can play well (U)

_____my best friend (P)

_____don't know

5. When I do something well, I should feel pleased because:

_____it shows I have learned correctly (U)

_____my family will approve (P)

_____I have done the right thing (U)

_____my friends will like me better (P)

_____don't know

6. If you were a school monitor and you caught your brother running in the hall, should you:

_____ask him not to do this again (P)

_____report him to one of the teachers (U)

_____get angry but not report him (P)

_____ask one of the other monitors to report him (U)

_____don't know

B. The questions below ask about what will happen. In each of these questions check the answer closest to what *you* think the people in the question will *really do*.

7. When the President does something and asks the people to do it also, it is best that they:

_____disagree with him if they think he is wrong but do as he does (H)

_____do as he does because he is the President (H)

_____check to make sure it is a law (A)

_____see if it agrees with what they themselves think is right before doing it (A)

_____don't know.

8. If I want to do a good job in school, the most important thing for me to do is:

_____know the school rules (A)

_____pay attention to the teacher (H)

_____listen to what the principal says (H)

_____know that I have done the best I can (A)

_____don't know

9. In school it is all right to get angry with:

_____friends but not with class leaders or teachers (H)

_____someone I think is wrong, no matter who it is (A)

_____students that the teacher says are bad (H)

_____students who don't do their work (A)

_____don't know

10. When I pay attention to what my parents do and say, it is because:

_____paying attention is a nice thing (A)

_____my parents will be hurt if I don't pay attention (H)

_____paying attention is expected of children (A)

_____my parents will scold me if I don't pay attention (H)

_____don't know

11. In deciding things at home my parents usually:

_____remember what the family needs (H)

_____think what the family would like best (H)

_____think what the right thing to do is (A)

_____remember what a good citizen should do (A)

_____don't know

12. For a spy the worst kind of punishment would be to:

_____show his picture to everyone on television (H)

_____send him out of the country (A)

_____hang a sign around his neck and show him to others (H)

_____punish him alone in a prison cell (A)

_____don't know

13. Here is a group of people. Who is the leader? Put an X on the one you think is the leader:

14. Parents are most likely to blame children when:
_____they have been against their parents (H)
_____they have not been loyal to the family (H)
_____they have done something wrong (A)
_____they have been disorderly (A)
_____don't know

15. When I help friends in school it is because:
_____helping is good (A)
_____my friends will like me better (H)
_____it is good for the class (H)
_____I feel it is the right thing to do (A)
_____don't know

16. If a policeman does something I think is wrong, I'd probably:
_____keep quiet but still disagree inside (H)
_____show him that I do not agree (A)
_____tell my parents or teacher (H)
_____tell him that I felt he was wrong (A)
_____don't know

17. In school, when I disagree with a class leader, I would probably;
_____keep quiet even though I don't agree with him (H)
_____tell him he is wrong and do what I think is right (A)
_____tell him nicely how I feel but do as he says (H)
_____tell him nicely how I feel and try to persuade the others I am right (A)
_____don't know

18. When I disagree with my parents I usually:
_____keep quiet and say nothing (H)
_____tell them straight out that I disagree (A)
_____speak quietly and let them know that I'm upset at them (A)
_____do not say much but feel cross inside (H)
_____don't know

19. A class is usually orderly because:
_____not being orderly hurts others (A)
_____all people should be orderly (A)
_____being orderly with teachers is expected of children (H)
_____there are very special ways a class acts toward each other (H)
_____don't know

20. Here are two groups. Which group would you like to be leader of? Draw a big circle all around the group you pick:

21. If I were a judge in a court and my brother was on trial, I would probably:

_____be a little easier on him (H)

_____stay as judge to make sure my brother is treated as fairly as possible (H)

_____treat him as the law says, the same as anyone else (A)

_____ask another judge to take my place (A)

_____don't know

22. In a country, most people try to:

_____obey the laws (A)

_____do as the policeman says (H)

_____do what they believe to be right (A)

_____obey the President (H)

_____don't know

23. If the Mayor decides to close a playground near home so that an apartment building can be built, I would probably:

_____write the newspaper and complain (A)

_____feel angry but do nothing (H)

_____go along with the Mayor because he knows what is best (H)

_____ask my parents and friends if anything can be done (A)

_____don't know

24. If I were scolded by my parents for going to bed too late, I would probably:

_____pay no attention to them (A)

_____argue with my parents about the bed time rule (A)

_____feel angry inside at my parents but do as they say (H)

_____go to bed (H)

_____don't know

25. If a class leader lines up in a certain way and tells me that I have been lining up in the wrong way but I am not sure I was wrong, I would probably:

_____do as the class leader does but ask the teacher if he is right (H)

_____do as the class leader does because he ought to know (H)

_____talk it over with the class leader telling him I think he is wrong (A)

_____line up my way and tell the class leader he is not correct about the rules (A)

_____don't know

26. In electing a person for a position, I would probably vote for:

_____someone who does well in his work (A)

_____someone who is powerful (A)

_____someone whom I think will like me (H)
_____someone whom I have known a long time (H)
_____don't know

27. If I could be the teacher in my class, I would probably:
_____be a little harder on children I don't like (H)
_____punish everyone the same way (A)
_____punish according to the rules (A)
_____be a little easier on children I like better (H)
_____don't know

28. The mayor of a town will generally treat the people well because:
_____it is the job of the mayor (A)
_____the law says that he must treat the people well (A)
_____the people expect him to be good to them (H)
_____the people are the mayor's friends (H)
_____don't know

29. Here are four groups of people. Which of these groups would you like to be a member of? Draw a big circle all around the group you pick.

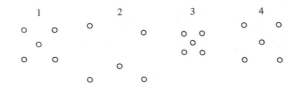

Selected Bibliography

Adelson, Joseph, "The Political Imagination of the Young Adolescent," *Daedalus*, Fall, 1971, pp. 1013–1050.

Agger, Robert E., Marshall N. Goldstein, and Stanley A. Pearl, "Political Cynicism: Measurement and Meaning," *Journal of Politics*, vol. 23, no. 3, August 1961, pp. 477–506.

Anderson, H. H., G. L. Anderson, I. H. Cohen, and F. D. Nutt, "Image of the Teacher by Adolescent Children in Four Countries: Germany, England, Mexico, United States," *Journal of Social Psychology*, vol. 50, First Half, August 1959, pp. 47–55.

Appleton, Sheldon, "Taiwanese and Mainlanders on Taiwan: A Survey of Student Attitudes," *China Quarterly*, no. 44, Oct.–Dec. 1970, pp. 38–65.

Aries, Philippe, *Centuries of Childhood: A Social History of Family Life*, Random House, Vintage Books, New York, 1962.

Aronfreed, Justin, "The Concept of Internalization," in David A. Goslin, ed., *Handbook for Socialization Theory and Research*, Rand McNally and Co., Chicago, 1969.

——, *Conduct and Conscience: The Socialization of Internalized Control over Behavior*, Academic Press, New York, 1968.

Baker, Hugh, D. R., *A Chinese Lineage Village: Sheung Shui*, Frank Cass and Co., London, 1968.

Bandura, Albert, "Social-Learning Theory of Identificatory Processes," in David A. Goslin, ed., *Handbook of Socialization Theory and Research*, Rand McNally and Co., Chicago, 1969.

Bandura, Albert, and Richard H. Walters, *Adolescent Aggression*, Ronald Press Co., New York, 1959.

Bandura, Albert, and Richard H. Walters, *Social Learning and Personality Development*, Holt, Rinehart, and Winston, New York, 1964.

Banfield, Edward C., *The Moral Basis of a Backward Society*, The Free Press, New York, 1958.

Barber, Bernard, *Social Stratification*, Harcourt, Brace and World, New York, 1957.

Barnett, A. Doak, ed., *Chinese Communist Politics in Action*, University of Washington Press, Seattle, 1969.

Baumrind, Diana, "Effects of Authoritative Parental Control on Child Behavior," *Child Development*, vol. 37, no. 4, December 1966, pp. 887–907.

Becker, Wesley C., "Consequences of Different Kinds of Parental Discipline," in Martin L. Hoffman and Lois W. Hoffman, eds., *Review of Child Development Research*, vol. 1, Russell Sage Foundation, New York, 1964.

Beloff, Halla, "Two forms of Social Conformity: Acquiescence and Conventionality," *Journal of Abnormal and Social Psychology*, vol. 56, no. 1, January 1958, pp. 99–104.

Benedict, Ruth, *The Chrysanthemum and the Sword*, Houghton Mifflin Co., Boston, 1946.

Berger, Peter L., and Thomas Luckman, *The Social Construction of Reality: A Treatise in the Sociology of Knowledge*, Doubleday and Company, Garden City, New York, 1966.

Berkowitz, Leonard, "Social Motivation," in Gardner Lindsey and Elliot Aronson, eds., *The Handbook of Social Psychology*, 2nd ed., vol. 3, Addison-Wesley Publishing Co., Reading, Mass., 1969.

Bezdek, William and Fred L. Strodtbeck, "Sex-Role and Pragmatic Action," *American Sociological Review*, vol. 35, no. 3, June 1970, pp. 491–502.

Brim, Orville G., Jr., "Family Structure and Sex Role Learning by Children: A Further Analysis of Helen Koch's Data," *Sociometry*, vol. 21, 1958, pp. 1–16.

Brim, Orville G., Jr., and Stanton Wheeler, *Socialization After Childhood: Two Essays*, John Wiley and Sons, Inc. New York, 1966.

Bronfenbrenner, Urie, "The Changing American Child—A Speculative Analysis," in Neil J. Smelser and William T. Smelser, eds., *Personality and Social Systems*, John Wiley and Sons, New York, 1963.

———, "Freudian Theories of Identification and Their Derivatives," in Celia Burns Stendler, ed., *Readings in Child Behavior and Development*, 2nd ed., Harcourt, Brace and World, New York, 1954.

———, *Two Worlds of Childhood: U.S. and U.S.S.R.*, Russell Sage Foundation, New York, 1970.

Brown, Roger, *Social Psychology*, The Free Press, New York, 1965.

Browning, Rufus P., and Herbert Jacob, "Power Motivation and the Political Personality," *Public Opinion Quarterly*, vol. 28, Spring, 1964, pp. 73–90.

Campbell, John D., "Peer Relations in Childhood," in Martin L. Hoffman and Lois W. Hoffman, eds., *Review of Child Development Research*, vol. 1, Russell Sage Foundation, New York, 1964.

Chin, Ai-Li S., "Family Relations in Modern Chinese Fiction," in Maurice Freedman, ed., *Family and Kinship in Chinese Society*, Stanford University Press, Stanford, 1970.

Clausen, John A., "Family Structure, Socialization, and Personality," in Lois W, Hoffman and Martin L. Hoffman, eds., *Review of Child Development Research*, vol. 2, Russell Sage Foundation, New York, 1966.

——, "Perspectives on Childhood Socialization," in John A. Clausen, ed., *Socialization and Society*, Little, Brown and Co., Boston, 1968.

Cohen, Myron L., "Developmental Process in the Chinese Domestic Group," in Maurice Freedman, ed., *Family and Kinship in Chinese Society*, Stanford University Press, Stanford, 1970.

Coser, Lewis, *The Functions of Social Conflict*, The Free Press, New York, 1956.

Cottle, Thomas J., "Self Concept, Ego Ideal, and the Response to Action," *Sociology and Social Research*, vol. 50, no. 1, October 1965, pp. 78–88.

Crowne, Douglas P., and David Marlowe, *The Approval Motive: Studies in Evaluative Dependence*, John Wiley and Sons, New York, 1964.

Dawson, Richard E., and Kenneth Prewitt, *Political Socialization*, Little, Brown and Co., Boston, 1969.

Dennis, Jack, Leon Lindberg, Donald McCrone, and Rodney Stiefbold, "Political Socialization to Democratic Orientations in Four Western Systems," *Comparative Political Studies*, vol. 1, no. 1, April 1968, pp. 71–101.

Devereux, Edward C., "The Role of Peer-Group Experience in Moral Development," in John P. Hill, ed., *Minnesota Symposia on Child Psychology*, vol. 4, University of Minnesota Press, Minneapolis, 1970.

De Vos, George, "Achievement and Innovation in Culture and Personality," in Edward Norbeck, Douglass Price-Williams, and William M. McCord, eds., *The Study of Personality*, Holt, Rinehart, and Winston, New Yorik, 1968.

——, "The Relation of Guilt toward Parents to Achievement and Arranged Marriage among the Japanese," *Psychiatry*, vol. 23, no. 3, August 1960, pp. 287–301.

Di Palma, Giuseppe, and Herbert McClosky, "Personality and Conformity: The Learning of Political Attitudes," *American Political Science Review*, vol. 64, no. 4, December 1970, pp. 1054–1073.

Dubin, Elizabeth Ruch, and Robert Dubin, "The Authority Inception Period in Socialization," *Child Development*, vol. 34, no. 4, December 1963, pp. 885–898.

Earle, Margaret J., "Bilingual Semantic Merging and an Aspect of Acculturation," *Journal of Personality and Social Psychology*, vol. 6, no. 3, July 1967, pp. 304–312.

Easton, David, and Jack Dennis, *Children in the Political System: Origins of Political Legitimacy*, McGraw-Hill Book Co., New York, 1969.

————, and Robert D. Hess, "The Child's Political World," in Leroy N. Rieselbach and George I. Balch, eds., *Psychology and Politics*, Holt, Rinehart, and Winston, New York, 1969.

Eberhard, Wolfram, "The Cultural Baggage of Chinese Emigrants," *Asian Survey*, vol. 11, no. 5, May 1971, pp. 445–462.

————, *Guilt and Sin in Traditional China*, University of California Press, Berkeley and Los Angeles, 1967.

Erikson, Erik H., *Identity, Youth, and Crisis*, W. W. Norton and Co., New York, 1968.

Eulau, Heinz, *The Behavioral Persuasion in Politics*, Random House, New York, 1963.

Finifter, Ada W., "Dimensions of Political Alienation," *American Political Science Review*, vol. 64, no. 2, June 1970, pp. 389–410.

Fleron, Frederic J., Jr., and Rita Mae Kelly, "Personality, Behavior and Communist Ideology," *Soviet Studies*, vol. 21, no. 3, January 1970, pp. 297–313.

Free, Lloyd A., and Hadley Cantril, *The Political Beliefs of Americans: A Study of Public Opinion*, Rutgers University Press, New Brunswick, N.J., 1967.

Freud, Sigmund, *Group Psychology and the Analysis of the Ego*, Bantam Books, New York, 1970.

Fromm, Erich, "Character and the Social Process," in Leroy N. Rieselbach and George I. Balch, eds., *Psychology and Politics*, Holt, Rinehart, and Winston, New York, 1969.

Gallin, Bernard, *Hsin Hsing, Taiwan: A Chinese Village in Change*, University of California Press, Berkeley and Los Angeles, 1966.

Gewirtz, Jacob L., "Mechanisms of Social Learning: Some Roles of Stimulation and Behavior in Early Human Development," in David A. Goslin, ed., *Handbook of Socialization Theory and Research*, Rand McNally and Co., Chicago, 1969.

Glidewell, John C., Mildred B. Kantor, Louis M. Smith, and Lorene A. Stringer, "Socialization and Social Structure in the Classroom," in Lois W. Hoffman and Martin L. Hoffman, eds., *Review of Child Development Literature*, vol. 2, Russell Sage Foundation, New York, 1966.

Goffman, Erving, *Behavior in Public Places*, The Free Press, New York, 1963.

————, "Embarrassment and Social Organization," in Neil J. Smelser and William T. Smelser, eds., *Personality and Social Systems*, John Wiley and Sons, New York, 1963.

Goffman, Irving, *Encounters*, Bobbs-Merrill Co., Indianapolis, Indiana, 1961.

Goodnow, Jacqueline J., "A Test of Milieu Effects With Some of Piaget's Tasks," *Psychological Monographs*, vol. 76, no. 36, whole no. 555, 1962, pp. 1–22.

Graham, Grace, *The Public School in the American Community*, Harper and Row, New York, 1963.

Greenstein, Fred I., "The Benevolent Leader: Children's Images of Political Authority," *American Political Science Review*, vol. 54, December 1960, pp. 934–943.

———, *Children and Politics*, Yale University Press, New Haven, 1965.

———, "New Light on Changing American Values: A Forgotten Body of Survey Data," *Social Forces*, vol. 42, no. 4, May 1964, pp. 441–450.

———, *Personality and Politics: Problems of Evidence, Inference, and Conceptualization*, Markham Publishing Co., Chicago, 1969.

———, issue ed., "Personality and Politics: Theoretical and Methodological Issues," *Journal of Social Issues*, vol. 24, no. 3, July 1968, pp. 1–156.

Greenfield, Patricia Marks, and Jerome S. Brunner, "Culture and Cognitive Growth," in David A. Goslin, ed., *Handbook of Socialization Theory and Research*, Rand, McNally and Co., Chicago, 1969.

Gregg, W. D., *Hong Kong Education Department Annual Summary, 1968–1969*, Government Press, Hong Kong, 1969.

Gross, Edward, and Gregory P. Stone, "Embarrassment and the Analysis of Role Requirements," in Gregory P. Stone and Harvey A. Faberman, eds., *Social Psychology through Symbolic Interaction*, Ginn-Blaisdell, Waltham, Mass., 1970.

Gurr, Ted R., *Why Men Rebel*, Princeton University Press, Princeton, N.J., 1970.

Hagen, Everett E., *On the Theory of Social Change*, Dorsey Press, Homewood, Illinois, 1962.

Handel, Gerald, "Psychological Study of Whole Families," *Psychological Bulletin*, vol. 63, no. 1, January 1965, pp. 19–41.

Haring, Douglas G., ed., *Personal Character and Cultural Milieu*, Syracuse University Press, Syracuse, N.Y., 1956.

Hartmann, Heinz, "Comments on the Psychoanalytic Theory of the Ego," *The Psychoanalytic Study of the Child*, vol. 5, 1950, pp. 74–96.

Hess, Robert D., and Judity V. Torney, *The Development of Political Attitudes in Children*, Aldine Publishing Co., Chicago, 1967.

———, "The Socialization of Attitudes Toward Political Authority: Some Cross-National Comparisons," *International Social Science Journal*, vol. 15, no. 4, 1963, pp. 542–559.

Hoffman, Martin L., and Herbert D. Saltzstein, "Parent Discipline and the Child's Moral Development," *Journal of Personality and Social Psychology*, vol. 5, no. 1, January 1967, pp. 45–57.

Horney, Karen, *Neurosis and Human Growth*, W. W. Norton and Co., New York, 1950.

Hsu, Chen-Chin and Tsung-Yi Lin, "A Mental Health Program at the Elementary School Level in Taiwan: A Six-Year Review of the East-Gate Project," in William Caudill and Tsung-Yi Lin, eds., *Mental Health Research in Asia and the Pacific*, East–West Center Press, Honolulu, 1969.

————, "A Study on 'Problem Children' Reported by Teachers," *Japanese Journal of Child Psychiatry*, vol. 7, no. 2, 1966, pp. 91–108.

————, Tsung-Yi Lin, Yung-ho Ko, and Sophia S. C. Lee, "Special Education for Mentally Subnormal Children in Taiwan," *American Journal of Orthopsychiatry*, vol. 38, no. 4, 1968, pp. 615–621.

Hsu, Francis L. K., "Chinese Kinship and Chinese Behavior," in Ping-ti Ho and Tang Tsou, eds., *China in Crisis: China's Heritage and the Communist Political System*, vol. 1, book 2, University of Chicago Press, Chicago, 1968.

————, *Clan, Caste, and Club*, D. Van Nostrand Company, Princeton, N.J., 1963.

Hu, Hsien-Chin, "The Chinese Concepts of Face," *American Anthropologist*, vol. 46, no. 1, pt. 1, January–March 1944, pp. 45–64.

Huang, I., ed., *Child Psychology*, (*Erh-t'ong Hsin-li-hsueh*), Li Chie, publisher, Taipei, Taiwan, 1969.

Huang, Te-Hsing, *Mental Hygiene and Individual Cultivation*, (*Hsin-li Wei-sheng yu Jen-ke P'ei-yu*), Chao Shou-cheng, publisher, Taipei, Taiwan, 1964.

Hui, Ching-Chao, *Dialogue of Family Education*, (*Chia-t'ing Chiao-yu Chiang-hua*), Nan Yang Book Co., Hong Kong, 1968.

Inkeles, Elex, and Daniel J. Levinson, "National Character: The Study of Modal Personality and Socio-Cultural Systems," in Gardner Lindzey, ed., *Handbook of Social Psychology*, Addison-Wesley Publishing Co., Cambridge, Mass., 1954.

————, "Social Structure and Socialization," in David A. Goslin, ed., *Handbook of Socialization Theory and Research*, Rand McNally and Co., Chicago, 1969.

————, "Society, Social Structure, and Child Socialization," in John A. Clausen, ed., *Socialization and Society*, Little, Brown and Co., Boston, 1968.

Janis, Irving L., George F. Mahl, Jerome Kagan, and Robert R. Holt, *Personality Dynamics, Development, and Assessment*, Harcourt, Brace and World, New York, 1969.

Jaros, Dean, Herbert Hirsch, and Frederic J. Fleron, "The Malevolent Leader: Political Socialization in an American Sub-Culture," *American Political Science Review*, vol. 62, no. 2, June 1968, pp. 564–575.

Jennings, M. Kent, and Richard G. Niemi, "Patterns of Political Learning," *Harvard Educational Review*, vol. 38, no. 3, 1968, pp. 443–467.

Kagan, Jerome, "Acquisition and Significance of Sex Typing and Sex Role Identity," in Martin L. Hoffman and Lois W. Hoffman, eds., *Review of Child Development Research*, vol. 1, Russell Sage Foundation, New York, 1964.

Kelman, Herbert C., "Compliance, Identification, and Internalization: Three Processes of Attitude Change," *Journal of Conflict Resolution*, vol. 2, no. 1, 1958, pp. 51–60.

Klineberg, Otto, "Emotional Expression in Chinese Literature," *Journal of Abnormal and Social Psychology*, vol. 33, no. 4, October 1938, pp. 517–520.

Kohlberg, Lawrence, and Carol Gilligan, "The Adolescent as a Philosopher: The Discovery of the Self in a Postconventional World," *Daedalus*, Fall, 1971, pp. 1051–1086.

Kohlberg, Lawrence, "Development of Children's Orientations toward a Moral Order," in Richard C. Sprinthall and Norman A. Sprinthall, eds., *Educational Psychology*, Van Nostrand–Reinhold Co., New York, 1969.

———, "Development of Moral Character and Moral Ideology," in Martin L. Hoffman and Lois W. Hoffman, eds., *Review of Child Development Research*, vol. 1, Russell Sage Foundation, New York, 1964.

———, "Stage and Sequence: The Cognitive Developmental Approach to Socialization," in David A. Goslin, ed., *Handbook of Socialization Theory and Research*, Rand McNally and Co., Chicago, 1969.

Kohn, Melvin L., "Social Class and the Exercise of Parental Authority," in Neil J. Smelser and William T. Smelser, eds., *Personality and Social Systems*, John Wiley and Sons, New York, 1963.

Lane, Robert E., *Political Thinking and Consciousness: The Private Life of the Political Mind*, Markham Publishing Co., Chicago, 1969.

Langton, Kenneth P., *Political Socialization*, Oxford University Press, London, 1969.

Langer, Jonas, *Theories of Development*, Holt, Rinehart, and Winston, New York, 1969.

LeVine, Robert A., "Culture, Personality, and Socialization: An Evolutionary View," in David A. Goslin, ed., *Handbook of Socialization Theory and Research*, Rand McNally and Co., Chicago, 1969.

———, *Dreams and Deeds: Achievement Motivation in Nigeria*, University of Chicago Press, Chicago, 1966.

Levy, Marion J., Jr., *Modernization and the Structure of Societies*, vol. 1, Princeton University Press, Princeton, N.J., 1966.

Lewis, John Wilson, *Leadership in Communist China*, Cornell University Press, Ithaca, N.Y., 1963.

Lin, Chi-sha, *Cultivation and Service of Youth (Ch'ing-nien Hsui-yang yu Fu-wu)*, Tai Fong Publishing Society, Hong Kong, 1967.

Lipset, Seymour M., "A Changing American Character?" in Seymour M. Lipset and Leo Lowenthal, eds., *Culture and Social Character: The Work of David Riesman Reviewed*, The Free Press, New York, 1961.

Lynd, Helen Merrell, *On Shame and the Search for Identity*, Science Editions, New York, 1961.

Maccoby, Eleanor E., "The Development of Moral Values and Behavior in Childhood," in John A. Clausen, ed., *Socialization and Society*, Little, Brown and Co., Boston, 1968.

———, "Effects of the Mass Media," in Martin L. Hoffman and Lois W. Hoffman, eds., *Review of Child Development Research*, vol. 1, Russell Sage Foundation, New York, 1964.

MacRae, Duncan, Jr., "A Test of Piaget's Theories of Moral Development," *Journal of Abnormal and Social Psychology*, vol. 49, no. 1, January 1954, pp. 14–18.

Marlowe, David, and Kenneth J. Gergen, "Personality and Social Interaction," in Gardner Lindzey and Elliot Aronson, eds., *The Handbook of Social Psychology*, 2nd ed., vol. 3, Addison-Wesley Publishing Co., Reading, Mass., 1969.

Maslow, Abraham H., *Toward a Psychology of Being*, D. Van Nostrand Co., Princeton, N.J., 1962.

McClelland, David C., *The Achieving Society*, D. Van Nostrand Co., Princeton, N.J., 1961.

McClelland, David C., "Motivational Patterns in Southeast Asia with Special Reference to the Chinese Case," *Journal of Social Issues*, vol. 19, no. 1, January 1963, pp. 6–19.

McClosky, Herbert, "Consensus and Ideology in American Politics," in Edward C. Dreyer and Walter A. Rosenbaum, eds., *Political Opinion and Behavior: Essays and Studies*, 2nd ed., Wadsworth Publishing Co., Belmont, California, 1970.

McGuire, William J., "The Nature of Attitudes and Attitude Change," in Gardner Lindzey and Elliot Aronson, eds., *The Handbook of Social Psychology*, 2nd ed., vol. 3, Addison-Wesley Publishing Co., Reading, Mass., 1969.

Mead, George Herbert, "Development of the Self through Play and Games," in Gregory P. Stone and Harvey A. Faberman, eds., *Social Psychology through Symbolic Interaction*, Ginn-Blaisdell, Waltham, Mass., 1970.

Merelman, Richard H., "The Development of Political Ideology: A Framework for the Analysis of Political Socialization," *American Political Science Review*, vol. 63, no. 3, September 1969. pp. 750–767.

Meyers, Samuel M., "The Role of Traditional Orientations toward Social Relations in Chinese Responses to Communist Military-Political Control," in Samuel M. Meyers and Albert D. Biderman, eds., *Mass Behavior in Battle and Captivity*, University of Chicago Press, Chicago, 1968.

Miller, Daniel R., and Guy E. Swanson, *Inner Conflict and Defense*, Henry Holt and Co., New York, 1960.

Miller, Neil E., and John Dollard, *Social Learning and Imitation*, Yale University Press, New Haven, 1941.

Moore, Wilbert E., *Social Change*, Prentice Hall, Englewood Cliffs, N.J., 1963.

Nash, Dennison and Louis C. Shaw, "Achievement and Acculturation: A Japanese Example," in Melford E. Spiro, ed., *Context and Meaning in Cultural Anthropology*, The Free Press, New York, 1965.

Notterman, Joseph M., *Behavior: A Systematic Approach*, Random House, New York, 1970.

Opler, Marvin, K., *Culture Psychiatry and Human Values*, Charles C. Thomas, Publisher, Springfield, Illinois, 1956.

Palmer, Francis H., "Inferences to the Socialization of the Child from Animal Studies: A View from the Bridge," in David A. Goslin, ed., *Handbook of Socialization Theory and Research*, Rand MacNally and Co., Chicago, 1969.

Parsons, Talcott, and Winston White, "The Link Between Character and Society," in Seymour M. Lipset and Leo Lowenthal, eds., *Culture and Social Character: The Work of David Riesman Reviewed*, The Free Press, New York, 1961.

———, "Social Structure and the Development of Personality: Freud's Contribution to the Integration of Psychology and Sociology," in Neil J. Smelser and William T. Smelser, eds., *Personality and Social Systems*, John Wiley and Sons, New York, 1963.

Patterson, Samuel C., "The Political Cultures of the American States," in Edward C. Dryer and Walter A. Rosenbaum, eds., *Political Opinion and Behavior: Essays and Studies*, 2nd ed., Wadsworth Publishing Co., Belmont, California, 1970.

Piaget, Jean, *The Moral Judgment of the Child*, Collier Books, New York, 1962.

Peck, Robert F., with Robert J. Havighurst, *The Psychology of Character Development*, John Wiley and Sons (Science Editions), New York, 1960.

Piers, Gerhart, and Milton B. Singer, *Shame and Guilt*, Charles C. Thomas, Publisher, Springfield, Illinois, 1953.

Pinner, Frank A., "Parental Overprotection and Political Distrust," *Annals of the American Academy of Political and Social Science*, vol. 361, September 1965, pp. 58–70

Price, R. F., *Education in Communist China*, Routledge and Kegan Paul, London, 1970.

Proshansky, Harold M., "The Development of Intergroup Attitudes," in Lois W. Hoffman and Martin L. Hoffman, eds., *Review of Child Development Research*, vol. 2, Russell Sage Foundation, New York, 1966.

Pye, Lucian W., *The Authority Crisis in Chinese Politics*, University of Chicago Center for Policy Study, University of Chicago, Chicago, 1967.

Pye, Lucian W., "Hostility and Authority in Chinese Politics," *Problems of Communism*, vol. 17, no. 3, May–June 1968, pp. 10–22.

———, *The Spirit of Chinese Politics*, Massachusetts Institute of Technology Press, Cambridge, Mass., 1968.

Riesman, David (in collaboration with Reuel Denney and Nathan Glazer), *The Lonely Crowd: A Study of the Changing American Character*, Yale University Press, New Haven, 1950.

Rodd, William G., "A Cross-Cultural Study of Taiwan's Schools," *Journal of Social Psychology*, vol. 50, 1st half, August 1969, pp. 3–36.

Rosenberg, Morris, *Society and the Adolescent Self-Image*, Princeton University Press, Princeton, N.J., 1965.

Rowe, Elizabeth, Y. P. Lau, G. H. Lee, A. K. Li, and W. G. Rodd, in collaboration with S. C. Hu, *Failure in School: Aspects of the Problem in Hong Kong*, Hong Kong Council for Educational Research, Publication No. 3, Hong Kong University Press, Hong Kong, 1966.

Schachter, Stanley, *The Psychology of Affiliation*, Stanford University Press, Stanford, California, 1959.

Schnaiberg, Allan, "Measuring Modernism: Theoretical and Empirical Explorations," *American Journal of Sociology*, vol. 76, no. 3, November 1970, pp. 399–425.

Schonfeld, William R., "The Focus of Political Socialization Research," *World Politics*, vol. 23, no. 3, April, 19671, pp. 544–578.

Scott, William A., "Attitude Measurement," in Gardner Lindzey and Elliot Aronson, eds., *The Handbook of Social Psychology*, Addison-Wesley Publishing Co., Reading, Mass., 1969.

Sears, Robert R., Eleanor E. Maccoby, and Harry Levin, *Patterns of Child Rearing*, Row, Peterson and Co., Evanston, Ill. and White Plains, New York, 1957.

———, Lucy Rau, and Richard Alpert, *Identification and Child Rearing*, Stanford University Press, Stanford, 1965.

Sigel, Roberta, "Assumptions About the Learning of Political Values," in Leroy N. Rieselbach and George I. Balch, eds., *Psychology and Politics*, Holt, Rinehart, and Winston, New York, 1969.

Slater, Philip E., "Parental Behavior and the Personality of the Child," *Journal of Genetic Psychology*, vol. 101, 1st half, September 1962, pp. 53–68.

Smith, Arthur H., *Chinese Characteristics*, Fleming H. Revell Co., New York, 1894.

———, *Village Life in China*, Fleming H. Revell Co., New York, 1899.

Solomon, Richard H., "Communication Patterns and the Chinese Revolution," *China Quarterly*, no. 32, Oct.–Dec. 1967, pp. 88–110.

———, "Mao's Effort to Reintegrate the Chinese Polity: Problems of Authority and

Conflict in Chinese Social Processes," in A. Doak Barnett, ed., *Chinese Communist Politics in Action*, University of Washington Press, Seattle, 1969.

Spiro, Melford E., "Religious Systems as Culturally Constituted Defense Mechanisms," in Melford E. Spiro, ed., *Context and Meaning in Cultural Anthropology*, The Free Press, New York, 1965.

Stendler, Celia Burns, "Possible Causes of Overdependency in Young Children," *Child Development*, vol. 25, no. 2, June 1954, pp. 125–146.

Stone, Gregory P., "Appearance and the Self," in Gregory P. Stone and Harvey A. Faberman, eds., *Social Psychology Through Symbolic Interaction*, Ginn-Blaisdell, Waltham, Mass., 1970.

Sun, Pang-cheng, *Education Guide Outline (Chiao-yu Shih-tao Ta-kang)*, Hsu Yu-shou, publisher, Taipei, Taiwan, 1965.

Taguiri, Renato, "Person Perception," in Gardner Lindzey and Elliott Aronson, eds., *The Handbook of Social Psychology*, 2nd ed., vol. 3, Addison-Wesley Publishing Co., Reading, Mass., 1969.

Tapp, June L., "A Child's Garden of Law and Order," *Psychology Today*, vol. 4, no. 7, December 1970, pp. 29–31, 62–64.

———, issue editor, "Socialization, The Law, and Society," *Journal of Social Issues*, vol. 27, no. 2, 1971, pp. 1–230.

Tasch, Ruth J., "The Role of the Father in the Family," *Journal of Experimental Education*, vol. 20, no. 4, June 1952, pp. 319.

Terhune, Kenneth W., "From National Character to National Behavior: A Reformulation," *Journal of Conflict Resolution*, vol. 14, no. 2, June 1970, pp. 203–263.

Trasher, Gordon, "Socialization," in David Edge, ed., *The Formative Years: How Children Become Members of Their Society*, Schocken Books, New York, 1968.

Triandis, Harry C., and Vasso Vassiliou, "Frequency of Contact and Stereotyping," *Journal of Personality and Social Psychology*, vol. 7, no. 3, November 1967, pp. 316–328.

Tomkins, Silvan S., *Affect Imagery Consciousness*, vol. 2: *The Negative Affects*, Springer Publishing Co., New York, 1963.

Tseng, Wen-Sheng, "A Paranoid Family in Taiwan," *Archives of General Psychiatry*, vol. 21, no. 1, July 1969, pp. 55–63.

Wallace, Anthony F. C., *Culture and Personality*, Random House, New York, 1961.

Wei, Ch'in-I, ed., *Psychology and Education (Hsin-li yu Chiao-yu)*, Ch'en Hsin-yin, publisher, Taipei, Taiwan, 1969.

Weinstein, Fred, and Gerald M. Platt, *The Wish to Be Free: Society, Psyche, and Value Change*, University of California Press, Berkeley and Los Angeles, 1969.

Whiting, John W. M., and Irvin L. Child, *Child Training and Personality: A Cross-Cultural Study*, Yale University Press, New Haven, 1953.

Whiting, John W. M., Eleanor Chasli, Antonovsky Hollenberg, Helen Faigin, and Barbara Chartier Ayres, "The Learning of Values," in Evon Z. Vogt and Ethel M. Albert, eds., *People of Rimrock*, Harvard University Press, Cambridge, Mass., 1966.

Wilson, Richard W., "A Comparison of Political Attitudes of Taiwanese Children and Mainlander Children on Taiwan," *Asian Survey*, Vol. 8, no. 12, December 1968, pp. 988–1000.

————, *Learning to be Chinese: The Political Socialization of Children in Taiwan*, Massachusetts Institute of Technology Press, Cambridge, Mass., 1970.

————, "The Learning of Political Symbols in Chinese Culture," *Journal of Asian and African Studies*, vol. 3, nos. 3–4, July and October, 1968, pp. 241–256.

Witkin, Herman A., Donald R. Goodenough, and Stephen A. Karp, "Stability of Cognitive Style from Childhood to Young Adulthood," *Journal of Personality and Social Psychology*, vol. 7, no. 3, November 1967, pp. 291–300.

Wolf, Margery, "Child Training and the Chinese Family," Maurice Freedman, ed., *Family and Kinship in Chinese Society*, Stanford University Press, Stanford, 1970.

Wrong, Dennis H., "The Oversocialized Conception of Man in Modern Sociology," in Gregory P. Stone and Harvey A. Faberman, eds., *Social Psychology Through Symbolic Interaction*, Ginn-Blaisdell, Waltham, Mass., 1970.

Yang, Martin C., *A Chinese Village: Taitou, Shantung Province*, Columbia University Press, New York, 1945.

Yap, P. M., "Phenomenology of Affective Disorder in Chinese and Other Cultures," in A. V. S. De Reuck and Ruth Porter, eds., *Transcultural Psychiatry*, Little, Brown and Co., Boston, 1965.

Yeh, Hou-Chung, *On Family Life (Chia-t'ing Sheng-huo Man-t'an)*, Tai Dei Publishing Society, Hong Kong, 1957.

Yin, Yun-Hua, *Family Education (Chia-t'ing Chiao-yu)*, Hu Yung-cheng, publishers, Taichung, Taiwan, 1970.

Yenger, J. Milton, "Modal Character," in Leroy N. Rieselbach and George I. Balch, eds., *Psychology and Politics*, Holt, Rinehart, and Winston, New York, 1969.

Zeigler, Harmon, *The Political Life of American Teachers*, Prentice-Hall, Englewood Cliffs, N.J., 1967.

Zigler, Edward and Irvin L. Child, "Socialization," in Gardner Lindzey and Elliot Aronson, eds., *The Handbook of Social Psychology*, 2nd ed., vol. 3, Addison-Wesley Publishing Co., Reading, Mass., 1969.

Index